T0271002

An Introduction to
Quantitative Finance
A Three-Principle Approach

An Introduction to
Quantitative
Finance
A Three-Principle Approach

Christopher Hian Ann Ting

Singapore Management University, Singapore

World Scientific

NEW JERSEY · LONDON · SINGAPORE · BEIJING · SHANGHAI · HONG KONG · TAIPEI · CHENNAI · TOKYO

Published by

World Scientific Publishing Co. Pte. Ltd.

5 Toh Tuck Link, Singapore 596224

USA office: 27 Warren Street, Suite 401-402, Hackensack, NJ 07601

UK office: 57 Shelton Street, Covent Garden, London WC2H 9HE

Library of Congress Cataloging-in-Publication Data
Ting, Christopher Hian Ann, author.
   An introduction to quantitative finance : a three-principle approach / Christopher Hian Ann Ting.
      pages cm
   Includes bibliographical references and index.
   ISBN 978-9814704304 (alk. paper)
   1. Finance--Mathematical models. I. Title.
   HG106.T56 2015
   332.01'5195--dc23
                                    2015025675

British Library Cataloguing-in-Publication Data
A catalogue record for this book is available from the British Library.

In-house Editor: Qi Xiao

Typeset by Stallion Press
Email: enquiries@stallionpress.com

Printed in Singapore

Dedicated to
Reiko, Eri, Ai, and Joshua.

In memory of
Mr. Lee Kuan Yew.

Contents

Foreword

Christopher Ting is an Associate Professor in the Quantitative Finance area at the Lee Kong Chian School of Business. He is a brilliant scholar who comes with a rich background in theoretical physics, scientific computing, and financial econometrics. He also spent time in the financial markets doing professional futures trading at a proprietary trading firm. Besides writing research papers in finance and quantitative areas of finance, Professor Ting now produces herewith a very interesting introductory book to the world of quantitative finance.

Being a course leader in this field and the director of the Master Program in Quantitative Finance, which is jointly organized with the Cass Business School, Christopher brings with him a clear perspective of how students in Quantitative Finance would benefit by tooling themselves with appropriate methods and technology in the new financial markets.

The book provides a quick access to the various classes of assets an investor would meet in the marketplace, and also shows how each type of asset should be analyzed to evaluate their profitability and correct pricing. Some degree of elegant mathematics is incorporated to illustrate the famous Black–Scholes model. The book is

well written with witty discussion and nice diagrams to follow. I
am sure students would enjoy reading this book and learning something out of it.

Lim Kian Guan
OUB Chair Professor
Singapore Management University

Preface

Quantitative Finance is a new field emerging from the intersection of finance, financial mathematics, and computing. Being practice- and market-oriented, the main applications of Quantitative Finance are to price assets, generate alpha, and manage risk.

In view of the financial crises in the capitalist markets, it is imperative to watch out for the chasm between the models on paper and the profit & loss in actuality. There are many financial and mathematical models of risk, but risk, in reality, is to see rickety investments snap kafkaesquely, causing your heart to skip a beat and your stomach to clench up in knots.

This book aims to provide an introductory overview of Quantitative Finance by marshalling a host of ideas and methods that are relevant to the goal of making sense out of what is happening in the financial markets. Parallel to Newton's three laws of motion, three principles of Quantitative Finance are put forward as buoys for navigating the treacherous waters of hypotheses, models, and gaps between theory and practice. It is often said that the gap between theory and practice is always wider in practice than in theory.

Advanced undergraduate and beginning postgraduate students are the target audience. Included also are practitioners who want to add understanding to their daily use of Quantitative Finance models, which are usually shrouded in the form of commercial or proprietary software black boxes. Hopefully, this book is helpful in guiding the audience to a level where more advanced Quantitative

Finance books and research papers become readable. Toward this end, the three principles of Quantitative Finance introduced in this book should be able to enable you to gain a categorized perspective on how the major models of Quantitative Finance fit together in a self-consistent framework. Essentially, the three principles of Quantitative Finance are applied to derive and examine the basic relationships among plain vanilla derivatives and their underlying assets.

The genesis of this book comes from years of teaching undergraduate and graduate courses related to Quantitative Finance. Many exercises designed for tutorials, homework assignments, and exam questions are selectively included to reinforce or supplement the key ideas expounded in the main text. Moreover, important concepts are also introduced in the exercises, and you are strongly encouraged to attempt the exercises to think deeper, and to develop mathematical reasoning skills.

The definition–lemma–theorem–corollary style used by financial mathematicians is more *poetic*, rigorous, and organized. However, in the real world where risk-adjusted P&L reigns supreme, making things less complex for non-quants to understand is at times more germane. That said, mathematics is critically essential and you are encouraged to learn and practise mathematics on the daily basis. After all, Quantitative Finance is about problem solving and applying the models described mathematically to the real world to see whether the numbers churned out fit the reality well enough.

I strive to strike a balance between mathematical rigor and intuitive accessibility to a wider audience. In this context, the adoption of a prose style is a decision made after having taken heed of Einstein's remark [Som70]:

> Since the mathematicians have invaded the theory of relativity, I do not understand it myself anymore.

Nevertheless, some concepts and theorems in financial mathematics are not only more general but also crucial for gaining a deeper understanding and mastery of Quantitative Finance. Hopefully, this book could pique your curiosity to go for more. Even Einstein was not spared from having to deal with difficult mathematics when he was developing his general theory of relativity:

> Do not worry about your difficulties in mathematics. I assure you that mine are greater.

To spice up the discourse, judicious inclusions of relevant historical accounts are deemed to be beneficial. Some of these historical stories may even shed new light on the financial markets and the securities traded therein. Quotes such as the ones by Einstein are also harnessed to enhance readability and motivation to press on.

The main focus, however, is on and for real-world applications rather than mathematics. As much as possible, I provide step-by-step derivations of key results (such as the Black–Scholes equation) that epitomize Quantitative Finance. The mathematics required for a thorough reading includes freshman (advanced) calculus and probability & statistics.

The truth is, mathematical difficulty is not the main challenge of learning Quantitative Finance. What is really challenging, however, is to reach a level of realization that many models in Quantitative Finance, like in any other social science such as economics, ought to be abandoned simply because the models are uglily wrong and useless. At the same time, of the many wrong models (such as the Black–Scholes model), some are beautifully useful when applied in ways different from what they are originally intended. So, depending on how you look at it, Quantitative Finance can be either practically incorrect, or incorrectly practical. That, in a nutshell, is the deadly ugliness and beauty of Quantitative Finance intertwined in *All is Vanity* (Ecclesiastes Chapter 1 Verse 2).

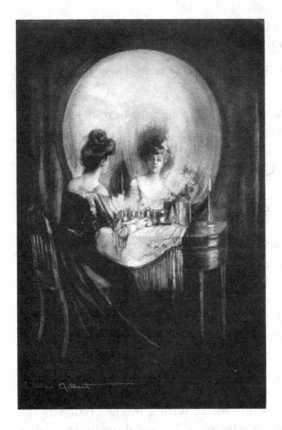

C. Allan Gilbert's *All is Vanity* (1892):
Intertwined Ugliness and Beauty
of Quantitative Finance

http://commons.wikimedia.org/wiki/File:Allisvanity.jpg

Christopher Ting
christophert@smu.edu.sg
Lee Kong Chian School of Business
Singapore Management University
April 2015

About the Author

Dr. Christopher Ting is an Associate Professor of Quantitative Finance Practice at the Lee Kong Chian School of Business, Singapore Management University. He serves as the area coordinator (department head) for Quantitative Finance, and he is also the founding director of SMU's Master of Science in Quantitative Finance (MQF) Program jointly offered by the Cass Business School.

He earned his bachelor degree in mechanical engineering and master degree in experimental physics (biophysics) from the University of Tokyo on two Japanese Government scholarships administered by the Public Service Commission (PSC) of Singapore. Upon returning from overseas study and having served the full-time National Service as an infantry officer, he was assigned by the PSC to work as a research scientist at the DSO National Laboratories. While working, and having published four research papers, he earned his PhD in theoretical physics from the National University of Singapore.

Dr. Ting rose to the rank of laboratory head and he had managed over 40 high-caliber research scientists and engineers in DSO. In 1999, he was conferred the title of Distinguished Member of Technical Staff. Moreover, Dr. Ting was awarded the Defence Technology Award (Team) twice and he holds a U.S. patent in natural language processing.

In 2009, Dr. Ting became a proprietary trader with a futures trading company, Promisedland (Simex Trader) Pte Ltd. He also applied quantitative finance methods to develop strategies for trading index futures subsequently.

As a result of his experience in conducting research and development in many fields as required by DSO and SMU, as well as his proprietary trading experience, he has published many papers in diverse disciplines of Physics, Computer Science, Finance, and Quantitative Finance. In addition, he has the experience of providing consultancy to the Singapore Exchange and May Bank (Singapore), among others.

Under his leadership, he revamped the Simulated Trading Room (STR) in SMU, equipped each terminal with trading software (CQG and Trading Technologies) used by professional traders, and brought trade and quote data streaming live from SGX, Eurex, and CME to STR through the exchanges' university outreach programs. He also spearheaded an initiative to elevate SMU's MSc in Quantitative Finance program to an academic partner of the Global Association of Risk Professionals (GARP).

Dr. Ting's current research interest includes quantitative trading & investment, and portfolio analytics & risk management.

Acknowledgments

The best part of writing a book is to acknowledge friends, colleagues, and people who had helped me to make the book into a reality.

To Mr. Ng Tee How, I want to say a big thank you for hiring me as a proprietary trader in his prop firm Promisedland (Simex Trader) Pte Ltd. Mr. Ng also taught me how to trade calendar and inter-market spreads. My experience in the electronic futures markets transformed my philosophical understanding of the hypotheses, models, and theories in the Economics & Finance textbooks and well-known journals. The textbooks and academic papers in Financial Economics are supposed to help practitioners understand what's going on in the market. But written without ever experiencing the pressure of bottom line, I began to see in many their superficiality and surreality in the real world — the jungle of hunger game. Being accountable for the realized P&L of my trades and risk exposures daily, I have developed a sense for models of which would work, and which would not. This is the most valuable asset (in addition to the small profit) that Tee How had helped me acquire.

Moreover, the camaraderie of traders in the trading firm and the arcade is the best I have ever experienced. Thank you, Amos, Charlie, and Jeffrey. Conversations with Stephen Tan, Wong Toon Luan, and Ian Loh are always refreshing and insightful.

Next, I would like to thank the late pioneers of post-colonial Singapore who institutionalized a system of meritocracy regardless of social status. With zero connection, I had a Monbukagakusho Scholarship opportunity to complete my university education in Japan. With his passing away in March 2015, it is timely to acknowledge Mr. Lee Kuan Yew, the leader of the pioneers, who dedicated his prime life building up a small nation where I grew up.

I am grateful to Professor Lim Kian Guan who hired me as a faculty member of Quantitative Finance. Without coming back to the academia, it would be impossible for me to write this book. Professor Lim's intellectual capacity to delve deep into many different topics of Finance and Quantitative Finance is truly inspiring. It is a great privilege to be his colleague and friend. I am really thankful and honored that he made time to write the foreword for this book.

I am also grateful to Professor Emanuel Derman and Professor Hui-Hsiung Kuo. Professor Derman went through several parts of the draft and Professor Kuo corrected a few mistakes concerning his personal relationship with the great mathematician, Kiyoshi Itô, the inventor of stochastic calculus. Professor Michael Benoliel, my SMU colleague, also helped me to verify the Jewish year of the first recorded forward contract and counterparty risk exposure in human history. I am thankful that they took the trouble to answer my emails, share their insightful thoughts, and pen words of encouragement.

I would also like to thank the anonymous reviewer who has provided good suggestions for topics to be included. Interestingly, the suggested topics coincide with much I have planned and drafted for the sequel to this book. My editor, Mr. Xiao Qi of World Scientific, has patiently provided professional guidance at various stages of the publication process. So to him, I want to say a big THANKS!

Last but not least, I want to thank my better half, Reiko, for taking up the lion share of the house chores, and for bearing with me for waking up at odd hours writing the book. The coffee she makes is the best to keep me awake.

Notations

$:=$	the left side is defined by the right side
$=:$	the right side is defined by the left side
$\triangle$	a change in
$\mathbb{P}(\ )$	probability operator
$\mathbb{E}(\ )$	expectation operator
$\mathbb{V}(\ )$	variance operator
$N(\mu, \sigma^2)$	normal distribution with mean μ and variance σ^2
$\widetilde{X}$	the tilde on top emphasizes that the variable X is a random variable
$\sim$	has the probability distribution of
$\mathfrak{R}$	set of real numbers
$\mathfrak{R}_+$	set of positive real numbers
PV	present value
FV	forward value
NPV	net present value
CF	cash flow
DF	discount factor
P&L	profit and loss

Chapter 1

Introduction

1.1 A Brief History of Quantitative Finance

Stories are usually a friendly way to start a conversation. Writing a book is perhaps no different. I start by telling the real story about how Quantitative Finance came to say "Hello World!"

It all happened in the 20th century.

When the American Association of Finance was founded in 1940, it was set up merely as a *special organization* of the American Association of Economics. The original goal was to focus on the major topics currently engaging the world of finance; and to develop the managerial and business aspects of finance (see Guthmann [Gut46]). Although the first issue of the *Journal of Finance* had already appeared in print by August 1946, Finance as an *academic* discipline did not quite exist until the 1950s, according to Miller [Mil99]. There was no framework, no paradigm, and no model with which to theorize the practice of finance.

A few years after the second World War, however, many researchers steeped in economics, better known as financial economists these days, made and continue to make inroad into Finance. Their thoughts, theories, hypotheses, models, and economic rationale permeate all Finance textbooks. Even to these days, Finance is still considered as a subfield of economics, but "distinguished by both its focus and its methodology" (see Ross [Ros08] and Summers [Sum85]). Therefore, it is not entirely unjustifiable to regard Finance as a new field that emerged from the well established discipline of economics.

Applied mathematicians can trace the origin of Financial Mathematics to 1900 when Bachelier published his highly original PhD thesis *Théorie de la spéculation* [Bac00]. But Quantitative Finance and Finance share the same defining moment when Markowitz's article entitled "Portfolio Selection" [Mar52] was published in 1952. This 15-page article is an offshoot of his doctoral thesis. Similar to Bachelier's experience during the defence of his thesis, the review committee did not know how to classify Markowitz's highly original dissertation. "It's not math, it's not economics, it's not even business administration" (see Bernstein [Ber92]). Despite this "isn't" concern, Markowitz earned his PhD anyway. Since this watershed defence of a purely theoretical dissertation, slowly but steadily, Finance — a concoction spewing out from a cauldron of accounting, business, economics, and econometrics — gained recognition as an academic discipline by itself.

Much like Finance emerged from the broader field of economics, Quantitative Finance took off in 1973 when stochastic calculus was first applied by Black and Scholes [BS73], and independently by Robert Merton [Mer73]. They succeeded in solving the option pricing problem. The analytical solution called the Black–Scholes formula is widely used by many option traders. The Black–Scholes partial differential equation is regarded as one of the 17 world-changing equations by some quarters (see Stewart [Ste12]). Black and Scholes were inspired by the idea of delta-hedging in a book entitled "Beat the Market: A scientific Stock Market System" written by Thorp and Kassouf [TK67]. The simple yet brilliant stroke of genius is their realization that by dynamically hedging away the volatility, "in equilibrium, the expected return on such a hedged position must be equal to the return on a riskless asset" [BS73].

Since the 1980s, mathematicians, physicists, and computer scientists made their ways to Wall Street, which began to beckon to them as the financial industry — investment banking in particular — was on the cusp of a series of fundamental transformations, driven by relentless competition, technological advancements, and new requirements to deal with volatility. Fischer Black of the Black–Scholes formula was among the earliest to join a Wall Street bank in 1984. Looking back 11 years later before he passed away, he recalled finding the investment bank, where he was made a partner, better for continual learning than a university (see Mehrling [Meh05]). This is indeed a first-hand testimony of the fact that Quantitative Finance was in the formative phase. Transforming ever so rapidly during Black's time in an investment bank, even he had to keep learning while developing new models to price and manage the risks of new financial products.

But what exactly is Quantitative Finance? Mathematical modeling, statistics, programming, a huge dose of clever ideas with which to examine the financial instruments in the financial markets, and all of these combined together, can be seen and illustrated in the life of a pioneering quant[1] on Wall Street: Emanuel Derman. His views on quants and Quantitative Finance are as follows [Der04]:

> Quants and their cohorts practice "financial engineering" — an awkward neologism coined to describe the jumble of activities that would better be termed *quantitative finance*. The subject is an interdisciplinary mix of physics-inspired models, mathematical techniques, and computer science, all aimed at the valuation of financial securities. The best quantitative finance brings real insight into the relation between value and uncertainty, and it approaches the quality of real science; the worst is a pseudoscientific hodgepodge of complex mathematics used with obscure justification.

The models built by the pioneering quants started to gain traction in the financial industry. In 1992, the International Association of Financial Engineers (IAFE)[2] was founded, and the first issue of IAFE's *Journal of Derivatives* appeared in fall 1993. Suddenly, Wall Street needed more quants to build pricing models.

---

[1]According to the Merriam-Webster online dictionary at http://www.merriam-webster.com/dictionary/quant, the first known use of the word "quant" is in 1979. The dictionary defines quant as an expert at analyzing and managing quantitative data.

[2]The association changed its name to International Association for Quantitative Finance in 2013.

To cater to this growing need, specialized master programs in financial engineering, computational finance, and the likes, started to sprout in the early 1990s, and rapidly spread across the North America, Europe, and Asia.

A second generation of quants and their stories on Wall Street are lucidly captured in "The Quants" [Pat10]. Here, statistical arbitrage, i.e., money making, the inner circle *business*, which eluded Derman and his friends, takes center stage. This time round, quants are math whizzes or computer scientists who develop sophisticated systems to trade securities around the world, or price financial instruments such as securities related to mortgages. On the back of the *huge* amount of profit generated, quants emerged as a very powerful group on Wall Street before the 2008 financial crisis.[3]

During the few years leading to the bursting of the housing bubble in the U.S., having quants within the sell-side division and at the buy-side front desks became an in thing. It was suspected that financial institutions sometimes employed quants to attract business because other banks were doing so profitably. Amid the feverish housing market, the demand for quants was so overwhelming that PhDs in engineering and actuary science were also enlisted to price the mortgage-backed securities, collateral debt obligations, and complex credit derivatives.

1.2   The 2008 Global Financial Crisis and Quantitative Finance

Not surprisingly, the blame for the near collapse of the global financial system fell on the quants. "The formula that felled Wall St" by Jones,[4] "Recipe for Disaster: The Formula That Killed Wall

---

[3]The article by Patterson "The Minds Behind the Meltdown" is available at http://online.wsj.com/news/articles/SB10001424052748704509704575019032416 477138 dated January 22, 2010.

[4]Jones' article is available at http://www.ft.com/cms/s/0/912d85e8-2d75-11de-9eba-00144feabdc0.html dated April 24, 2009.

Street" by Salmon,[5] "Maths geniuses and meltdown" by Witzel,[6] "Do Blame The Quants" by Portela,[7] just to name a few, dramatize how the models completely failed to reflect the risks in complex credit derivatives. Obliquely, the arrows of blame were shot at the model builders, namely, the quants, who had not been professional in their work and ethical conduct. Two quant models, in particular, Gaussian copula and value-at-risk metric, ran the gauntlet of severe criticism by acrimonious antagonists and detractors.

Taleb, one of the most vocal critics, put himself in the shoes of a philosophical birder. He spotted the metaphorical Black Swans *before* the 2008 financial crisis [Tal07] and cried out as a lone voice in the wilderness:

> Globalization creates interlocking fragility, while reducing volatility and giving the appearance of stability. In other words it creates devastating Black Swans. We have never lived before under the threat of a global collapse. Financial Institutions have been merging into a smaller number of very large banks. Almost all banks are interrelated. So the financial ecology is swelling into gigantic, incestuous, bureaucratic banks — when one fails, they all fall. The increased concentration among banks seems to have the effect of making financial crises less likely, but when they happen they are more global in scale and hit us very hard.

The concentration and contagion risks in Taleb's warning and prediction[8] were eerily spot on. Taleb was an option trader and intriguingly, a quant as well, but of a different kind. To a critical thinker and trader like him, no model is better than wrong model; all Gaussian models are deadly wrong, useless, and dangerous.

---

[5]Salmon's article is available at http://archive.wired.com/techbiz/it/magazine/17-03/wp_quant dated February 23, 2009.

[6]Witzel's article is available at http://www.ft.com/intl/cms/s/0/341d5432-76d6-11de-b23c-00144feabdc0.html dated July 22, 2009.

[7]Portela's article is available at http://www.forbes.com/2008/12/08/shreve-quants-derivatives-oped-cx_ptp_1209portela.html dated December 9, 2008.

[8]On Taleb's official website at http://www.fooledbyrandomness.com, a post with the title "The Black Swan: Quotes & Warnings that the Imbeciles Chose to Ignore" (http://www.fooledbyrandomness.com/imbeciles.htm) states that the Black Swam was written between 2003 and 2006. Other quotes that fit the description of the 2008 crisis are also highlighted in that post.

In an op-ed article published in October 2007 (The pseudo-science hurting markets[9]), Taleb took on almost all Nobel laureates who are deemed by the main stream to have accomplished breakthrough contributions to Quantitative Finance for advancing what he considers at best a pseudo-science. In Taleb's mind, his black swan model or philosophy is not compatible with modern portfolio theory and capital asset pricing model. These two frameworks of risk and return have, in his words, "the empirical and scientific validity of astrology (without the aesthetics)." He also took issue with the option pricing formula of Robert Merton and Myron Scholes (and Fischer Black but he passed away), as well as Engle's ARCH model of volatility forecast, for which they were awarded the Nobel prize. Taleb asserted that option traders never used these formulas and models in day-to-day trading. In a diatribe, he also accused the IAFE for partaking of the cover-up and for promoting the pseudo-science of these models of Quantitative Finance (see Taleb's foreword for Triana's book [Tri09]). Surely Taleb had given and continues to give these Nobel laureates a run for their prize money.

Traders are trained and conditioned daily by the rigor (which is an understatement) of P&L (profit & loss). They know instinctively that the market is almost always right, because it is *real* and their money is at stake. On the other hand, quants, financial mathematicians especially, are trained to abide by the mathematical rigor. Their original models, methodologies, and solutions are their intellectual babies. But majority of pragmatic investors probably have more faith in a senior trader with years of market experience to advise them than to attempt to understand quants' models that amount to nothing more than gibberish.

1.3   Fallacy of Prediction: White Kiwi

To present a balanced perspective, it is educational to read an op-ed by Taleb and Spitznagel in the *Financial Times*: Time to tackle the real

---

[9]Taleb's article is available at http://www.ft.com/intl/cms/s/0/4eb6ae86-8166-11dc-a351-0000779fd2ac.html dated October 23, 2007.

evil: too much debt.[10] On July 13, 2009 7:11 pm, they sounded the alarm bell and warned:

> But running a government deficit is dangerous, as it is vulnerable to errors in projections of economic growth. These errors will be larger in the future, so central bank money creation will lead not to inflation but to hyper-inflation, as the system is set for bigger deviations than ever before.

But their prediction in 2009 of an apparently imminent hyper-inflation caused by central bank money creation did not materialize despite three rounds of quantitative easing by the Federal Reserve and other G7 nations. Since the beginning of the financial market turmoil in August 2007, the Federal Reserve's balance sheet has grown in size. Total assets have increased significantly from $2,005,627 million on July 1, 2009 to $4,377,031 million on July 2, 2014 (see the statistics published by the Board of Governors of the Federal Reserve System[11]). But over these 5 years, the annual inflation rates were 2.7%, 1.5%, 3.0%, 1.7% and 1.5%, respectively. By all account, these figures are no way near the description of a hyper-inflation. No wonder defectors started to appear.[12]

Like the 2008 crisis prediction, Taleb–Spitznagel's prediction does not have an "expiry" date. If you wait long enough, may be 10 to 50 years from 2014, hyper-inflation in the U.S. may occur. But that does not mean that they have correctly predicted hyper-inflation. Otherwise, it is no different from any man on the street can predict a big earthquake or volcano eruption. If a black swan is spotted, it could well be luck.

Given the aggressive quantitative easing to tackle the fall-out from the U.S. housing market, Taleb had joined some other economists to forecast hyper-inflation. But the market reality is that

---

[10]Their article is available at http://www.ft.com/intl/cms/s/0/4e02aeba-6fd8-11de-b835-00144feabdc0.html dated July 13, 2009.

[11]The balance sheet statistics are available at http://www.federalreserve.gov/monetarypolicy/bst_recenttrends.htm.

[12]See an article "Nassim Taleb used to be my hero. But today, he's just plain wrong" by John Aziz at http://theweek.com/article/index/254694/nassim-taleb-used-to-be-my-hero-but-today-hes-just-plain-wrong dated January 6, 2014.

inflation in the U.S. 5 years after the forecast remains low even though money creation has climbed to the historical record of astronomical $4.4 trillion, and was projected to climb even higher. It seems that the boomerang of "astrology" allegation has come a full circle to the black swan birder.

Low inflation is generally good for the main street. The low interest rate environment despite astronomical quantitative easing presents an upside surprise to the hyper-inflation sayers. As an opposite analogy to the black swan for unexpected downside extreme event, you might as well have a *white kiwi* for unexpected *upside* extreme event in this episode of "hyper-inflation" prediction.

What can we take away from this story that unfolds before us? Bradford Hill, a statistician in the clinical research field, quips [Roy56],

> Alas, it is always dangerous to prophesy, particulary, as the Danish proverb[13] says, about the future.

By definition, rare, extremal events are few. Most if not all statistical tools are powerless to capture its very nature and essence. It follows that any claim to a "correct" warning of black swan or white kiwi cannot be validated statistically.

That said, and to make it absolutely clear, we are not saying that all predictions are futile astrological pursuits for attention. Like weather forecasts, there is value for economists and strategists to make *quantitative* predictions such as earnings per share, 12-month price targets, non-farm payrolls, inflation, and so on. These forecasts come with a time frame and definite numbers for the market to form a consensus on an accounting or economic number to be announced in due course. In this light, qualitative prophesies of events such as financial crisis or hyper-inflation are scientifically meaningful if a time horizon and the probability of happening are also provided.

---

[13]An aphorism attributable to a few people including the Danish physicist, Niels Bohr. He is supposed to have said, "It is difficult to make predictions, especially about the future."

Otherwise, it is better to leave black swans and white kiwis to birders and ornithologists.

1.4   Beat the Market

If there is any holy grail in Quantitative Finance, it has got to be the ultimate investment and trading system to beat the market systematically and consistently. There are at least two ways to go about doing it; either somehow obtain private information about the company, or forecast the price direction and magnitude of change. The private information way is illegal. The forecasting way is impossible, according to the devotees of efficient market hypothesis, because prices fully reflect all available information at any given time.

To demonstrate a counterexample to this hypothesis, suppose it is equally likely to make or lose money every year for 1,024 institutional funds. By pure chance over 10 years, one of these funds might have all 10 years making money since the probability is

$$\left(\frac{1}{2}\right)^{10} = \frac{1}{1024}.$$

Moreover, since there are 10 possible options to choose one of the 10 years to be a losing year, 10 funds might have 9 winning years. Similarly, 45 funds might have 8 profitable years. Regardless of skills and investment strategies, like coin flipping, 56 out of 1,024 funds might have at least 8 good years out of 10 years. Are these 56 funds simply lucky? Do they really have an edge to beat the market?

On this basis, 10 years may not be enough to distinguish skill from luck. What about 25 years? Consider the legendary Medallion Fund, which was started in March 1988 by a decorated mathematician of pure math background — James Simons.[14] The Medallion

---

[14]Read "Seeker, Doer, Giver, Ponderer: A Billionaire Mathematicians Life of Ferocious Curiosity" at http://www.nytimes.com/2014/07/08/science/a-billionaire-mathematicians-life-of-ferocious-curiosity.html?_r=0, which is a brief biography of James Simons.

Fund's money sucking performance is considered the best in the hedge fund industry. From 1988 to 2012 (inclusive), only 1 out of these 25 years is a down year, albeit marginally. What are the odds for a hedge fund such as the Medallion Fund to achieve the feat? Assuming again equal likelihood to make or to lose money, the probability is 7.45×10^{-7}, i.e., less than 1 in 1.3 million funds. In other words, the probability of wrongly rejecting the efficient market hypothesis is less than one in a million.

Two possibilities of this extremal phenomenon come to mind. Either Medallion Fund is a well cover-up scam, or James Simon and his Renaissance Technologies really have that something to beat the market. In a 2007 plenary speech,[15] James Simons vaguely revealed the secrets behind the success of Renaissance Technologies. He made the following points:

> We began to bring in some mathematicians and scientists and built models. And then more people came in and we built more models. Then the business got better and better, and over the years, we have been enormously successful and made a ton of money — I have to confess.

If the competitiveness and stellar records of Renaissance Technologies are anything to go by, it seems that investing and decision making can be improved by Quantitative Finance.

On the other hand, the misfortune of funds that are forced to become defunct prematurely may be due to either bad luck — as the fund founders and sympathizers are prone to lament — or the failure of risk management under extreme stress. Perhaps the investment strategies may need a little bit more time to pan out. But time is not on their side when financial distress mounts. Take the Long Term Capital Management (LTCM) for example. This is quite a black swan story. LTCM touted itself as "the financial technology" company. It was founded by John W. Meriwether, a skillful, seasoned trader who rose to the rank of vice chair and head of bond trading at an investment bank (Salomon Brothers). Two Nobel

---

[15]The transcript is downloadable from http://www.nga.org/files/live/sites/NGA/files/pdf/2007NGAWinterMeeting.pdf.

laureates and five PhDs from MIT were among the LTCM partners. Based on their luminary credentials, experience, and *galáctico* status, LTCM sure had no lack of skills and prowess. For the first 4 years since inception in 1994, the cumulative gain was more than 300%. By all standards, 300% was a great run. But LTCM came to a drastic halt when the Russian Government defaulted on its government bonds.

The trading strategies LTCM primarily used were based on statistical arbitrage, which is essentially finding and picking up nickels scattered on the railroad tracks. Although details differ, one of LTCM's trading strategies was similar to Edward Thorp's scientific system to beat the market [TK67]. Thorp is a Professor of mathematics, gambler, trader, and fund manager, all in one person. He developed probabilistic and statistical models to beat the market. Putting theories into practice, his hedge funds and personal portfolio were profitable in *each* of the 42 years from 1966 to 2008, according to his brief biography.[16] Thorp's white kiwi is a solid counterexample to the conjecture of market efficiency. The probability of this counterexample falsely rejecting the efficient market hypothesis is less than 1 in a trillion. Mathematically and scientifically, a hypothesis or conjecture must be rejected if a counterexample is found.

What can we learn from these three short stories about the Medallion Fund, LTCM, and Thorp? One takeaway is that despite the LTCM saga, mathematical modeling remains a useful approach to create an edge for trading and investment. In fact, majority of the people in the three stories are mathematicians with the desire to experiment with their theories in the jungle out there. Descending from the ivory tower, they voluntarily subject their ideas and models to, as it were, the survival test in the hunger game.

But mathematical modeling, though necessary, is not sufficient to guarantee success. Worst of all, as the example of LTCM demonstrates, mathematical models and financial economics may provide

---

[16]Thorp's biography is obtainable from his own website http://edward othorp.com/sitebuildercontent/sitebuilderfiles/bio.doc.

a greater sense of security than warranted. On this note, it is educational to hear what a legend of futures markets, Leo Melamed, has to say.[17]

> Listen, academics, as a rule, make terrible traders. So for me, to think that I'm gonna listen to their theories about trading, I beg to differ.

Despite the "terrible trader" remark, Melamed had a friend in the academia: Milton Friedman, a famous economics Professor and Nobel laureate. Melamed is better known not so much as the market beater. But his best trade was to pay Friedman $7,500 to write a paper, so that it could and did help him to *create* an exchange market for futures on foreign currencies.[18] Melamed was one of the driving forces that transformed the butter-and-egg Chicago Mercantile Exchange into the CME Group today. By any measure, CME Group is the largest and most diverse futures exchange in the world. Its market value is about $25 billion as of August 2014. For a fee of $7,500 to pave the way for creating the entirely new markets for trading futures on financial products, Melamed, the market creator, had surely gotten a "yummy" trade.

1.5 Topics and Prospects of Quantitative Finance

The real stories told thus far set the tone for this book. One common thread connecting these stories is the fact that the main characters in the stories are experts in different fields and backgrounds: Economist, financial economist, mathematician, physicist, quant, and yes, industry-leading practitioner. This connection of diversity speaks volume of the multi-disciplinary nature of Quantitative Finance.

---

[17]See the transcript of BBC documentary "The Midas Formula" at http://www.bbc.co.uk/science/horizon/1999/midas_script.shtml, broadcast on December 2, 1999. The documentary is viewable on youtube at http://www.youtube.com/watch?v=4auzn4bK1bM.

[18]See Melamed's speech, "If It's Good Enough for Milton" at http://www.leomelamed.com/essays/07-Friedman-oral.htm dated January 29, 2007.

As an additional evidence, a check on the *Encyclopedia of Quantitative Finance*[19] turns up a list of topics, including

- Asset pricing models
- Financial econometrics
- Asset allocation and portfolio management
- Option pricing: fundamentals
- Derivatives
  — Credit derivatives
  — Energy and commodity derivatives
  — Equity derivatives
  — Foreign exchange derivatives
  — Interest rate derivatives
- Risk management
- Market microstructure

These topics overlap substantially with Finance. That said, derivatives, option pricing models, and risk management these days are not as popular in Finance as before. The reasons are many, multifaceted, and intertwined. We offer two plausible ones.

First and foremost, a vast majority of the *fundamental* derivative pricing models have already been proposed. What ensues is mopping-up operation. In the preface of his book [Duf01], Darrell Duffie assesses the situation as follows:

> To someone who came out of graduate school in the mid-eighties, the decade spanning roughly 1969–1979 seems like a golden age of dynamical asset pricing theory.
>
> ⋮
>
> Theory developments in the period since 1979, with relative few exceptions, have been a mopping-up operation.

This frank assessment by an accomplished financial economist — winner of 2003 Financial Engineer of the Year — did take the sheen off the glamor of theorization in Finance. In its place, three subfields

---

[19]The outlines are available at http://onlinelibrary.wiley.com/book/10.1002/9780470061602/topics.

of corporate, empirical, and behavioral finance take center stage, and to a lesser degree, market microstructure.

Second, risk management *per se*, more like a cost center than generating revenues, has never been in the mainstream to begin with. From the business perspective, however, risk management is the necessary evil, thanks to the regulatory requirements. Regarded more as an operational unit of a financial institution, risk management is not a popular research topic among academics.

By contrast, it is not an overstatement that pricing derivatives and managing their risks are the bread and butter of Quantitative Finance. Practitioners deal with pricing and risk models on the daily basis, and apply them in the commercial setting. Moreover, for asset management, there can be no consistent profit generation without a proper risk management framework, processes, and effective enforcement.

The topics in the *Encyclopedia of Quantitative Finance* that really set the Quantitative Finance apart from Finance include

- Arbitrage theory
- Mathematical tools (mainly stochastic processes)
- Actuarial methods
- Partial differential equations and computational methods
- Simulation methods in financial engineering

Arbitrage theory and mathematical methods have been, and still are being developed by financial mathematicians and mathematical economists. The subject matters covered under these two topics are rarely treated in the mainstream Finance textbooks. Actuarial methods and partial differential equations are truly applied mathematics, which are almost absent in Finance. Finally, the topic on computational and simulation methods exemplifies the practice-oriented nature of Quantitative Finance.

The mathematical frameworks, models, and methods in Quantitative Finance illustrated in the Encyclopedia are used by quants regularly. What roles do quants fulfill in practice? More importantly, what are the quant jobs out there for quant wannabes? Probably this is the burning question that need to be addressed adequately first. We organize the quant jobs into four major categories:

- Quantitative researcher/analyst/strategist
- Quantitative risk analyst/manager
- Quantitative developer
- Quantitative associate (such as sales, trading, and consultancy)

Obviously, the *Encyclopedia of Quantitative Finance* is not meant to cover the programming languages used by quantitative professionals. As far as industry practice is concerned, most big firms have their own proprietary systems to price derivatives and fixed income securities, and to manage their exposures. Nevertheless, for quantitative developer, knowledge and mastery of general-purpose programming languages such as C and C++ are critical. On top of that, the ability to write codes on Unix-like systems such as Linux is crucial too. But for quantitative researchers and risk analysts, higher level languages such as R, Python, and MATLAB are the ones typically used during the research and development stage. Finally, Excel and VBA programming are the basics for any quants.

Being introductory in nature, it goes without saying that this book by no means offers to cover all these topics and programming languages. Instead, it provides an entry-level pathway to Quantitative Finance for senior undergraduates, specialized master program students, and practitioners who want to deepen their knowledge on how models actually work, beyond using them as black boxes. The pre-requisites for this book is a working knowledge of probability & statistics and calculus, at the college level.

Compared to Finance, the learning curve for Quantitative Finance is steeper because of its mathematical and computational nature. To provide you with the motivation to get started, let us hear what James Simons had said about the trends of quants in his 2007 plenary speech:

> Now, a lot has happened since Sputnik went up and the days of the National Defense Education Act. The world's whole economic engine now is not just defense, but increasingly based on math and science.

> You know, from Genentech to Google to Goldman (Sachs), math & science is becoming king ...
>
> Now, there at Goldman Sachs, these scientific types are called "quants," and some of you may have heard of quants, but at Google, they're just called employees, because they're all quants ...
>
> And that's a wave of the future. I think it's THE wave of the future.

Indeed, the trend in the financial industry is increasingly dependent on high-tech information systems and networks. With this dependence comes an enormous amount of data. Demand for talents to make full use of data through the lens of quantitative models has become more entrenched than ever before. With no shortage of models to price and hedge the existing products, it is therefore necessary to be well trained in Quantitative Finance to windsurf THE wave of the future.

1.6 Exercises

Q1. Professor Nouriel Roubini, nicknamed Dr. Doom, is another prominent economist who had forecasted correctly the 2008 financial crisis. On September 7, 2006, to the laughter and scepticism from an audience of economists at the International Monetary Fund, he made a bold prediction that in the *coming months and years*, the housing market bubble would burst, mortgage-backed securities would become insecure, and the global financial system shuddering to a halt (see an article Dr. Doom[20] by Stephen Mihm).

   (a) Discuss the quality of Roubini's crisis prediction *vis-à-vis* Taleb's.
   (b) The 2008 crisis is now at our rear mirror. Since March 2009, S&P 500 index has risen dramatically, reaching record high day after day, and month after month. In an interview with

---

[20]Mihm's article is available at http://www.nytimes.com/2008/08/17/magazine/17pessimist-t.html dated August 15, 2008.

Yahoo Finance[21] on December 5, 2014, Roubini's key message, as shown in his twitter[22] remark, is as follows:

We are in an asset bubble but it won't pop till 2016.

In the same breadth, with a line in the same tweet, Roubini asks, "When will the bubble burst?" What is your opinion concerning this prediction or prophesy of Dr. Doom?

Q2. How many combinations are there in picking k unordered outcomes from n possibilities? The answer to this question is known as the binomial coefficient, which is the number of combinations in choosing k items from n items. Denoted by $\binom{n}{k}$ or $_nC_k$, the number of "n choose k" is computed by the following formula:

$$\binom{n}{k} := \frac{n!}{k!(n-k)!} =: {}_nC_k.$$

Assuming equal likelihood to make or to lose money, verify that the probability of Medallion Fund's performance is 7.45×10^{-7}.

Q3. The legendary fund manager Peter Lynch was in charge of an actively managed mutual fund called the Magellan Fund between 1977 and 1990. Over the decade of 1980, the asset under management (AUM) increased phenomenally from $18 million to $13 billion, almost a thousand fold.

(a) In these 13 years, only one year had a negative total return. Assuming equal likelihood of positive and negative returns, what is the probability of his feat?

(b) For the 52 quarters during the tenure of Lynch, 14 quarters were in the red. Again, assuming equal likelihood of positive and negative returns, what is the probability of his quarterly performance?

---

[21]The interview is available at http://finance.yahoo.com/video/roubini-u-equities-strong-until-135802011.html, dated December 4, 2014.
[22]Roubini's twitter account is https://twitter.com/Nouriel/status/540953369557610496.

  (c) Is quarterly performance more impressive than the annual performance? Explain.

Q4. Over the same period from 1977 to 1990 when Peter Lynch was in charge of the Magellan Fund, the total return of S&P 500 index had only three negative annual returns. In other words, the whole stock market was in a bull run.

  (a) A fund manager adopts the follow-the-market approach. Assuming that the market is equally likely to move up and to move down, what is the probability of the annual performance delivered by this follow-the-market strategy?

  (b) Is the assumption of equal likelihood of positive and negative returns still valid?

  (c) In light of the bull run, was Peter Lynch (see Q3) lucky to be the fund manager at the right time, or was he skillful in picking stocks?

Q5. A stock mutual fund's performance is usually measured relative to a stock index such as the S&P 500 index. For a start, consider simply the difference between the return on the fund and the return on the S&P 500 index over the same period of time. If the difference is positive, the fund is said to have out-performed the market, and vice versa. Suppose N years of annual differences d_i are collected since the fund inception. Let us compute the sample average of these N differences and also their standard deviation. First, you look at the ratio of the sample average over the standard deviation, which measures the variability in each difference from the sample average.

$$\rho := \frac{\text{sample average}}{\text{sample standard deviation}}.$$

The sample average is computed by the formula:

$$\text{sample average} = \frac{1}{N} \sum_{i=1}^{N} d_i =: \bar{d},$$

and the sample standard deviation is computed as follows:

$$\text{sample standard deviation} = \sqrt{\frac{1}{N-1} \sum_{i=1}^{N} (d_i - \bar{d})^2}.$$

Next, we compute the t statistic:

$$t = \sqrt{N} \times \rho.$$

As a rule of thumb in practice, a t statistic greater than 2 would indicate that the fund has consistently beaten the market, which is based on skill and not luck. Suppose 35 years of differences are obtained. The sample average difference is 2.49% with a standard deviation of 8.21%.

(a) What is the value of the t statistic?

(b) With the same ρ value, how many more years are needed for the fund to qualify as a skillful fund?

Q6. Suppose one in 100 actively managed mutual funds in the database is truly based on skill and not luck. Moreover, suppose a statistical test can diagnose the difference between skill and luck. If a fund's return is due to skill, there is a 99% chance of testing positive. If a fund's return is not based on skill but luck, the probability of testing negative is also 99%. A mutual fund is randomly drawn from the database.

(a) It is tested positive. What is the probability that the mutual fund manager is skillful?

(b) It is tested negative. What is the probability that the mutual fund manager is lucky?

Chapter 2

Brief Introduction to Four Major Asset Classes

2.1   Introduction

In simple terms, financial assets endow monetary values and utilities to the asset owners, giving them the freedom to re-invest, spend, donate, and whatsoever the owners want to do. A financial asset is either cash itself, or a legal contract called security, which mandates cash and other benefits to be transferred from one party to the other party according to the contractual terms and conditions. To own or hold an asset, the buyer typically has to pay for it. The seller, on the other hand, receives cash for liquidating the asset. With the advancements in information technology, zillions of asset transactions can now take place in the financial markets all over the world.

There are many types of financial securities but the following four asset classes are the major ones:

A. Equity or stock;
B. Currency or foreign exchange;
C. Commodity;
D. Fixed income or debt instrument.

A criterion used for selecting these four asset classes is that they are primarily the underlying assets on which derivatives are written. Derivatives are securities whose values depend on or derive from

other securities. By contrast, the values of these four asset classes
in general depend on the economic, financial, social, political, technological, weather, and many other external conditions directly.
Another criterion is the volume of transactions and liquidity. These
four asset classes are liquid, investable and tradable by both institutional and retail investors/traders.

It goes without saying that a detailed discourse of each of these
asset classes requires a separate book; by no means will the following sections do justice to the subject matter. Nonetheless, they provide an overall picture and pave the way for understanding the data
characteristics of different asset classes.

2.2   Stocks

A stock is a form of capital raised by a corporation through the issue
of shares entitling holders to a partial ownership of the firm. Being
co-owners of a company, shareholders typically have one vote per
share to exert their influence over the company affairs. Shareholders
are also entitled to receive dividends in proportion to the number of
shares held. By construction, owning a company through common
stock comes with zero liability. If the company fails, shareholders
are not answerable to the liabilities of the company. From the standpoint of financial accounting, a common stock provides ownership
over the equity (rather than asset) of the firm, which is whatever
leftover of the asset after liability is subtracted.

The stock market facilitates the transfer of company ownership.
Without the stock market, the world would be very different from
what it is now. Start-up companies would be greatly hampered by
the lack of sufficient funds to expand and grow their businesses.
Entrepreneurial ventures would be much less active. Wealth and job
creation would be at a much lower level and slower pace. Therefore,
stocks are powerful financial instruments, providing incentives to
would-be entrepreneurs to work toward their goals. Stocks are the
necessary ingredients to advance the development and adoption of
new and appropriate technology, which leads to superior goods and
services for consumers.

Shareholders who need cash urgently can give up their ownership by selling their shares in the stock market. For every seller, there is a buyer. Therefore, trading is possible only if market participants have opposing needs and views. Everything else being equal, buyers strive to buy at the lowest possible price and sellers seek to sell at the highest price possible. This tug-of-war between buyers and sellers brings forth a stock price at any given time.

The myriad transactions in the stock markets may be regarded as many "experiments" to assess the value of a tradable stock by its price. It turns out, however, that the value of a stock is rather elusive if not ghostly. In an article entitled *Noise*, Fischer Black [Bla86] writes:

> All estimates of value are noisy, so we can never know how far away price is from value.

Being noisy, no wonder many "experiments" have to be repeatedly performed day after day to estimate and re-estimate the value.

Moreover, a quote generally attributed to Keynes goes like this:

> The market can stay irrational longer than you can stay solvent.

By using the word "irrational," presumably Keynes is alluding to the situation where the current market price is distant from some kind of "fundamental" or "intrinsic" value. In a monumental book [Key36], Keynes goes further. He argues that even "professional" investment is like, in his days, those newspaper competitions to select six prettiest faces from a hundred photographs. To win, the competitors must have their selected faces most nearly correspond to the average preferences of the competitors as a whole. Keynes writes,

> It is not a case of choosing those that, to the best of one's judgment, are really the prettiest, nor even those that average opinion genuinely thinks the prettiest. We have reached the third degree where we devote our intelligences to anticipating what average opinion expects the average opinion to be. And there are some, I believe, who practice the fourth, fifth and higher degrees.

According to Keynes' insight, stock selection transcends beyond ascertaining the fundamental value of a stock. In Keynes' beauty contest analogy, investment based on "fundamental analysis" corresponds to the first-degree strategy: The prettiest in your own view. A more sophisticated investor will consider also the crowd's consensus of the fundamental value, which is the second-degree strategy. And the third-degree strategy is to also anticipate whether most investors will adopt the second-degree approach to select stocks. Most likely, investors have different levels of sophistication and the value of a stock is a stochastically moving target. This complex system of heterogeneous belief formation processes with differing investment horizons inevitably results in stock price fluctuation.

From the investment and trading perspective, the profit and loss (P&L) for a round-trip transaction per share is simply the difference between the selling price and the buying price.

$$\text{P\&L per share} = \text{selling price} - \text{buying price}.$$

For a start, dividends, commissions, taxes, and other costs associated with the trade are omitted. If the P&L is positive, the investor gains from capital appreciation. Conversely, if the P&L is negative, capital depreciation is said to have occurred, as the selling price is less than the buying price.

How economically significant is the P&L, say $0.5 per share? To answer this question, it is natural to consider the P&L relative to the buying price paid for the investment, and we define the simple return as the ratio

$$\text{simple return} := \frac{\text{P\&L}}{\text{buying price}} = \frac{\text{selling price} - \text{buying price}}{\text{buying price}}.$$
(2.1)

Depending on the buying price, the simple return will be different even for the same amount of P&L. For example, a P&L of $0.5 will be 10% when the buying price is $5 per share, whereas it is a mere 0.1% when the buying price is $500.

Suppose the number of shares invested is N. The P&L in dollars is

$$\text{P\&L} = N \times \text{selling price} - N \times \text{buying price}.$$
(2.2)

In this expression, the total amount invested in dollars is $N \times$ buying price, and the proceeds from sale is $N \times$ selling price. The P&L is said to be amplified by N, literally. By contrast, the simple return is invariant to the trade size N:

$$\frac{N \times \text{selling price} - N \times \text{buying price}}{N \times \text{buying price}} = \frac{\text{P\&L}}{\text{buying price}}.$$

The two formulas (2.1) and (2.2) may seem trivial. But you shall see in the next section that it is not as straightforward when you want to compute the P&L and the simple return from round-trip forex transactions.

2.3 Currencies

In comparison to the stock market, modern-day foreign exchange market emerged relatively recently in August 1971 when the Bretton Woods system of exchange rates broke down. Currencies of the developed nations began to be floated rather than pegged to the U.S. dollar.

Since then, the volume of foreign exchange transactions has grown tremendously. In the first triennial central bank survey by the Bank for International Settlement (BIS), the average daily volume of spot forex transactions was $123 billion in 1986. In the eighth triennial survey 24 years later, the volume was $1,832 billion every day.[1] In terms of this nominal trade value, the forex market is the largest of all financial markets. Operating round the clock throughout the week, the forex market is very active, and each transaction between two financial institutions is typically well over a million dollars.

The phenomenal growth of spot forex transactions could be driven by increasing world trades and cross-border investments. For instance, importers are required to pay for the foreign goods and services in foreign currency. They need to convert their domestic currency into a currency specified by their counterparts.

---

[1] Average daily volume in 1986 is reported in Table 2B of a BIS report [BIS96]. The corresponding 2010 statistic is taken from another BIS report [vKMMG10] authored by von Kleist *et al.*

Trans-national flows of investment funds also require foreign exchange to settle the deal. Furthermore, investors and speculators trade currencies directly to profit from the movements in the currency exchange rates. Commercial and investment banks trade currencies as a service for their customers. These financial institutions also generally participate in the currency market for hedging and proprietary trading purposes. Last but not least, attempting to adjust economic or financial imbalances, governments and central banks trade currencies to intervene in the forex market. Countries such as Singapore use foreign exchange as a monetary policy tool to balance inflation and economic growth.

The forex market is typically made by dealers who stand ready to trade and thereby provide liquidity to the consumers and institutions. As an over-the-counter (OTC) market, transactions are conducted between any two parties who agree to trade via the telephone and other electronic network. Dealers often "advertise" their exchange rates using a communication network, which recently includes internet on computers and mobile devices.

To the dealers, currencies are like goods. They commit their own money to raise an inventory of currencies so that they can sell at a higher price. Institutional dealers such as banks and small-time money changers are market makers. The standard practice in this market is that the exchange rate is quoted for immediate delivery of the currency (within two working days). For this reason, the quoted exchange rate for spot delivery is therefore called the spot rate.

The forex market is a quote-driven market. Acting as market makers, dealers quote the exchange rates for a currency pair using ISO codes. For example, EUR/USD refers to euro and U.S. dollar, respectively. The first currency before the slash is referred to as the base currency, and the second as the quote currency.

Base Currency/Quote Currency.

According to this format or market practice, dealers make the market by buying one unit of base currency at a lower bid price quoted before the slash. They sell one unit of base currency at a higher ask price quoted after the slash. The rates are denominated in the quote currency.

For example, suppose a dealer bids to buy one euro by paying $1.0923 and offers to sell one euro by asking for $1.0927. The quotes published by the dealer will be

$$EUR/USD = 1.0923/27.$$

The bid price before the slash is the price for every euro that the dealers are buying from their customers. Up to four decimal points, the customers obtain $1.0923 per euro. The second currency after the slash is dealers' ask price. This price is the amount the customer pays in dollars when buying one euro. Under this abbreviated convention, the ask price is obtained by increasing the bid price until the last two decimal places are equal to the digits after the slash. In this example, the ask price is $1.0927. In another example, suppose the quotes are published as

$$EUR/USD = 1.0998/03.$$

The bid price is now $1.0998. The ask price is not $1.0903 but $1.1003 instead. Dealers' ask price is always higher than the bid price.

The market practice is that USD is always the base currency except for the following four currencies:

- Euro: EUR;
- British Pound: GBP;
- Australian Dollar: AUD;
- New Zealand Dollar: NZD.

Interestingly, dealers trade these currencies by their nicknames: Fiber for EUR, Sterling for GBP, Aussie for AUD, and Kiwi for NZD. The U.S. dollar is nicknamed the Greenback or Buck, Swiss franc the Swissy, Canadian dollar the Loonie, and so on.

Now, the notion of currency is something akin to trading a "share" of an asset. Each country or a region has its own currency. From the standpoint of an investor domiciled in a particular country, the currencies of all the other countries can be considered as "stocks." In fact, the foreign exchange rate is the *price* of one unit of foreign currency. Suppose you are an investor in Singapore, and you think that the Japanese yen will appreciate against the Singapore dollar. So you buy 1 million Japanese yens. Suppose ¥100 costs 1.45

Singapore dollars. You pay S$14,500 for a million yens. In a sense, you buy 10,000 "shares" of JPY in units of 100 yens. A few months later, the exchange rate becomes ¥100 for S$1.52, which suggests that the Japanese yen has appreciated against the Singapore dollar. You sell your holding of Japanese yens, and the profit is, according to (2.2),

$$¥1,000,000 \times (0.0152 - 0.0145) = S\$700.00.$$

The return you have realized in Singapore dollars is, according to definition (2.1),

$$\frac{0.0152 - 0.0145}{0.0145} = 4.8276\%.$$

Next, suppose you anticipate the British pound to depreciate against the Singapore dollar. Though you do not have any British pound, you can easily "short sell" GBP through your online forex trading account. In this case, you are said to have taken a short position on GBP. Suppose a pound is selling for S$2.05 and you short sell £10,000 to obtain S$20,500. Suppose the British pound indeed depreciates against the Singapore dollar and drops to S$1.99 per pound. You buy back the British pound at this rate. The selling price is S$1/1.99 in this transaction and the buy-back price is S$1/2.05. In this example, the transaction volume is S$20,500 from the short seller's viewpoint because the buying and selling rates are in pounds per Singapore dollar. Hence, the P&L is, in pounds

$$S\$20,500 \times \left(\frac{1}{1.99} - \frac{1}{2.05} \right) = £301.51.$$

In contrast to the earlier example involving the Japanese yens, you sell first and then buy back the British pound. To compute the P&L, the order of transaction (buy first or sell first) does not matter. All that is needed, is to know the volume, and what the buying and selling prices are. Correspondingly, the return realized in British pounds is

$$\frac{\frac{1}{1.99} - \frac{1}{2.05}}{\frac{1}{2.05}} = 3.0151\%.$$

What about the P&L in Singapore dollars? To answer this question, first we note that short selling GBP is equivalent to buying SGD. Recognizing this fact, the trade volume is no longer S$20,500 but £10,000. So, the P&L is

$$£10,000 \times (2.05 - 1.99) = S\$600.$$

Applying (2.1), the return in Singapore dollars is computed, and as anticipated, we obtain

$$\frac{2.05 - 1.99}{1.99} = 3.0151\%.$$

As shown earlier, the P&L in pounds is £301.51 and the amount of £10,000 is involved. The ratio of these two numbers in pounds is 3.0151%, which coincides with the earlier return calculation. Interestingly, however, in Singapore dollar terms, the P&L of S$600 divided by S$20,500 is 2.9268%. Which of the two ratios is correct? It turns out that 2.9268% corresponds to the ratio of P&L divided by the selling price of 2.05 rather than the buying price of 1.99 and hence incorrect. To avoid making this mistake, it is therefore important to use the earlier paradigm of short selling the British pound.

2.4 Commodities

The markets for commodities date back to the dawn of civilization. As the history unfolds, and progresses in technologies give birth to new marketplaces, investments in commodities become not only a possibility but also a thriving business. In contrast to stocks and currencies, commodities as an asset class are much less homogeneous. These days, in practice, commodities are classified into vastly different sectors as follows:

- Metals;
  - Precious metals,
  - Industrial metals,
- Energy;

- Agriculturals products;
  - — Grains and Oilseeds,
  - — Softs,
- Livestock;
- Exotics.

In stark contrast to stocks, commodities are not capital assets; they do not generate cash flows like stocks do. Moreover, commodities need warehouses for storage, and the logistic infrastructure to transport the commodities from one place to another. Being affected by weather conditions, distance, production, storage, transportation availability and costs, etc., physical delivery of a commodity is by no means trivial. To complicate matters, commodities in the agricultural sector are subject to putrefaction, and livestock is also vulnerable to diseases. Dealers, who purchase the commodities directly from producers bear these risks for a presumably high chance of a profit.

Prices of commodities are *qualitatively* determined by the economics of supply and demand. At the macro level, rising world population and more crucially, rising standard of living are the impetus that confines the prices of commodities on the upward trajectories in the long run. In the absence of technological breakthroughs and fundamental changes in the world economy, supply of a commodity tends to be limited relative to demand. The resulting effect is inflation.

For illustration purpose, consider the precious metal, gold, which is regarded as a hedge against inflation by some investors. It is intriguing that many cultures, both ancient and modern as well as east and west, ascribe a high value to gold, the 79th element in the periodic table with a density about 19 times that of water. Gold is not a financial contract *per se* but it stores value so long as people around the world agree that it has value beyond its industrial use as material. In the form of bullion, gold is money that becomes more valuable during the state of anarchy. It serves as cross-border money even today, as it was in the past.

In September 1717, the renowned physicist Newton, in his capacity as the Master of the Royal Mint, determined that the official price

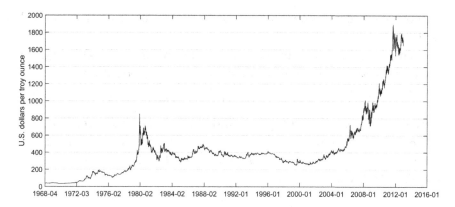

Fig. 2.1   Historical prices of gold in U.S. dollars per troy ounce since April 1968.
Source: London Bullion Market Association.

of gold was 3 pounds 17 shillings and 10 1/2 pence per troy ounce, or £3.17s.10$\frac{1}{2}$d. in short. This official price was used for about 200 years in England. The fixing of gold price by the English monetary authority became the precursor to the gold standard, which pegged currency to gold at a fixed rate. In 1816, Britain adopted the gold standard with the passing of the Coinage Act. Many countries also adopted the gold standard by the early 20th century, as cross-border trades flourished. It was not until April 1, 1968 before the gold price was allowed to float freely in the gold markets.[2] The time series of gold prices since then is shown in Figure 2.1.

On each business day, the gold price is determined by a procedure conducted by the market making members of the London Bullion Market Association (LBMA) known as Gold Fixing at 3.00 pm GMT.[3] At the year end of 1968, the gold price was $41.9. An

---

[2]A concise history of gold standard can be found on the World Gold Council's website, http://www.gold.org/.

[3]Five LBMA members conduct the Gold Fixing by telephone. Orders are placed by clients in dealing rooms of members of the Fixing who net all orders before communicating that net interest to their representative at the Fixing. The gold price is then adjusted up and down until demand and supply is matched, at which point the price is declared "Fixed" and all business is conducted on the basis of that Fixing Price. Transparency at the Fixing is served by the fact that counterparties may be kept advised of price changes, together with the level of interest, while the

explosive price increment saw the gold price reach $1,531 at the end of 2011.

What is the average growth rate r per annum over 43 years? To answer this question, we consider the following equation:

$$\$41.9 \times (1+r)^{43} = \$1,531.$$

Solving this equation for r, we find that the growth rate is about 8.7285%. From a reverse perspective, in order to receive $1,531 after 43 years and given the interest rate of 8.7285%, the principal required today is

$$\$41.9 = \frac{\$1,531}{(1+0.087285)^{43}}.$$

These calculations are numerical illustrations of the time value of money.

2.5   Fixed Income

Fixed income or debt instruments are contracts between or among borrowers and lenders. Suppose a borrower has all the credit worthiness to borrow $41.9 for 43 years at the interest rate of 8.7285% per annum. Obviously, 43 years is a long time and things will change before repayment. How much must the borrower repay the lender after 43 years? The answer is, as anticipated, $1,531. This simple example illustrates a very important concept underpinning the fixed income instruments: Credit. It is the level of trust that the creditor or the lender has for the borrower.

Without credit, it is virtually impossible to borrow money. An entity such as a bank or a sovereign state with poor credit rating need to pay investors a high interest rate. Otherwise, from the investment standpoint, the return from interest payments does not adequately compensate them for the high default risk they bear. The irony here is that when an entity is in need of money to turn around, it has to pay more money in order to borrow the money needed.

Fixing is in progress and may cancel, increase or decrease their interest dependent on this information.

The higher interest rate may aggravate the financial distress and increase the probability of default.

Another distinguishing feature of the fixed income asset class is maturity or expiration. In contrast to stock, currency, and commodity, a fixed income security has a definite date of expiration when the liability of the borrower is fully discharged. Thanks to this feature, it is much easier to estimate the value of a fixed income instrument compared to stock.

As an illustration, consider the 5-year note issued by the U.S. Treasury. This fixed income instrument has a maturity of 5 years. Before maturity, the U.S. Treasury pays the investors semi-annually a fixed amount of interest called coupon. At maturity, the investors will receive the last coupon payment and the principal sum. An investor of the 5-year note is in fact lending money to the U.S. federal government for 5 years.

After the second World War, market participants generally regard the debt securities issued by the U.S. Treasury to be virtually free of default risk. Therefore, the probability of receiving the coupons plus the repayment of principal amount A on time is very close to 100%. If the 5-year note is held to maturity, the value of the guaranteed stream of future cash flows (coupons) can be found by discounting the cash flows by a rate of return known as the yield to maturity, which is denoted by y. The present value (PV), i.e., the value today, is the sum of all the discounted future cash flows:

$$PV = \frac{C/2}{(1+y/2)^1} + \frac{C/2}{(1+y/2)^2} + \cdots + \frac{C/2}{(1+y/2)^9}$$
$$+ \frac{C/2}{(1+y/2)^{10}} + \frac{A}{(1+y/2)^{10}}.$$

In this equation, the amount in dollars invested in the 5-year note is A. Like interest rate, coupon rate c is quoted on the annualized term. So $C = Ac$ is the dollar amount of coupon payment per year for A dollars invested. The yield to maturity is annualized. Since the U.S. Treasury pays coupon semi-annually, each half year's return is $y/2$.

When the yield is given, the present value is truly the value of the 5-year note, for all market participants know and use the same formula to value the 5-year note. As a result, the price today of the 5-year note is none other than the present value PV. More generally, for an n-year default-free note or bond with a constant coupon rate c, the price P is

$$P = \frac{C}{2} \sum_{t=1}^{2n} \frac{1}{(1+y/2)^t} + \frac{A}{(1+y/2)^{2n}}. \qquad (2.3)$$

In this form, the bond price has a deceptive look of being determined entirely by the yield y. But what truly happens in the bond market is a matter of supply (seller) and demand (buyer). More sellers than buyers will see the bond price become lower, and vice versa. The formula (2.3) is merely a price-to-yield translator. Given the market price P, the yield y backed out by applying (2.3) is simply the return to the buyer if the bond is held to maturity. These days, financial calculators specially designed to solve the polynomial equation (2.3) for y are widely used. For Treasury bonds, users just need to key in the present value P, coupon cash flow per period $C/2$, and the number of periods $2n$.

An important implication is that when the bond is held till maturity, the rate of return y is known at the point of purchase by (2.3). This property is a result of the fact that all cash flows $C/2$ and A are contractually scheduled and the borrower is 100% trustworthy in paying these cash flows. By contrast, the return is not knowable for stocks, currencies, and commodities because the future prices of these asset classes are random variables.

In the fixed income market, the borrower is also known as the issuer. The standard practice is that when a n-year coupon-bearing bond is freshly issued, it is selling at the par value of 1, or 100%. To illustrate, suppose the issuer wants to raise $5 million with 5,000 certificates of this security. Then each certificate must have the face value of $1,000. Investors have to pay $1,000 for each certificate, or 100% of the face value printed on the certificate. Therefore, for every dollar of face value and given the semi-annual payment convention, the present value p in percentages is

$$p = \frac{c}{2} \sum_{i=1}^{2n} \frac{1}{(1+y/2)^i} + \frac{1}{(1+y/2)^{2n}} \times 1. \tag{2.4}$$

This par bond pays coupon at the fixed interest rate of c annually and is selling at $p = 1$.

Being a geometric series, we rewrite the pricing formula (2.4) as

$$p = \frac{c}{y} \left(1 - \frac{1}{(1+y/2)^{2n}} \right) + \frac{1}{(1+y/2)^{2n}}.$$

Note that $p \approx c/y$ when n is large. After multiplying both sides by $(1+y/2)^{2n}$ and shifting the 1 obtained from the right side to the left side, the result is

$$p(1+y/2)^{2n} - 1 = \frac{c}{y}\left((1+y/2)^{2n} - 1\right).$$

This expression is interesting. It shows that when the bond is selling at par with $p = 1$, the coupon rate c and the yield to maturity y must be equal for this equation to hold. In other words, when a bond is selling at par, there is no need to use a financial calculator to solve for y, because the coupon rate c *is* the yield to maturity y.

Depending on the original maturity at the time of issue, the market of fixed income securities is broadly divided into two main sectors: Money market and capital market.

The money market is where short-term (up to 12 months) fixed income instruments are traded over the counter. By all account, the most liquid instruments in this market are the U.S. Treasury bills, which are sold at public auctions every week, at a discount to their face value at maturity. Also known as the par amount, the face value is the amount paid by the U.S. Treasury at maturity in units of $1,000 to the investors. The bills are sold at a discount in the sense that the purchase price is less than the face value. The interest earned is simply the face value minus the purchase price. For example, if you buy a $1,000 bill at a price of $99.7621 per $100, then you pay $997.62 ($1,000 × 0.997622 = $997.621). The interest earned is $2.38.

As a matter of fact, the liquid instruments such as T-bills in the money market are classified as cash. Financial institutions will deposit the sales proceeds in the money market accounts when assets such as stocks and currencies are liquidated.

In the capital market, debt instruments of original maturities longer than 12 months are offered. The availability of an efficiently functioning capital market is crucial to the federal and local governments, as well as corporations. The federal government issues long-term notes and bonds to fund the national debt. State and municipal governments also issue long-term fixed income securities to finance, for instance, infrastructure projects. Corporations raise funds from the bond market to finance their business and investment activities, or to preserve their capital against unexpected needs.

An example of a corporate bond is a 100-year debt security issued by Walt Disney. Maturing on July 15, 2093, the bond's coupon rate is 7.55%. As in Figure 2.2, the last traded price of this bond was \$131.471 per \$100 on December 26, 2012. According to the

```
 DD530097     Corp  DES
WALT DISNEY CO   DIS7.55 07/93-23    131.471/131.471   (4.08/4.08) TRAC @12/26
 DIS 7.55 07/15/93 Corp        99) Feedback                    Page 1/11 Description: Bond
                            90 Notes   ·    95) Buy      96) Sell      97) Settings  ·
 2I) Bond Description    22) Issuer Description
Pages            Issuer Information                    Identifiers
 1)Bond Info     Name    WALT DISNEY COMPANY/THE       BB Number   DD5300973
 2)Addtl Info    Industry Media Non-Cable              CUSIP       254687AH9
 3)Covenants     Security Information                  ISIN        US254687AH95
 4)Guarantors    Mkt of Issue Domestic MTN             Bond Ratings
 5)Bond Ratings  Country    US        Currency  USD    Moody's     A1
 6)Identifiers   Rank   Sr Unsecured  Series    MTN    S&P         A
 7)Exchanges     Coupon  7.55          Type     Fixed  Fitch       A
 8)Inv Parties   Cpn FreqS/A                            DBRS        NR
 9)Fees, Restrict Day Cnt 30/360      Iss Price 100.00000 Issuance & Trading
 10)Schedules    Maturity 07/15/2093                   Amt Issued/Outstanding
 11)Coupons      CALL 07/15/23@103.02                  USD        300,000.00 (M) /
 Quick Links     Issue Spread   95.00bp vs T 7 ⅛ 02/23 USD        201,169.00 (M)
 32)ALLQ Pricing Calc Type  (1)STREET CONVENTION       Min Piece/Increment
 33)QRD Quote Recap Announcement Date         07/21/1993           25,000.00 / 1,000.00
 34)TDH Trade Hist Interest Accrual Date      07/15/1993 Par Amount           1,000.00
 35)CACS Corp Action 1st Settle Date          07/28/1993 Book Runner         MLPFS,MS
 36)CF  Prospectus 1st Coupon Date            01/15/1994 Reporting              TRACE
 37)CN  Sec News
 38)HDS Holders  SETTLEMENT: NEW YORK FUNDS. CO ACQ'D CAPITAL CITIES/ ABC INC FFF 2/12/96.
 66)Send Bond
Australia 61 2 9777 8600 Brazil 5511 3048 4500 Europe 44 20 7330 7500 Germany 49 69 9204 1210 Hong Kong 852 2977 6000
Japan 81 3 3201 8900    Singapore 65 6212 1000    U.S. 1 212 318 2000    Copyright 2012 Bloomberg Finance L.P.
                                        SN 775309 HKT  GMT+8:00 H440-4672-0 28-Dec-2012 09:40:29
```

Fig. 2.2 Description of a bond issued by Walt Disney with an original maturity of 100 years.

Source: Bloomberg.

Prospectus dated August 18, 1992, Disney intends to use the net proceeds for general corporate purposes, such as repayment of debts, capital expenditures, and the repurchase from time to time outstanding shares of Disney's common stock.

Compared to the U.S. Treasury bonds, this 100-year security issued by Walt Disney comes with a substantial risk of default. In fact, all corporate bonds are defaultable. The biggest-ever U.S. bankruptcy is the collapse of Lehman Brothers in 2008, resulting in as much as $639 billion of unpaid debts. According to the CRSP (Center for Research in Security Prices) database, 679 publicly listed companies domiciled in the U.S. went bust between 1931 and 2012. Over the recent 30 years from 1983 to 2012, the number of bankrupt companies was, on average, 19.17 per year. These sobering statistics suggest that default risk must be taken into account seriously when investing in corporate bonds (and stocks).

Thus far, the risk-free nature of fixed income securities issued by the U.S. Treasury was taken for granted. The general consensus and market practice indeed is to assume that the U.S government will not default on its debt obligations. The billionaire investor Warren Buffett went so far as to say during an interview that the U.S. merits a quadruple A rating, right after the U.S. rating was cut one notch from the highest triple A rating to AA+ by the Standard & Poor's. He said,

> In Omaha, the U.S. is still triple A. In fact, if there were a quadruple-A rating, I'd give the U.S. that.

If a consistently successful investor like Buffett had said so on August 5, 2011,[4] what could stop market participants from following his thought leadership?

But nothing is more deceiving and further from the truth than the "security" of fixed income. Constitutionally, the U.S. government cannot borrow more than a debt ceiling, although it could

---

[4]See the article "Buffett to FBN: S&P Downgrade 'Doesn't Make Sense' in FOX Business (FBN) at http://www.foxbusiness.com/markets/2011/08/05/buffett-to-fbn-sp-downgrade-doesnt-make-sense/ dated August 5, 2011.

raise the ceiling by passing a bipartisan bill to do so. More crucially, the Federal Reserve can help mint more U.S. dollars to "secure" payments for the massive debts. But as any seasoned traders know, "anything can happen in the market." Though the probability of U.S. defaulting on its debt obligation may be slimmer than seeing 10 tossed coins standing on their edges at the same time, the financial market will react violently, and even melt down completely when the event of U.S. default becomes more likely to happen.

2.6　Other Investments

Thus far, we have discussed four major asset classes that are actively traded, either on public exchanges or on OTC markets. A common characteristic of these four asset classes is their transparency, because their prices are readily and freely obtainable from mass media such as newspapers and financial websites. Much less transparent asset classes include real estates and collectables. They are also much less accessible to retail investors.

Historically, real estate was the single most important asset class. Ownerships of land and castles were reserved only for the most wealthy of society: Kings, nobles, and aristocrats. Over the past few hundred years, ownership of property had changed to the ownership of legal entity. As a result, residential properties became available for ordinary households and billionaires alike. Beyond residential properties, commercial properties are another entities that may provide an alternative to diversify the portfolio made up of one or more of the four major asset classes.

Collectables are antiques, paintings, sculptures, manuscripts of famous persons, stamps, coins, or any unique items that are valued by collectors. From the investment standpoint, artists such as Pablo Picasso, Francis Bacon, and Daqian Zhang are like stocks and the volume of the artists' artworks is measured in "lots sold" and in dollars. Interestingly, a composite price index can be constructed for an artist based on the latest auction price of each artist's artwork. By extension, market-wide price indexes are constructed to gauge the ever changing trends and fashions in the circles of collectors.

In the markets of collectables, the economics of supply and demand does not quite apply. Each collectable item is unique and cannot be manufactured to increase the supply when demand increases. The artwork, in particular, is valued for its authenticity and whatever aesthetic criteria used by the connoisseurs. Even so, its utility may well be derived from the social status that comes with owning an extravagantly priced piece of art created by a renowned artist. On May 2, 2012, the pastel-on-board version of "The Scream" by the famous Norwegian painter Edvard Munch, set a world record for an artwork at auction when it sold for $119.9 million. The buyer was Mr. Leon Black,[5] a prominent investment banker. Far from economics, it appears that the beauty and value of a painting are truly in the eye of the beholder.

2.7 Exercises

Q1. Suppose you are a forex trader domiciled in the U.S. and you hold the view that the euro is going to weaken against the Greenback. The exchange rate GBP/USD is nicknamed cable. You decide to short the cable when quotes are 1.5591/92 to obtain $1 million (i.e., sell the pound). When the quotes become 1.5580/81, you square off your position by buying back the pound (i.e., sell the dollar).

   (a) How many pounds can you short for $1 million?
   (b) What is the P&L in Sterling?
   (c) What is the return realized in Sterling?
   (d) What is the P&L in Greenback?
   (e) What is the return in Greenback?

Q2. An investor from the eurozone bought 500 shares of Microsoft a year ago for $38.13 per share. The exchange rate was $1.3591 per euro then. Today, Microsoft is traded at $47.74 and the exchange rate is $1.2460.

---

[5]See the online article, "An Art Mystery Solved: Mogul is 'Scream' Buyer" by Kelly Crow in the *Wall Street Journal* dated July 11, 2012.

(a) What is the simple return in dollars?

(b) What is the simple return in euros?

Q3. The simple return (2.1) can be rewritten as

$$r := \text{simple return} = \frac{\text{selling price}}{\text{buying price}} - 1.$$

The ratio R defined by

$$R := \frac{\text{selling price}}{\text{buying price}}$$

is known as the simple gross return. The natural logarithm of R is called the log return. Often, we are interested to know how long does it take for an asset's price to double. Namely,

$$\ln(R) = \ln\left(\frac{2 \times \text{buying price}}{\text{buying price}}\right) = \ln(2) \approx 0.70.$$

(a) Suppose r is the annual rate of simple return. Show that the number of years T needed for an asset's price to double is well approximated by

$$T \approx \frac{70\%}{r\%}.$$

This simple relation is called the rule of 70.

(b) Suppose the average inflation is 3.5%. To watch a movie in the cinema costs $10 today. How many years ago could you watch the movie at half the price?

Q4. Total return is simple return with the inclusion of dividends received. In the typical long first and short later setting, let P_t be the selling price and P_{t-1} be the buying price one period ago. The total return $\check{r}_t$ is

$$\check{r}_t := \frac{P_t + D_t - P_{t-1}}{P_{t-1}},$$

where D_t is the sum of all dividends received up to time t. The current dividend yield is defined as the ratio

$$y_t := \frac{D_t}{P_t}.$$

(a) Show that

$$y_t = \frac{\check{r}_t - r_t}{1 + r_t},$$

where r_t is the simple return:

$$r_t = \frac{P_t - P_{t-1}}{P_t}.$$

(b) Most companies declare their dividend payments quarterly. One important date is called the ex date. It is the date on or after which a security is traded without the declared dividend. A seller who sells the stock on ex date is entitled to receive the dividend. The buyer, on the other hand, will not receive the dividend. Show that, everything else being equal, the stock price must drop by the amount equivalent to the dividend.

Q5. Given a sample r_t, $t = 1, 2, \ldots, T$, of simple returns or total returns over one period, say, a year. The arithmetic mean a is defined as

$$a := \frac{1}{T} \sum_{t=1}^{T} r_t.$$

The geometric mean g is an average return that takes into account the compounding nature of growth. Mathematically, we write

$$\prod_{t=1}^{T} (1 + r_t) =: (1 + g)^T.$$

Though r_t may be different for each t, the forward value of a dollar invested from $t = 0$ grows at an average rate of g per period, resulting in $(1 + g)^T$ at time $t = T$. The geometric mean is obtained as

$$g = \left(\prod_{t=1}^{T} (1 + r_t) \right)^{\frac{1}{T}} - 1.$$

(a) Show that when $|r_t| \approx 0, t = 1, 2, \ldots, T$, the geometric mean is approximately equal to the arithmetic mean:

$$g \approx a.$$

(b) Show that the geometric mean return is always equal or smaller than the arithmetic return. Namely,

$$g \leq a.$$

(c) Let P_t, $t = 0, 1, 2, \ldots, T$, be the prices of an asset. Show that

$$g = \left(\frac{P_T}{P_0} \right)^{\frac{1}{T}} - 1. \tag{2.5}$$

Q6. Incorporated in 1974, Temasek is a sovereign wealth fund based in Singapore. Temasek manages a portfolio (asset under management (AUM)) valued at S$223 billion as of March 31, 2014. The 1-year total returns (TR) of this investment company over the years, and for comparison, the 1-year TR on Singapore MSCI Free Index in Singapore dollars are tabulated as follows:

Year	2004	2005	2006	2007	2008	2009	2010	2011	2012	2013	2014
AUM	90	103	129	164	185	130	186	193	198	215	223
Total Return (%)	46.0	16.0	24.0	27.0	7.0	−30.0	42.0	4.6	1.5	8.9	1.5
SIMSCI TR (%)	32.5	13.8	18.2	26.9	−2.3	−75.2	42.4	9.8	−1.7	10.4	−0.8

Source: Temasek Review.[6]

(a) In the 2014 annual report called the *Temasek Review*, it is stated that the 5-year total return (by market value), i.e., the geometric mean return over the last 5 years, is approximately 11% per annum. Verify this statement.

(b) Do likewise for the claim in the 2014 *Temasek Review* that the 10-year total return is 9% per annum.

(c) Using the AUM numbers, calculate the geometric mean return of Temasek.

(d) Why is the 10-year geometric mean return g computed based on AUM different from that computed based on the 1-year total returns?

---

[6]The annual reviews are downloadable from http://www.temasek.com.sg/ investorrelations/investorlibrary/temasekreview.

(e) 2004 is the year when Temasek started to make public its annual report. In the 2004 *Temasek Review* (p. 7), the 2-year geometric mean is about 8%. With the 1-year total return for 2004 being 46%, what is the 1-year total return you can infer for 2003?

(f) According to the 2004 *Temasek Review*, the 3-year geometric mean is also 8%. Having answered Q. 6(e), infer the 1-year total return for 2002.

(g) Use all the 1-year total returns in the table and the two inferred returns for 2003 and 2002, compute the standard deviation (denoted by s) of these returns. As at 2014, the total return reported by Temasek is 16% per year since inception. Assuming that s also applies across the entire 40-year history of Temasek, what is the t statistic of Temasek's performance measured by the total return? (The null hypothesis is that the total return is zero.)

(h) The MSCI Singapore Free (SIMSCI) Index is probably not a good benchmark to measure the performance of Temasek. But since Temasek's portfolio is at least 1/3 invested in the Singapore market over the last 12 years, the total return on the SIMSCI Index is not too bad a yardstick either. To be compatible with Temasek's financial year closing month, end of March's total return index values are obtained from Bloomberg (ticker: GDDLSGF), which allows us to compute the annual total returns and tabulate them in the table. We hypothesize that Temasek's total return and SIMSCI's total return are two samples drawn independently from the same population. Conduct a two-sample t-test to examine whether this null hypothesis should be accepted or rejected. In other words, compute the t-statistic:

$$t = \frac{\bar{x} - \bar{y}}{\sqrt{\dfrac{s_x^2}{n} + \dfrac{s_y^2}{m}}},$$

where n is the number of observations to estimate the sample average $\bar{x}$ and the unbiased variance s_x^2 for x. Similarly, m is the number of observations for estimating $\bar{y}$.

Q7. In addition to the arithmetic and geometric means, another average is called the harmonic mean. These three means were proposed and studied by Pythagoras. The harmonic mean h of T positive real numbers $x_1, x_2, \ldots, x_T$ is defined as

$$h := \frac{T}{\frac{1}{x_1} + \frac{1}{x_2} + \cdots + \frac{1}{x_T}}.$$

(a) Compute the arithmetic, geometric, and harmonic means of AUM in Q. 6. Which average makes most sense?

(b) Consider an investment strategy called dollar-cost averaging. Financial planners or advisors like to recommend this strategy to their unsophisticated clients. Instead of timing the market, why not invest a fixed dollar amount on a regular basis? Suppose the exchange traded fund (ETF) is recommended. Moreover, suppose the share price is $100 now, $40 a month later, and $30 two months later.

   i. Compute the harmonic mean of these three share prices.

   ii. Consider the dollar-cost averaging approach with a fixed dollar amount of $1,200 to invest in the ETF each month. Compute the number of shares acquired for each of the three rounds of shares purchase.

   iii. Compute the volume-weighted average price (VWAP) of investing in the ETF.

$$\text{VWAP} := \frac{1}{V} \sum_{i=1}^{N} p_i v_i.$$

   In this definition, V is the total number of shares acquired, v_i is the number of shares bought in the ith round when the share price is p_i per share. The number of rounds is denoted by N.

   iv. Why is the harmonic mean equal to the VWAP?

Q8. Show that, for the three averages of Pythagoras, namely, arithmetic mean a, geometric mean g, and harmonic mean h, they satisfy the following inequality:

$$h \leq g \leq a.$$

That is,

$$\frac{T}{\frac{1}{x_1} + \frac{1}{x_2} + \cdots + \frac{1}{x_T}} \leq \left(x_1 x_2 \cdots x_T\right)^{\frac{1}{T}} \leq \frac{1}{T}\sum_{i=1}^{T} x_i.$$

Q9. An investor buys a Treasury bond at 103% of the par value and holds it to maturity, which is two years later. The coupon rate is 6%.

(a) What is the return on this investment for holding the bond to maturity?

(b) The current yield is the ratio obtained from dividing the coupon amount by the bond price. What is the current yield of this bond at the point of purchase.

(c) Instead of holding to maturity, suppose six months later, the investor sells the bond immediately after collecting the semi-annual coupon. The liquidation price is 101%. What is the return to the investor in this case?

(d) Suppose a year later, the Treasury bond is traded at 104% of the par value. What is the yield to maturity?

Q10. A Treasury bond has one year left before maturity. The annual coupon rate is c and the coupon is paid semi-annually. An investor has invested an amount of A for this bond at the price of P.

(a) Solve the quadratic polynomial to express the yield to maturity y in terms of P, $C = Ac$, and A.

(b) Since $y > 0$, show that $P < A + C$.

Chapter 3

Principles of Quantitative Finance

3.1 Introduction

Financial markets of equities, currencies, and fixed income securities, and to some extent commodities, constitute the backbones of the globalized financial system. The proper functioning of these markets is crucial to the economic well being of the increasingly integrated economies around the world. Buyers and sellers, and oftentimes intermediaries such as banks, brokerage firms, and clearing houses, are the major players in this complex, constantly evolving and growing web of networks.

The myriad transactions in the financial markets may be regarded as many "experiments" to assess the value of a tradable asset by its price. It turns out, however, that the value of an asset is rather elusive if not ghostly. Instead of being preoccupied with the value of each security, a more pragmatic perspective is to treat prices as reflections of buying and selling pressures at any given moment. When more people want to buy for whatever reasons, the price will go up, even when the "fundamentals" do not change.

It is important to recognize that the chronological order of financial transactions matters. Looking at the record of each transaction in isolation does not profit. Many market participants know that the manner by which a particular price P is reached makes a lot of difference. If it is from a price higher than P, and moreover if the speed at which P is reached is rapid, then it is quite likely that the subsequent price at a slightly later time is going to be lower than P. Conversely, if P is reached rapidly from a lower price, then the subsequent price tends to be higher. This observation is particularly applicable to intra-day price movements, and it is widely known as "price momentum."

Another important market regularity is the spill-over effect. A security is seldom traded in isolation from the other security. For instance, suppose Bank B reports good earnings and its share price goes up. Oftentimes, Bank A, though not reporting for that day, is likely to see its share price go up as well.

3.2   Uncertainty and Risk

For the price moves described above, it is practical to consider these movements as, rightly or wrongly, reflections of the market expectations, or something deemed likely to happen in the near future. In this regard, prices are prices, and not so much the *exact* values that analysts arduously obtain from their research. Like all expectations in life, many surprises will spring up. Any market participant will attest to the fact that extreme surprises typically drive the price to move rapidly in the direction that the surprises are pointing to.

Events in the future are inherently uncertain. It is impossible to know which of the possible outcomes will be realized. But uncertainty is not necessarily a risk in itself. Consider the outcome of tossing a coin. This event is uncertain but there is no risk. The uncertain event presents a risk only when a financial payoff is contingent on it, as in a wager.

As an example, suppose an investor buys 1,000 shares of a stock at \$5 per share and holds the shares for a year. Suppose the share price turns out to be \$6 a year later. Moreover, if the stock does not pay dividends, then the realized return after selling the shares will be, according to (2.1),

$$\frac{6-5}{5} = 20\%.$$

Having pocketed the gross profit of $1,000, the capital gain of 20% is the return realized over a year.

If the round-trip transaction fees in the form of brokerage commission, clearing and settlement, and any other costs amount to $0.2 per share, the return net of these costs will be less than 20%:

$$\frac{6 - 5 - 0.2}{5} = 16\%.$$

The profit after fees is $800, and the resulting 16% is referred to as the net return. Moreover, if the investor has to pay tax on the capital gain, the net return after tax is even smaller, say, 12%.

The bottom line is, stock return is uncertain, and the downside aspect of this uncertainty is the risk that the investor takes. In this example, if the shares can only be sold below $5, then the investor's money after transaction costs will be less than this initial cash. Uncertainty that may trigger financial losses is risk. If the stock price declines to $4 a year later, then the net return will become

$$\frac{4 - 5 - 0.2}{5} = -24\%.$$

Accordingly, the investor losses 24%, i.e., every $1.00 the investor had a year earlier is reduced to $0.76. But a stock analyst who does not invest in the stock will have no risk, though the analyst recognizes that the stock return is uncertain and risky too.

The alternative to investing in stock is to deposit the money at a *totally* trustworthy bank. In this case, there is no uncertainly whatsoever and hence risk-free. This is because the depositor is guaranteed to receive the money deposited plus interest at the point of time when fund is deposited. The realized return, which is the interest rate quoted by the bank, is known in advance. By contrast, the realized return on a stock can only be known a year later in the example above.

Suppose the totally trustworthy bank pays 3% interest annually. The investor has to decide between the risky stock and the risk-free time deposit. If the choice is to invest in stock, the investor must have speculated that the share price will rise from the current price. More importantly, the investor *expects* the 1-year stock return to be higher than the risk-free 3%. Otherwise, where is the incentive to take the chance when a 100% certain gain of 3% is already at hand?

3.3   Principles of Quantitative Finance

In placing a deposit with a 100% trustworthy bank, the investor is in fact buying a bond from the bank. The bond is backed by the full faith of the bank, and as an asset to the investor, it is risk-free. In general, a risk-free asset is a financial instrument for which the future cash flow is guaranteed and exactly predictable today. There is absolutely no uncertainty whatsoever, and the value of such asset increases at a constant risk-free rate. An example of, or more appropriately, a proxy for such risk-free asset is the Treasury bills issued by the U.S. government, which will not, in all likelihood, default on its obligation to pay back T-bill investors plus interest on time. As the interest rate or the yield is determined at the beginning of the T-bill purchase, the value of this risk-free asset increases at a constant rate by the amount of interest accrued over time.

3.3.1   *First principle: Return is fixed*
in the absence of risk

The first principle of Quantitative Finance states that a risk-free asset whose value is zero remains zero, or when non-zero, increases at a constant risk-free rate. It is known more widely as the time value of money, i.e., a dollar received today is more valuable than a dollar received in the future. Cash is king.

Suppose the risk-free rate is r_0 per annum. By lending out an amount C at this rate today, after T years, the lender will surely receive

$$FV = C(1 + r_0)^T, \tag{3.1}$$

because the borrower is 100% credit worthy. It is worth emphasizing that this future cash flow is known today, and (3.1) is aptly named the forward value (FV).

The first principle also applies in the opposite direction. Suppose a cash flow C is guaranteed T years in the future. To receive this cash flow, the price to pay today is

$$PV = \frac{C}{(1 + r_0)^T}. \tag{3.2}$$

This price is better known as the present value of future cash flow. The first principle provides a one-to-one mapping between the future value and the present value via the risk free rate.

$$PV \xleftrightarrow{r_0} FV.$$

Also, any portfolio that is risk-free must earn only risk-free interest rate r_0.

More generally, when the cash flow in (3.2) is the expected value of some payoff function in the future time T instead, the present value at time 0 is

$$PV = \frac{\mathbb{E}\left(\text{payoff function}\right)}{(1 + r_0)^T}. \tag{3.3}$$

The symbol $\mathbb{E}(\cdot)$ indicates the expectation of the random variable within the brackets.

It is important to emphasize that the functional form of the payoff function must be known, and the investment horizon or expiration date T must be fixed. When discounted by the risk-free rate, the expectation is taken under the so-called risk-neutral probability. It is risk-neutral in the sense that investors are indifferent to risk because the payoff function can be replicated exactly, at least in principle, by a combination of other financial instruments. As a result of this replication possibility, investors can lay off the risk associated with the payoff of a financial instrument by an off-setting or neutralizing replication and thus becoming neutral to the payoff.

3.3.2 *Second principle: Expected return is directly proportional to risk*

The second principle of Quantitative Finance states that the return on a risky asset is expected or required to be at a higher rate than that of a risk-free asset. Moreover, when the risk is higher, the expected return must be higher too. We write

$$\mathbb{E}(r_a) \geq \mathbb{E}(r_b), \quad \text{if asset } a\text{'s risk} \geq \text{asset } b\text{'s risk.}$$

Here, r_a and r_b are, respectively, the return on asset a and on asset b.

In light of the second principle, the first principle provides the baseline framework to examine risk and how risk alters the expected rate of return required by investors. Suppose the expected return on a stock is 10% per year and the risk-free rate is 3%. The spread or the difference of 7% between the risky asset and the risk-free asset is the risk premium. It compensates investors for exposing themselves to risk. Generically, we write

$$\text{risk premium} = \mathbb{E}(r_a) - r_0. \tag{3.4}$$

Here, it is implicitly assumed that both the risky and the risk-free assets share a common investment horizon. Since the risk of asset a is necessarily higher than that of the risk-free asset, by the second principle, the risk premium must be positive.

The risk premium is, in lack of a better term, the "reward" for taking risk. Consider a financial institution that is 100% trustworthy. It borrows money at the risk-free rate, and the fund raised is invested in risky asset, for the expected return from the risky asset is deemed to be greater than the risk-free rate. Given that the investment produces the expected return, the net return after paying the debt at the risk-free rate is the risk premium "earned" by the investor for taking risk.

A popular type of risky asset is the market portfolio. It comprises all tradable stocks. Equation (3.4) suggests that the expected return on the market portfolio less the risk-free rate is known as the market risk premium. Moreover, as alluded to in Chapter , the brilliant, revolutionary idea of Black and Scholes [BS73] is that the hedged portfolio, being free of risk, should earn the expected return equal to the risk-free rate r_0. Since there is no risk premium, from (3.4), we must have $\mathbb{E}(r_a) = r_0$.

It is noteworthy that, in stark contrast to price, expected return is just a concept, and it is unobservable.[1] Models are needed to act as proxies for the expected return. Despite all the shortcomings highlighted in the papers by Fama and French [FF04], as well as Mandelbrot and Hudson [MH04], and many others, the Capital Asset Pricing Model (CAPM) first proposed by Treynor [Tre61] and Sharpe [Sha64] remains the most widely used model for the expected return on a stock, provided the expected return $\mathbb{E}(r_m)$ of market portfolio itself is known in the first place. CAPM suggests that the risk premium of a stock is directly proportional to the market risk premium. Hence,

$$\mathbb{E}(r_a) - r_0 = \beta_a(\mathbb{E}(r_m) - r_0). \tag{3.5}$$

In this model, r_0 is the risk-free rate and r_m is the return on market portfolio. The proportional constant β_a is interpretable as the sensitivity of stock a's risk premium to the market portfolio's risk premium.

To develop an intuition for β_a, consider two values that are associated to two assets already discussed. If $\beta_a = 0$, then the risk premium is zero, and the expected return of stock a is the risk-free rate r_0; there is no risk and no uncertainty. If $\beta_a = 1$, then the risk premium of stock a is no different from that of the market portfolio. Thus, a smaller β_a has lesser risk compared to a larger β_a. Accordingly, for stock a and stock b with positive β_a and β_b, respectively,

$$\mathbb{E}(r_a) \geq \mathbb{E}(r_b), \quad \text{if } \beta_a \geq \beta_b.$$

An implicit assumption of this model is that the investment horizon of the risky assets and that of the risk-free asset are the same.

---

[1]Strictly speaking, expected return $\mathbb{E}(r)$ is the population mean. As long as the entity such as a company is still operating, the average of the past returns on the stock is at best the *sample* mean. So the usual disclaimer of "past performance is not a guarantee of future return" must be uttered as a reminder. The expected return of an exchange-traded stock can only be obtained when the company ceases to be listed for a variety of reasons. But if the company is de-listed, then the stock is no longer investable for the vast majority of investors, and knowing its expected return is of little practical use.

Another model is in the form of Modigliani–Miller Proposition II (see Modigliani and Merton Miller [MM58] and Miller [Mil88]). In this model, a company may decide to be completely free of debt (unlevered) or to take on a debt for leverage (levered). In the unlevered scenario, the rate of return on the equity E required by the shareholder is $\mathbb{E}(r_u)$, which becomes $\mathbb{E}(r_l)$ when the company is levered with debt D. The creditor evaluates the company's financial health and demands the rate of return $\mathbb{E}(r_d)$ for lending money to the firm. The risk-return proposition of Modigliani and Miller is remarkably similar to CAPM (3.5):

$$\mathbb{E}(r_l) - \mathbb{E}(r_u) = \gamma(\mathbb{E}(r_u) - \mathbb{E}(r_d)). \tag{3.6}$$

Here, γ is the debt-to-equity ratio D/E.

Typically, the expected return on equity $\mathbb{E}(r_u)$ is higher than the expected return on debt $\mathbb{E}(r_d)$. This is because equity or stock has a higher market risk as the stock price may exhibit large fluctuation. On the other hand, if a debt or bond is held to maturity, investors are not exposed to the price risk but mainly the default risk, which occurs less frequently compared to the occurrence of stock price fluctuation. Therefore, by the second principle of Quantitative Finance, the spread between the two required rates, $\mathbb{E}(r_u) - \mathbb{E}(r_d)$, is necessarily positive.

On the left side of (3.6), $\mathbb{E}(r_l) - \mathbb{E}(r_u)$ is the return that remains after the return on equity is subtracted away. What the Modigliani–Miller model (3.6) suggests is that given the spread between the two rates of return on equity and on debt, a higher debt-to-equity ratio leads to a higher required return spread $\mathbb{E}(r_l) - \mathbb{E}(r_u)$, which is the return sought by creditors to compensate themselves for their exposure to a higher credit risk. Intuitively, holding the equity constant, the required return for bearing the credit risk should increase with the level of debt D. Indeed the Modigliani–Miller model (3.6) agrees with this intuition.

It is interesting to note that the debt-to-equity ratio γ plays the same role as β does in CAPM. They are the constant or parameter that makes reward proportional to a risk factor, which is the market factor $\mathbb{E}\left(r_m\right) - r_0$ in CAPM and the equity-debt factor $\mathbb{E}\left(r_u\right) - \mathbb{E}\left(r_d\right)$ in the second proposition of Modigliani and Miller.

3.3.3 Third principle: Every willing buyer has a willing seller

The third principle of Quantitative Finance states that in the financial market, for every willing buyer who pays a price for an asset, there is a willing seller who sells that asset at the same price.

This principle is inspired by Bachelier, who is widely regarded as the father of Financial Mathematics. In his doctoral thesis [Bac00] published in 1900,[2] Bachelier reveals an insightful epigram:

> Il semble que le marché c'est-à-dire l'ensemble des spéculateurs, ne doit croire à *un instant donné* ni à la hausse, ni à la baisse, puisque, pour chaque cours coté, il y a autant d'acheteurs que de vendeurs.

This original French text conveys an interesting, avant-garde idea:

> It seems that the market, i.e., the ensemble of speculators, must believe *at a given instant* neither a rise, nor a fall, since, for every quoted price, there are as many buyers as sellers.

In this one-sentence paragraph, Bachelier crystalizes the concept of equilibrium *at a given instant* when neither price increment nor price decrement occurs. Since there are "as many buyers as sellers" at the *quoted* price, which may not necessarily be the *true* price, the quoted price is the market clearing price at each given point in time when "supply" (selling) equals "demand" (buying). The equilibrium is presumably attained only for that particular instant of time for a given financial security.[3]

---

[2]Louis Bachelier was a rather obscure mathematician when alive. Bernstein [Ber05] shows how Bachelier's ideas and formulas in his doctoral thesis are directly linked to the theory of Brownian motion of Einstein [Ein05]. This is one of the many examples of "great minds think alike."

[3]"Equilibrium" is a term used in thermodynamics to describe the eventual stable state of identical temperature attained when two liquids of different temperatures mix. Economists use "equilibrium" as a metaphor to connote the state where suppliers and demanders adjust their prices ("thermostat") so that eventually transactions take place at a single price.

The quoted or market price of Bachelier is none other than the price in the law of one price. This fundamental "law" of economics[4] asserts *normatively* that a good must sell for the same price at all locations of an economy. Otherwise, there would be opportunities for profit left unexploited. In Quantitative Finance, to prevent such arbitrage opportunity, portfolios that yield the same payoff must have the same price, no matter how that portfolio is constructed. In light of this market price of Bachelier, the third principle is largely — but not completely — synonymous to the "law" of one price. Moreover, this one price is achieved collectively by profit-oriented arbitrageurs. They are a breed of supposedly more sophisticated speculators, who are always on a constant look-out for any risk-free money-making opportunities left unexploited. In this regard, the "law" is enforced by arbitrageurs swiftly stepping up to exploit the opportunities for a risk-free gain (see Billingsley [Bil06]). The third law, therefore, also encompasses the principle of no risk-free arbitrage opportunity *at a given instant*.

Moreover, the third principle leaves open the possibility that one party of the transaction may have more information than the other, i.e., information asymmetry among buyers and sellers. Also, neither does the third principle require material information to transmit *instantaneously* to all market participants by way of trades in the open market. Some traders may obtain information ahead of others, i.e., bandwidth asymmetry among traders, prompting traders who have an information advantage to front-run others to exploit their information to the fullest for profits.

Despite the information and bandwidth asymmetries, an important aspect of the third principle concerns the market participants' willingness to trade at the quoted price. The willingness to trade should *not* be taken for granted, because it is directly contrary to

---

[4] Strictly speaking, laws such as Kepler's three laws of planetary motion of natural science describe natural phenomena that are absolutely true and not breakable. By contrast, Quantitative Finance is not about the natural world but the financial world inhabited by all kinds of people. The "law" of one price may break down. Futures traders in a large pit would attest to the fact that those standing at the outer fringes of a large crowded pit may trade at prices different from those standing near the center.

the "no trade" theorem expounded in a seminal paper by Grossman and Stiglitz [GS80]. In essence, the Grossman–Stiglitz theorem indicates that if a rational buyer is prepared to buy at a price P, then the buyer must have expected that the asset value will exceed P. But if the rational buyer's valuation is to be believed, the rational seller will become unwilling to sell. Hence, no trade will happen.

In reality, of course, trades occur so very frequently in the financial market. To overcome the Grossman–Stiglitz no-trade theorem, an important ingredient need to be included: different types of traders. The profit-motivated traders (speculators and dealers) in Harris' taxonomy [Har03] trade on their rational expectation to profit; the futile traders believe that they are profit-motivated traders but their expectations are not realistic because they have no advantage or "edge" that would make their trades profitable; and utilitarian traders trade on the expectation that they would obtain some benefit from trading besides trading profits. Together, these three broad types of traders collectively overcome the Grossman–Stiglitz no-trade theorem by their differing expectations to trade for profits. They enter willingly into a transactional relationship over a particular security based on their expectations, rightly or wrongly.

More often than not, a select group of profit-motivated informed traders are more knowledgeable and market savvy, also faster to obtain and analyze material information. A prime example of an informed trader is none other than the legendary investment banker, Nathan Mayer Rothschild (1777–1836). He had a proprietary "network" of carrier-pigeons and of fast-sailing boats to obtain news from the Europe Continent to England much faster than anybody else. He was thus able to "utilize to the best advantage his special sources of information, while no one was a greater adept in the art of promoting the rise and fall of the stocks." For example, during the battle of Waterloo, "being able to transmit to London private information of the allied success several hours before it reached the public," Rothschild "effected an immense profit."[5]

---

[5]The quotes are taken from the 11th Edition *Encyclopedia Britannica*, first published in 1911. In the *Jewish Encyclopedia*, which was originally published between

All other traders who think they are informed but actually not add noise to prices. They are named duly as noise traders. The third principle of Quantitative Finance suggests that the informed traders and the noise traders willingly take sides opposite to each other for any given transactions. More often than not, informed traders emerge as winners. Their winnings come at the expense of noise traders.

Moreover, the third principle requires informed traders to compete among themselves to transact with noise traders. Informed traders such as Rothschild are motivated to pay for a faster if not the fastest access to superior information. They want to stay ahead of the curve all the time, so as to render even their informed competitors into noise traders. On the other hand, noise traders eventually learn from their "mistakes" by knowing the information imparted by the informed traders.

The ideal strategy for every arbitrageur who aspires to beat the market is to seek out any risk-free arbitrage opportunity and exploit it to the fullest. Despite starting with absolutely nothing and taking no risk, the risk-free arbitrage strategy creates a possibility to end up with a positive amount of money without incurring debts and risks. The third principle suggests that such risk-free arbitrage opportunity, when really is without any risk, does not exist in a market populated by fiercely competitive arbitrageurs and fast learning noise traders. In the absence of risk-free arbitrage opportunity, the market price is fair to both the buyer and the seller. In this regard, the third principle is the well-known principle of no risk-free arbitrage opportunity.

As an illustration, suppose the security is traded simultaneously at multiple exchanges. When capital and information flows are not impeded, its market price at Exchange A must be identical to the market price at Exchange B eventually. Otherwise, there will be money on the table for arbitrageurs to snatch freely over

---

1901 and 1906, Rothschild's usage of carrier-pigeons is also recorded. But whether Rothschild did indeed profit from buying the depressed stocks before the news on allied's victory became public information is not mentioned.

and over again from noise traders. Whenever price discrepancies arise, competing arbitragers will step in quickly to buy from the market that trades the security at a lower price from noise traders, and simultaneously sell the same security to other noise traders at another market trading at a higher price. Such "free" money from location arbitrage will be quickly arbitraged away as noise traders learn from their losing trades, and one price eventually prevails. This kind of straightforward risk-free arbitrage opportunities rarely occur and if they do, will disappear almost instantaneously.

Less straightforward, however, is that two assets or portfolios providing the same cash flow in the future will have the same price today. As an illustration, suppose two portfolios are judiciously constructed in such a way that they have exactly the same expected payoff. Although the compositions of the portfolios may be different, both assets provide the same expected payoff in the future. Accordingly, holding everything else constant, they are perfect substitute of each other and investors should be indifferent in their choice of which of the two to trade on. Again, whenever price differential arises, arbitrageurs will rush in to make these two securities trade at the same price or present value eventually.

In sum, at any given time, for every willing buyer who pays for a security at a certain price, there is a willing seller who sells it at that single price. Owing to the heterogeneity of traders and competition in the market, the third principle is effectively a statement about the principle of no risk-free arbitrage opportunity. Figure 3.1 provides a summary of the relationships between the no risk-free arbitrage opportunity, law of one price, and the third principle of Quantitative Finance.

3.4 Relative Valuation

The three principles of Quantitative Finance are both descriptive and prescriptive (normative) in laying out a framework to understand what is going on in many financial markets. The first principle prescribes a deterministic formula to connect, given the absence of risk, the present value to the guaranteed future cash flow receivable.

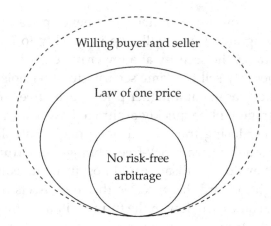

Fig. 3.1   No risk-free arbitrage opportunity is the most restrictive form of the third principle.

The second principle requires the market participants to be capable of assessing the risk of an asset *relative* to the risk of another asset, at least qualitatively. Then it goes on to describe the general market behavior, namely, a relatively higher risk is rewarded with a relatively higher *expected* return. The third principle lays the axiomatic foundation for a transaction to take place, willingly, between buyers and sellers at one price that leaves little room for arbitrageurs to take advantage of.

Moreover, investors and traders in general are also capable of comparing different portfolios' future payoffs and determine which should be priced relatively higher today. If portfolio A's future value is almost surely higher (lower) than the future value of portfolio B, then competing arbitrageurs and learning noise traders interact through transactions in such a way that the price of portfolio A will almost surely be higher (lower) than the price of portfolio B today.

For any two portfolios A and B generating, respectively, future values or cash flows of $V_A(T)$ and $V_B(T)$ that are *relatively* comparable at time t, i.e.,

$$V_A(T) \leq V_B(T),$$

then the third principle of Quantitative Finance suggests that their current prices $P_A(t)$ and $P_B(t)$ must also abide by the same relative relationship, i.e.,

$$P_A(t) \leq P_B(t).$$

Otherwise, whenever $P_A(t) > P_B(t)$, the arbitrageurs will step in to sell asset A and buy asset B at time t, and unwind this long–short position at time T to capture the free money. To be specific, we write $P_A(t) = P_B(t) + \tilde{Y}_t$, where $\tilde{Y}_t$ is a positive random variable. Also, since $V_A(T) \leq V_B(T)$ as assumed, we write $V_B(T) = V_A(T) + \tilde{Y}_T$ where $\tilde{Y}_T$ is a positive random variable too. The cash flows of the long–short strategy at times t and T are analyzed in Table 3.1. From the table, it is clear that a total of $\tilde{Y}_t + \tilde{Y}_T$ is obtainable almost surely.

When all the arbitrageurs get to know about the free money on the table, they will compete ferociously — much like a vulture will do over a carcass — to snatch the free money by trying to buy portfolio B at a price higher than their competitors and sell portfolio A at a price lower than their competitors. Eventually, $P_A(t)$ will become lower and $P_B(t)$ will become higher, so much so that $P_A(t) \leq P_B(t)$ ensues.

In sum, the resulting relative valuation rule implied by the third principle of Quantitative Finance is stated as

$$V_A(T) \leq V_B(T) \implies P_A(t) \leq P_B(t), \qquad \text{almost surely for } t < T. \tag{3.7}$$

It is important to emphasize once again that for this relationship to hold, both $V_A(T)$ and $V_B(T)$ must be relatively valuable, i.e., the relationship $V_A(T) \leq V_B(T)$ can be ascertained at time t. Separately or individually, however, their absolute values $V_A(T)$ and $V_B(T)$ need not necessarily be knowable at time t.

Table 3.1 Arbitrage opportunities generating cash flows at times t and T for the arbitrageurs.

Time t	Cash flow at time t	Time T	Cash flow at time T
Sell portfolio A	$P_B(t) + \tilde{Y}_t$	Buy portfolio A	$-V_A(T)$
Buy portfolio B	$-P_B(t)$	Sell portfolio B	$V_A(T) + \tilde{Y}_T$
Net cash flow	$\tilde{Y}_t$	Net cash flow	$\tilde{Y}_T$

3.5   An Application of the Principles of Quantitative Finance

The three principles described thus far are rather extract. It is time to put flesh on the bones. Consider two parties entering into an agreement to trade an asset. The actual transaction, however, does not take place immediately. Both parties nevertheless agree today on the forward price to be traded, say, a year down the road. In other words, the exchange of cash for asset takes place in a year's time, and both parties are obligated to trade at the pre-determined forward price. Regardless of the market price of the asset then, the seller must deliver the asset to the buyer, who must pay for it by cash. This kind of agreement and arrangement is called the forward contract.

Intriguingly, probably the first recorded forward contract can be found in *The Book of Genesis*, the first book of *Torah* and also of *The Bible*. As early as 1575 BC, Jacob said,[6] "I will serve thee seven years for Rachel thy daughter," and Laban agreed to give his daughter to Jacob as wife in exchange for Jacob's labor. After slaving out for 7 years, Jacob and Laban's daughter consummated the agreement by marriage. In this forward contract, the maturity is 7 years; the transactional settlement is by physical delivery; the forward price is 7 years of slavery; and the underlying asset is Rachel.[7]

Jacob paid the price of 7 years working as a slave for Laban. Did he get a good deal? Was the price fair? What should the forward price be so that both parties can strike a deal today?

The key idea to ascertain the forward price is to execute a simple strategy. Immediately after entering into the forward contract at the forward price of F_0, the seller in this deal borrows cash S_0 from a bank today to buy the asset at the price of S_0 from the market.

---

[6]Genesis Chapter 29 Verse 18, King James Bible.

[7]After 7 years of hard labor and in violation of the forward contract, Laban did not deliver Rachel, the younger daughter but Leah, the older daughter instead. Thus, Jacob had to work another 7 years for Rachel. This is the first recorded incident of counter-party risk in the forward market.

The net cash flow today is zero, as the cash borrowed is used to pay for the asset, and the forward contract involves no cash flow. This simple zero-cash strategy is said to be self-financing because seller's own fund is not incurred for entering the forward contract. Moreover, the seller is deemed to be 100% trustworthy by the bank and the bank is willing to lend money to the forward seller at the risk-free rate of r_0.

What is the net cash flow to the seller a year later? By delivering the asset he bought a year ago to the buyer, the seller receives the pre-determined F_0. The seller is also required to pay back the borrowed sum S_0 to the bank plus interest. Applying the first principle of Quantitative Finance, the seller pays the bank S_0 along with the risk-free interest amount of $S_0 r_0$. Therefore, the net cash flow to the seller a year later is

$$F_0 - S_0(1 + r_0).$$

The cash flows are depicted in Figure 3.2. Upward arrows mean incoming cash flows and downward arrows indicate outgoing cash flows. At time $t = 0$, the seller's asset is a share, and a liability of S_0. The seller is also liable to sell the asset a year later to the buyer. At time $t = 1$, the seller honors the forward contract by selling the asset at the pre-determined price F_0. After paying off the debt, the seller is free of both asset and liability.

It is important to note that the quantities r_0, S_0, and F_0 are known today by both the seller and the buyer. The interest rate r_0 is obtained from the bank, and the asset price S_0 is observed from the market. The forward price F_0 must be determined and agreed by both parties today. Therefore, the seller has no uncertainty whatsoever concerning the net cash flow $F_0 - (1 + r_0)S_0$ a year later. Since

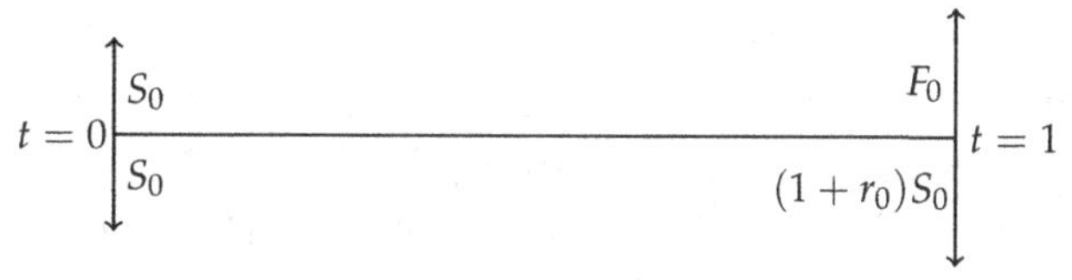

Fig. 3.2   The cash flows of forward seller.

there is no uncertainty, there is no risk to the seller, and according to the second principle of Quantitative Finance, there should not be any risk premium. By applying the first principle of Quantitative Finance, the net cash flow a year later must be zero since the net cash flow today is zero. Otherwise, according to the third principle, if $F_0 - (1 + r_0)S_0 > 0$, the seller is sure to make a gain and the buyer will not be willing to seal the deal today. Conversely, if $F_0 - (1 + r_0)S_0 < 0$, the seller ends up losing money for sure and therefore will be unwilling to sign the forward contract. Accordingly, the net cash flow must be

$$F_0 - (1 + r_0)S_0 = 0.$$

Hence, the forward price that is fair to both parties at time 0 should be

$$F_0 = (1 + r_0)S_0. \tag{3.8}$$

Next, we examine a self-financing strategy from the forward buyer's perspective. Since the buyer can and must buy the asset a year later, the buyer sells the security in possession today at the price of S_0. The buyer then deposits the sale proceeds at the risk-free rate of r_0. Therefore, the net cash flow today is zero, as the cash obtained from selling the asset is converted into a time deposit at a risk-free bank. A year later, by the first principle, the time deposit matures and the buyer obtains $(1 + r_0)S_0$ cash from the bank. The forward buyer pays the seller F_0 for the asset. The net cash flow a year later is $(1 + r_0)S_0 - F_0$. Again, this net cash flow in the future is precisely known today. Therefore, there is no uncertainty and thus no risk, and according to the second principle, no risk premium. The forward buyer gets back the asset eventually and no additional cash flow is involved. By the third principle, the future cash flow $(1 + r_0)S_0 - F_0$ must be zero to prevent risk-free arbitrage. It follows that $F_0 = (1 + r_0)S_0$ as anticipated.

This simple example shows that the three principles of Quantitative Finance are useful in ascertaining the forward price F_0 that are fair to both the seller and the buyer. It follows that when F_0 is equal to $(1 + r_0)S_0$ for the forward contract, the resulting forward price can be called the fair price.

At this juncture, it is timely to re-visit Bachelier's thesis again. In the section entitled "The Probabilities in the Operations of Stock Exchange", Bachelier highlights his postulate in one italicized sentence concerning the *true* price (as opposed to the quoted price):

Le marché ne croit, à un instant donné, ni à la hausse, ni à la baisse du cours vrai.

The literal translation of Bachelier's maxim is as follows:

The market does not believe, at a given instant, neither a rise, nor a fall in the true price.

The true price of Bachelier corresponds to our fair price, as neither an increment nor a decrement of F_0 is to be believed in as being fair to either side of the transaction. In other words, the fair value of F_0 must be $(1 + r_0)S_0$ in this example.

In his proclamation for the true price, curiously enough, Bachelier omits "as many buyers and sellers" he has earlier written for the quoted price. We could only speculate that perhaps Bachelier wants to leave the option open for the quoted or market price to be different from the true price at a given instant.

3.6 Violations of Three Principles?

Indeed, intriguing as it may seem, securities that are essentially the same may be traded at different prices for a protracted period of time. A well-known example is the Royal Dutch/Shell Group, which was 60% owned by Royal Dutch Petroleum and 40% by Shell Transport & Trading. The Royal Dutch shares were traded in Amsterdam and Shell shares in London as separate entities. In theory, the Royal Dutch stock should worth 1.5 times the Shell stock, because all adjusted cash flows and dividends to investors were split in the proportion of 60:40. However, Froot and Dabora [FD99] find that from January 1980 through December 1995, these twin shares were traded at a disparity from the 60:40 ratio by as much as 9.5% on average. Lamont and Thaler [LT03] attribute this deviation from theoretical parity as the failure of the law of one price.

The Royal Dutch/Shell Group is not an isolated case. It is one of the many so-called dual-organization companies. Also referred to as Siamese twin, a dual organization involves two companies incorporated in different countries contractually agreeing to operate their businesses as if they were a single enterprise, yet retaining their separate legal identity and existing stock exchange listings. De Jong *et al.* [DJRVD09] evaluate investment strategies that exploit the deviations from theoretical price parity in a sample of 12 dual-organization companies. They find that simple trading rules are able to generate arbitrage net returns of almost 10% per annum.

By sharing the business yet remaining as separate entities, do Siamese twins really have the same expected return and risk? If they do, by the third principle, they should trade at or near theoretical parity. Given the well documented deviations from parity, is it then a failure of the third principle instead?

Though less pronounced, similar phenomenon is also observed in futures trading. Like the forward contract, a futures is a simple derivative security, and it has a one-to-one relationship with the underlying asset it is written on. As shown in Section 3.5, a theoretical value is associated with the futures. But every seasoned trader knows that throughout the trading session, the futures can persistently trade above its theoretical price, and at times, below. In principle, this disparity presents arbitrage opportunity. Buy the underlying security when the futures market price is higher than the theoretical value and concurrently, sell an equivalent amount of futures contracts. Do the reverse when the futures market price is lower than the theoretical price. These arbitrage trades, if many of them occur, will make the futures price converge to its theoretical value.

But when will the convergence happen, nobody has a clue — not even the master strategists of Long Term Capital Management (LTCM), which is defunct now. LTCM took a massive position in Shell versus Royal Dutch, to the tune of $2.3 billion. Long before this pair of Siamese twin eventually converged, their prices diverged even more. Owing to the leverage nature of that "arbitrage" strategy, LTCM was forced to unwind its position, resulting in a big loss.

The partners of LTCM, along with two Nobel prize winners on its board, learnt a painful lesson that markets could remain irrational longer than LTCM could remain solvent.[8]

Is it pointless then, to establish the relationship between two securities, such as Shell *vis-à-vis* Royal Dutch, and futures *vis-à-vis* the underlying asset? Does this empirical evidence negate the three principles of Quantitative Finance? Imagine for a moment, risk-free arbitrage and the law of one price are not in the vocabulary of Quantitative Finance. Then there will be no theoretical prices to begin with and by extension no anomalies like the Siamese twin.

"Anything can happen in the market," this hackneyed saying on the street downplays the deviation from fair value any more serious than the unscientific notion of market sentiment. Traders care less about the scientificness of the price than the bottom line. When the market price is not in sync with the theoretical price, for example, when the futures price is lower, it may suggest that, going forward, the sentiment in the market is cautious and less optimistic.

Rather than denouncing the principles, the takeaway in this section is that theoretical values derived from the three principles are useful in serving as reference prices in the market. When market prices deviate from the theoretical prices, there must have been willing buyers and sellers, who value the two securities involved asymmetrically. For instance, it is typically easier and less costly to trade futures contracts than to trade the underlying assets. In particular, it is less costly to trade the equity index futures, which is a forward contract written on a basket of many stocks, compared to trading the underlying component stocks as one aggregate order. As for the Siamese twin, the crux of the matter is that the two stocks are not entirely fungible. You cannot buy 200 shares of Royal Dutch in Amsterdam cheaply and sell them as 300 shares of Shell Transport in London, and vice versa. Similarly, futures as a derivative security and the underlying security are also not interchangeable directly.

---

[8]See Lowenstein [Low00] for an illustrious account on the LTCM debacle.

3.7   Principles versus Models

The three principles of Quantitative Finance are not models. Suggesting what investors and traders ought to do, they are more normative than descriptive. The first principle lays out a totally risk-free framework. With reference to the risk-free rate of return, a risk premium should be demanded by investors for investing in risky assets. The second principle is a statement about risk. When risk is appropriately defined and measured, investors should demand a higher expected return from asset that has more risk. The third principle suggests that the price at which a trade occurs should be fair to the buyer and seller at the point of transaction. Here, fairness means that ideally, the price leaves no room for risk-free arbitrage.

These three principles of Quantitative Finance are broad. Being the basis for reasoning, the principles, however, do not provide details on how the expected return and risk should be defined and measured. The details are provided by models instead. For example, CAPM is a model for expected returns and risks. It is a popular model used by the practitioners to price the market risk.

As mentioned in Section 3.6, even the principles are subject to violation. It should therefore come as no surprise that models may behave badly. Derman [Der11] writes,

> A model is a metaphor of limited applicability, not the thing itself.

To Derman, a model is no more than "a caricature that overemphasizes some features at the expense of others." In this context, CAPM is quite limited, for there are other types of risks, such as credit risk, liquidity risk, operational risk, and even model risk, which are not addressed by CAPM.

Perhaps it is pertinent to visualize a model as a shooting game in an amusement park. Against a prop of forest, the game is to shoot down 10 mock birds perching on the tree branches. When one bird is gunned down, the model will produce the number '9' to answer the question of how many birds are still left. In the market of real jungle, however, if one of the birds is shot down, no bird will be left perching on any branches. Drawing upon this analogy, when markets operate normally, '9' may be the correct answer. But during financial crisis or abnormal times, the mini-amusement park suddenly morphs into a real jungle. The answer '9' turns out to be an overstatement of '0', which unfortunately, becomes obvious only after the fact.

To sum up, in Quantitative Finance, the three principles are normative axioms and models are specific relationships among different financial quantities of interest to the academics and practitioners. But as far as models are concerned, an insightful reminder from Box [Box79] — a prominent statistician — is helpful:

> All models are wrong, but some are useful.

In light of what Box has said, CAPM is a wrong model. But practitioners find CAPM to be an extremely useful model for a variety of applications ranging from the estimation of the cost of capital to stock picking.

3.8   Physics Envy?

Astute readers by now might smell rats that the three principles of Quantitative Finance are paraphrasing the three laws of motion enunciated by Sir Isaac Newton. Having defined *vis inertiæ* and *vis impressa* in the Mathematical Principles of Natural Philosophy [New86], Newton inscribes the renowned three fundamental laws of motion (*leges motus*) concerning these two forces and their effects on the state and acceleration of a body, as well as the interaction between a pair of bodies.

First Law:
Every body perseveres in its state of rest, or of uniform motion in a right line, unless it is compelled to change that state by forces impressed thereon.

Second Law:
The alteration of motion is ever proportional to the motive force impressed, and is made in the direction of the right line in which that force is impressed.

Third Law:
To every action there is always opposed an equal reaction; or the mutual actions of two bodies upon each other are always equal, and directed to contrary parts.

By the first law of motion, Newton postulates an inertia system of coordinates when the force is absent. In essence, the first law asserts the existence of an inertial frame of reference in an empty space by which a physical body is observed to be either stationary or moving in a straight line at constant speed. The first principle of Quantitative Finance also states categorically that there is a risk-free frame of reference, in which the value of a risk-free asset increases by the constant yield till maturity.

The second law of motion postulates that any acceleration (alteration of motion) is due to the force exerted on it. Everything else being constant, the larger the force is, the higher is the acceleration. According to the second principle of Quantitative Finance, the value of a risky asset in the future is expected to increase at a higher rate than that of a risk-free asset. Moreover, when the risk is higher, the expected return is higher too.

Interestingly, there is almost an exact parallel in the context of CAPM, which suggests that the expected return of a risky asset in excess of the risk-free rate is proportional to the market risk premium. In other words, the expected return of a risky asset is accelerated relative to the risk-free rate by the market risk premium (force). The so-called beta is the proportional constant (inverse of the mass). The larger the beta is, or the smaller the mass is, the expected rate of return will be higher or faster, which is intuitive indeed.

Newtonian third law is often called the law of action and reaction. In the financial market, for every buyer who pays a price for an asset, there is a seller who sells that asset at the same price. It follows that two assets of the same expected return and risk will have the same present value. Otherwise, there will be a risk-free arbitrage opportunity, which is the same as saying that there is money on the table for people to snatch. Surely, "free" money will be quickly arbitraged away and one price eventually prevails at any given time.

Risk-free arbitrage opportunities rarely occur and if they do occur, will disappear almost instantaneously, so as to abide by the "law" of one price.

There is yet another way to see the parallel between the third law of motion, which is about the net action–reaction being zero, and the third principle of Quantitative Finance. Namely, a financial position established with zero net cash flow today cannot give rise to a non-zero net cash flow in the future, and vice versa.

The three laws of Newtonian physics, in conjunction with Newton's law of gravity, govern how the moon orbits around the earth, and pave the way for mankind to imprint "small steps" on it 283 years after the Principia was first prefaced on May 8, 1686.

As far as the earthly experience is concerned, what goes up must come down. However, the man on whose giant shoulders many scientists after him stand, apparently forgot about gravity in the speculative stock market. Newton chased after the South Sea Company's stock. As plotted in Figure 3.3, the stock price rose rapidly from about £150 per share to the peak of £950 per share in six months. When the bubble burst, he was said to have lost about £20,000, or a few million pounds in today's term (see Reed [Ree99]).

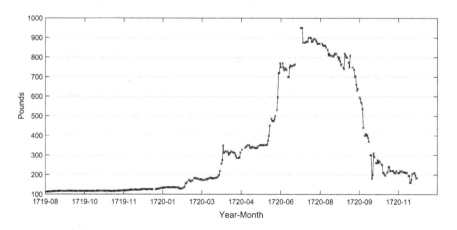

Fig. 3.3   Stock prices of South Sea Company in British pounds.
Source: Frehen *et al.* [FGR12].

Intriguing as it may appear, stock prices do not follow the three principles of Quantitative Finance. One of the main reasons is that in contrast to fixed income securities and forward contracts, stocks do not have maturity dates, and hence their future prices are — despite the best efforts of chartists, analysts of company's fundamentals, and even quants — random variables, which are unknown before they are realized. Though bounded from below, in principle, stock prices are not theoretically bounded from above. They can climb as high as the irrational exuberance can take them to the blue sky, as if to defy the gravity of economic fundamentals. Newton, the greatest scientist of gravity then, should have known better. According to Francis' account [Fra49], when asked what he thought of the market frenzy, Newton replied,

> I can calculate the motions of erratic bodies, but not the madness of a multitude.

Newton's laws of physics work extremely well in describing the motions of celestial bodies. By contrast, the three principles of Quantitative Finance are no more than distilled reflections of common human behaviors, serving as general *guides* to answer the question of what could be expected. Applicable only on what is to be expected of the known unknown, these three general guides are certainly not as profitable in forecasting what will surely happen.

The principles may not even be applicable when risks are being swept deliberately under the carpet by excessive greed, outright dishonesty, and ignorance. Rightfully so, de la Vega, the author of Confusión de Confusiones [dlV57], cautioned as far back as 1688,

> What really matters is an awareness of how greed and fear can drive rational people to behave in strange ways when they gather in the marketplace.

But when sanity is restored, the three principles of Quantitative Finance plus a host of mathematical and statistical models can be expected to work beautifully in pricing financial products, taming risks, and designing quantitative strategies to trade on statistical arbitrage.

3.9 Market Friction

In line with the practice to lay bare the assumptions at the onset, a discussion of the assumptions underlying the three principles is in order. Even here, physics envy lingers on. To begin with, Newton's three laws of physics assume that point particles move in the vacuum, a space within which absolutely nothing exists, i.e., the pure absence of matter. The first law suggests that a body will continue to move in a straight line with constant speed *forever* in the vacuum. After all, Newton is interested in finding out how the celestial bodies move in the outer space. Friction, the resistance encountered when a body is moving in contact with other matter, is the natural stopper to the perpetual motion. A by-product in the form of heat is generated as a result.

In the same vein, the three principles of Quantitative Finance assume the absence of any form of market "friction." But financial transactions such as buying or selling shares invariably incur transaction costs. Stoll [Sto00] speaks of trading friction and provides as many as seven ways to measure it. As a matter of fact, the law of one price ought to be called the law of one pair of best bid-and-ask prices. When you want to buy (sell) shares, currencies, commodities, or fixed income securities immediately, you have to buy (sell) at the higher (lower) ask (bid) price. Relative to the midquote, which is the average of the bid and ask prices, you always pay a higher price for buying and receive a lower price when selling.

As an example, suppose the best bid-and-ask prices prevailing in the market are \$10.1 and \$10.9, respectively. The midquote is \$10.5. To buy immediately, the price is \$10.9. Suppose the bid-and-ask prices do not change and you want to sell immediately. You can sell only at the price of \$10.1. The resulting loss is the quoted spread, \$10.9−\$10.1 = \$0.8. With respect to the buying price, the loss amounts to 7.34%, which is substantial.

In an influential paper [Per88], Perold proposed the notion of implementation shortfall. The key idea is that the performance of a stock on paper is always superior to the performance of actually buying and selling a stock. Clearly, on paper, it is assumed that you can transact any quantity "at the stroke of the pen" without price impact and free of all commissions. But in reality, there are not only execution costs for trading such as the bid-ask spread discussed earlier, but also opportunity costs for *not* trading. These costs are "frictions that flow from transacting in large amount." In essence, the shortfall from implementing the paper trade drags down the performance, much like the friction does in slowing down a moving vehicle.

Other sources of market friction include the capital gain tax, service tax, dividend income tax, commission, all sorts of chargeable fees, and so on. These are direct costs that are known or estimable before trades. By contrast, the implicit cost of trading comes in the form of price impact created by trading itself, as discussed in Perold's paper. The market somehow has this uncanny sense to sniff out traces of a big liquidity demand or "shock." When fund managers are about to re-balance their portfolios, the market tends to move, at least temporarily, against their trading. This is also a kind of market friction, which lowers the portfolio return.

Short sale restriction in trading stocks is a knockout of market friction stemming from regulatory requirements. A short sale is the selling of a stock that a seller does not own or a sale consummated by the delivery of a stock borrowed by, or for the account of, the seller.[9] The restrictions vary from the so-called up-tick rule to a complete ban. What are the effects of this market friction on investor's asset allocation preference? DeGennaro and Robotti [DR07] examine the performances of portfolios with and without a short-sale ban. They find that the risk-adjusted expected return that embeds the no-short-sale constraint is lower than that of the unconstrained. They conclude that market frictions do indeed impose utility costs on investors by making preferable investment portfolios unattainable.

---

[9]This definition is taken from the U.S. Securities and Exchange Commission.

3.10 Exercises

Q1. Consider the following FX quotes:

	Bid	Ask
EUR/USD	1.3501	1.3502
USD/SGD	1.2711	1.2734
EUR/SGD	1.7077	1.7100

A trader has spotted a triangular arbitrage opportunity starting with SGD. The trader who is based in Singapore has S$1,710.

(a) How much will the trader make from one round of triangular arbitrage in Singapore dollars?

(b) How should the quotes for US$/SGD be changed in order to prevent this risk-free arbitrage?

Q2. The adjective "uncertain" from which "uncertainty" is derived has many different meanings in different contexts. In Quantitative Finance, uncertainty refers to the state of limited knowledge to adequately identify the existing state or a future outcome. Risk is uncertainty qualified by an additional condition of possible financial loss. In a lecture before the Prussian Academy of Sciences, January 27, 1921. Einstein spoke about Geometry and Experience. A famous statement from that lecture goes as follows:

> As far as the propositions of mathematics refer to reality, they are not certain; and as far as they are certain, they do not refer to reality.

This interesting quip embodies the notion of model risk discussed in Section 3.7.

(a) In the case of tossing a coin with a probability of p for the head to turn up, we define a function

$$f(p) := p \ln p + (1 - p) \ln(1 - p).$$

In fact, $f(p)$ is known as the entropy of a statistical system. It is the expected value of the log of probabilities. Show that when $p = 1/2$, the entropy $f(p)$ is at its maximum.

(b) Could the entropy function, at least for the binary system of tossing a coin, be a measure of the degree of uncertainty? Discuss.

Q3. The risk-free rate r_0 is a key ingredient of the first principle of Quantitative Finance. Consider a frictionless world — absolutely no taxes, transaction costs and so on. In this idealized economy, not only is the risk of default absent, but also the regulatory risk (such as changes in the regulations, which might prohibit altogether the lender from collecting on a loan, or would require the lender to pay more in taxes on the interest earned than originally estimated). However, inflation risk still remains because prices of goods and services are likely to increase, leading to the erosion of lender's purchasing power.

The price of a basket of goods and services is p_0 today (time 0). A year later, it is $\tilde{p}_1$, a random variable. We denote the anticipated price of $\tilde{p}_1$ by $\pi_1 := \mathbb{E}_0(\tilde{p}_1)$. It follows that we can define the expected inflation i_0 for next year as

$$i_0 := \frac{\pi_1 - p_0}{p_0}.$$

It is akin to the simple return generated by buying the basket today at the price of p_0 and selling it a year later at the anticipated price of π_1.

Now, instead of buying the goods and services today, lend the money equal to the amount of p_0 at the risk-free rate r_0 to a 100 percent trustworthy bank. Lending money to the bank is equivalent to buying a debt security from the bank. Consider

$$h_0 := \frac{p_0(1 + r_0) - \pi_1}{\pi_1}.$$

This time round, the amount $p_0(1 + r_0)$ is the selling price because the investor liquidates or sells the bond security for cash, so as to buy the goods and services at the anticipated price of π_1. The rate h_0 takes the expected inflation into account because the purchase price is π_1 rather than p_0. It is called the real interest rate or the real rate. With h_0 being the real rate, the risk-free r_0 is then correspondingly referred to as the nominal interest rate or simply the nominal rate.

(a) Show that

$$1 + r_0 = (1 + h_0)(1 + i_0). \qquad (3.9)$$

This relation between the real and nominal interest rates, h_0 and r_0, respectively, and the expected inflation rate i_0, is known as the Fisher equation.[10]

(b) What are the possible interpretations of the Fisher equation (3.9) in the context of this book from the beginning up to (3.9)?

(c) Derive the following approximation from (3.9) when both the inflation rate i_0 and the real interest rate h_0 are small:

$$h_0 \approx r_0 - i_0.$$

Q4. A futures contract is a standardized forward contract traded through a futures exchange rather than bilaterally over the counter. An index futures is a derivative product for investors trading and hedging in the equity market.

Take the Dow Jones Industrial Average (DJIA) index as an example. Being a price-weighted index, you can simply buy 1 share for each of the 30 component stocks to replicate the DJIA index.

(a) Consider a round-trip of buying and selling. Suppose all the component stocks are liquid and always quoted at one penny ($0.01) apart for the best bid and the best ask. What is the total transaction cost incurred by the bid-ask spread?

(b) The mini Dow futures traded on CME has a price multiplier of $5, and a minimum tick size of one index point. What is the minimum transaction cost incurred by the bid-ask spread in a round trip?

---

[10] Irving Fisher is one of the earliest *mathematical* economists. The Fisher equation appears in Chapter 5 of his monograph "The rate of Interest" [Fis07], in the form of an illustration.

(c) There is an exchange-traded fund called SPDR Dow Jones
Industrial Average ETF, which is nicknamed the Dow Diamonds. Traded on the stock exchanges, suppose the bid-ask
spread of Dow Diamonds is also one penny. Which of these
three options — ETF, futures, and a basket of 30 stocks — is
the most liquid in terms of the bid-ask spread?

Chapter 4

Interest Rates

4.1 Introduction

The first principle of Quantitative Finance introduced in Chapter 3 postulates a frame of reference where risk is absolutely absent, just like a vacuum, completely void of uncertainty. It is purely a mathematical construct, for in reality, none of the financial assets qualifies to be categorized as having zero uncertainty. The market practice today is to take the debt securities issued by the U.S. Treasury as a proxy for risk-free instruments. This practice is derived from the current world order after the second World War, which saw the U.S. emerge as the "greatest nation on earth." It has the largest economy (and military), and the Greenback is the most widely used currency in cross-border trades, settlements of financial transactions, collateral postings, and so on.

Nevertheless, if a debtor is 100% creditworthy and pays back the principal plus interests *on time*, then to the creditor, there is zero uncertainty and thus risk-free for this loan. In other words, the first principle postulates the existence of a hypothetical financial institution with *absolute* credibility and ability to repay its creditor on schedule. The sole purpose of the first principle is to provide the risk-free framework, wherein the absolutely credible financial institution issues debt securities to investors on a regular basis.

In the risk-free framework, the yield-to-maturity r of the risk-free debt security is called the risk-free rate. It connects the present value

and the future value when the security matures at time T determin-
istically.

$$FV = PV \times (1+r)^T. \tag{4.1}$$

If the present value is 0, the future value remains 0. Otherwise, the
value increase steadily as time T increases, which is the time value
of money.

A crucial aspect of (4.1) is that, by virtue of the absolute cred-
itworthiness of the issuer, no uncertainty whatsoever is present in
all the quantities involved. Moreover, the future value is already
guaranteed at the time of purchasing the risk-free security, with the
present value PV being the security's price.

4.2   Compounding Schemes

From the operational standpoint, however, there is an ambiguity
concerning how the present value is to be compounded to yield
the future value. Implicit in (4.1) is that r is the interest rate per
annum and T is the number of years, and thus annual compounding is assumed. What if compounding occurs every half year? In
this case, we have

$$FV = PV \times \left(1 + \frac{r}{2}\right)^{2T}.$$

By the same argument, quarterly, monthly, and daily compounding
schemes are, respectively,

$$FV = PV \times \left(1 + \frac{r}{4}\right)^{4T};$$

$$FV = PV \times \left(1 + \frac{r}{12}\right)^{12T};$$

$$FV = PV \times \left(1 + \frac{r}{365}\right)^{365T}.$$

Obviously, for the same PV, r, and T, the future value is different when the compounding methods differ. The more frequent is

the compounding, the larger will be the future value, which is intuitively straightforward to understand. As an illustration, consider a quarter or 3 months, which means that $T = 1/4 = 3/12$. Let $r = 4\%$ and PV = \$10 million. Under quarterly compounding, the future value is \$10,100,000. By contrast, when monthly compounding is applied, the future value is \$10,100,333.70, which is \$333.70 more.

The first principle of Quantitative Finance is equally applicable to all the compounding schemes, which can be written generically as

$$FV = PV \times \left(1 + \frac{r}{n}\right)^{nT},$$

where n is the compounding frequency. What if $n \to \infty$? In other words, what if the interest is being compounded infinite number of times?

To answer this question, we note that $x^{nT} = (x^n)^T$, and consider only the term involving n as follows:

$$y(n) := \left(1 + \frac{r}{n}\right)^n.$$

Since the function $y(n)$ is positive for $n \geq 0$, you can take the natural log on both sides of the equation, yielding

$$\ln\left(y(n)\right) = n \ln\left(1 + \frac{r}{n}\right) = \frac{\ln\left(1 + \frac{r}{n}\right)}{\frac{1}{n}}.$$

Note that $\ln\left(y(n)\right)$ is indeterminate, being of the form $0/0$ as $n \to \infty$. Hence, the l'Hôpital's rule applies and we obtain

$$\lim_{n \to \infty} \ln\left(y(n)\right) = \lim_{n \to \infty} \frac{r}{1 + \frac{r}{n}} = r,$$

which implies that

$$\lim_{n \to \infty} y(n) = \lim_{n \to \infty} \left(1 + \frac{r}{n}\right)^n = e^r.$$

Consequently, when interest is being compounded infinitely many times, or compounded continuously over time, the first principle of

Quantitative Finance is written as

$$FV = PV \times e^{rT}.$$

The takeaway here is that knowing the interest rate alone is not sufficient. It is also absolutely necessary to have the compounding scheme disambiguated. To underscore this point, consider two risk-free interest rates, 10% versus 9.55%. Intuitively, the higher the risk-free rate is, the larger will be the amount of interest. If the annual compounding scheme applies for 10%, but continuous compounding is adopted for 9.55%, after a year, the former combination of larger interest rate will result in an interest amount *smaller* than that of the latter combination.

The annual compounding rate is also known as the simple interest rate. To compare different compounding schemes, a common practice is to entertain the notion of effective annual rate $\hat{r}$, which is the interest rate that would be obtained if the forward value were to be calculated under the annual compounding scheme. By equating the forward values, the effective interest rate can be backed out. For example, the rate r of continuous compounding is equivalent to $\hat{r}$ via the following equation:

$$FV = PV \times e^{rT} = PV \times (1 + \hat{r})^T.$$

In other words,

$$\hat{r} = e^r - 1.$$

Since $e^r = 1 + r + \frac{1}{2}r^2 + \cdots$, to obtain the same forward value, the effective annual rate $\hat{r}$ must be larger than r. An insight gleaned from this exercise is that the continuously compounding interest rate is the smallest among all the interest rates of the same tenor to produce the same FV.

4.3 Zero-Coupon Yield Curve and Risks

So far, we have not made any distinction between the risk-free rates of debt securities maturing in 1 month, 3 months (a quarter),

6 months (a half year), 1 year, and many years. If you plot the risk-free rates against the times to maturity, you will find that the so-called term structure of interest rates is a flat line. In other words, the yield-to-maturity curve, or yield curve in short, is assumed to be flat with r being the same yield across all maturities at any given point of time t.

Everything else being equal, however, there is no *a priori* reason to believe that a 10-year risk-free bond should have the same yield as a 1-year risk-free security. The risk-free nature of these yields is premised upon the assumption that investors hold these securities to maturity. If the decision to buy and hold till maturity has been made and cast in stone, in addition to the absence of default risk, price risk is absent too. Moreover, the risk-free yield r_0, which provides the link between the future value and the present value, is known at time 0 when the security is purchased, and remains unchanged till maturity.

The marked-to-market value of the fixed income security, however, changes as the interest rate r_t varies on the daily basis to reflect changes in the supply and demand of funds, which translate to price risk. Before maturity, therefore, the risk-free bond will experience paper gain or loss as the interest rate r_t fluctuates from time to time.

4.3.1 *Zero-coupon bonds and interest rate risks*

The yield on the yield curve refers to the return obtained from a zero-coupon bond, also known as the discount bond. From (4.1), and for convenience, let the forward value be fixed at $1. The present value then becomes the price paid to receive $1 in the future. Namely, the dollars amount payable at time t is

$$P_t = \frac{1}{(1 + r_t)^{T-t}}. \tag{4.2}$$

This is the price of a zero-coupon bond at time t. To receive every dollar at the future time T when the bond matures, the price to pay today $t = 0$ is P_0.

Given that the future value of $1 is already determined at the beginning of the investment horizon, it is therefore not possible for the zero-coupon bond to produce an annual yield better than r_t if the bond is held to maturity.

If the risk-free interest rate r_t increases, the price of the zero-coupon bond will decrease, and the marked-to-market value P_t of the zero-coupon bond will also decrease. It might not be optimal to sell the zero-coupon bond at a lower price before maturity when interest rate is increasing. On the other hand, if the interest rate decreases, the bond price increases. But when the hold-until-maturity decision has already been made and cannot be changed, the investor misses out the opportunity to sell the bond at a higher price. It might be optimal for the investor to seize the opportunity to realize a return higher than r_t and thereafter reallocate the proceeds to other asset classes.

Intuitively, compared to the short-term 1-year horizon, long-term investment has more opportunities to see the price of a zero-coupon bond appreciate beyond its purchase price P_0. Therefore, 10-year or long-term fixed income securities have a higher risk of opportunity cost than short-term securities have. Also, long-term bonds face more uncertainty than securities of shorter maturities do. Inherently, the future is uncertain; the further into the future, the greater will the uncertainty be. For example, the investment landscape may transform drastically; the regulatory environment, tax regime, and inflation expectations, just to name a few, may change in a much less predictable way, which is potentially harmful to the investment strategy. Besides these external factors, internally, the investment policies may need an overhaul, or cash may become badly needed, or for some other unforeseeable reasons, the long-term assets may need to be liquidated prematurely under unfavorable market conditions and thus realizing a loss.

On the other hand, short-term investments are subject to reinvestment risk. When short-term securities mature, the resulting proceeds may need to be reinvested at the interest rate on the day of maturity, which is uncertain and could be unfavorable. To the investors of long-term assets, however, the reinvestment risk is of a lesser concern. If there is no better reinvestment opportunity than the current yield-to-maturity r_0, which has already been locked in, investors of long-term securities simply keep holding their long-term bonds. Nevertheless, it does not mean that long-term securities are not completely without reinvestment risk. But compared to the 1-year securities, which mature each year to face the reinvestment risk, a 10-year security matures once in 10 years to face the reinvestment risk. In other words, everything else being equal, a 10-year bond has $1/10$ reinvestment risk of a 1-year bond.

In sum, the opportunity cost risk and the uncertainty risk work against the long-term bond whereas the reinvestment risk is more pronounced for the short-term security. On balance, opportunity cost risk plus uncertainty risk is usually greater than the reinvestment risk. Although uncertain, interest rates of the immediate future are comparatively easier to forecast, and hence the uncertainty is lesser with regard to reinvestment. Another possible reason is that upon maturity of the short-term security, the investor may want to use the proceeds for other purposes (such as consumption), in which case the notion of reinvestment does not even apply in the first place.

Given these considerations, the second principle of Quantitative Finance expects the long-term securities to provide a higher expected return or higher yield to compensate investors of long-term bonds for bearing the relatively higher risk. It follows that the yield curve should be upward sloping under normal market conditions. Two examples of upward sloping yield curve are plotted in Figure 4.1.

At this juncture, it is timely to present an example that makes use of the term structure of zero rates. In our previous introduction to fixed income instruments in Section 2.5, we have used the same interest rate as a basis to discount all the future cash flows of a coupon-bearing bond. In light of the term structure, (2.3) constitutes a very special case where the yield curve is perfectly flat.

In general, it makes sense to use the different zero rates along the term structure to discount the cash flows receivable at different

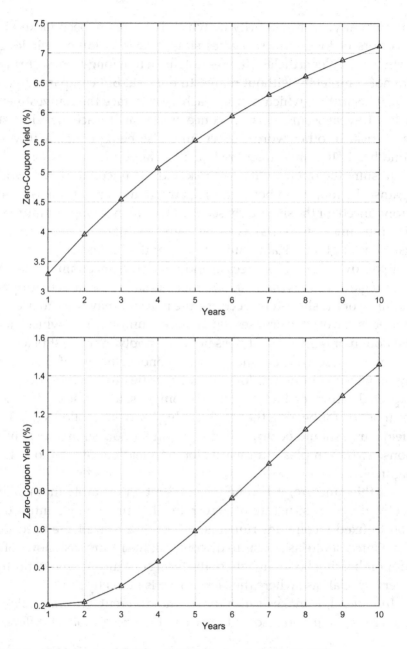

Fig. 4.1   Yield curves of October 7, 1992 (top) and of July 25, 2012.

Source: Dataset created and maintained by Gurkaynak *et al.* [GSW06].

future dates as follows:

$$P = \frac{C/2}{\left(1 + \frac{z_{\frac{1}{2}}}{2}\right)^1} + \frac{C/2}{\left(1 + \frac{z_1}{2}\right)^2} + \cdots + \frac{C/2}{\left(1 + \frac{z_{n-\frac{1}{2}}}{2}\right)^{2n-1}}$$

$$+ \frac{C/2}{\left(1 + \frac{z_n}{2}\right)^{2n}} + \frac{A}{\left(1 + \frac{z_n}{2}\right)^{2n}}. \tag{4.3}$$

In fact, an n-year coupon-bearing bond is practically a portfolio of $2n + 1$ zero bonds. Each coupon to be paid at the jth period (half year) can be regarded as a zero coupon bond of $j/2$ years to maturity. Hence, its price is given by $1/\left(1 + z_j/2\right)^j$. Accordingly, (4.3) is the overall price of $2n + 1$ zero bonds. One of these zero bonds is invested with a larger amount of A, while the other $2n$ zero bonds are identically allocated with $C/2$, where $C = Ac$ and c is the annualized coupon rate. Dividing both sides of (4.3) by A, we obtain the price p for every \$1 of face value:

$$p = \frac{c}{2} \sum_{j=1}^{2n} \frac{1}{\left(1 + \frac{z_j}{2}\right)^j} + \frac{1}{\left(1 + \frac{z_n}{2}\right)^{2n}}. \tag{4.4}$$

4.3.2 *Gurkaynak–Sack–Wright (GSW) dataset*

The two zero-coupon yield curves plotted in Figure 4.1 are taken from a sample in a dataset constructed and maintained by Gurkaynak, Sack, and Wright (GSW) [GSW06]. In the GSW dataset, the zero-coupon yields are continuously compounding interest rates. The yield curve that they construct is based on a large set of outstanding Treasury notes and bonds, which are similar in terms of their liquidity, and plain vanilla. Excluded are

1. Securities with option-like features such as callable bonds and tax-related bonds.
2. Securities with less than three months to maturity, since the yields on these securities often seem to behave oddly.
3. Treasury bills, out of concern about segmented markets.

4. Twenty-year bonds from 1996 onwards, because those securities often appear cheap relative to 10-year notes with comparable duration.

5. The two most recently issued securities with maturities of 2–5, 7, 10, 20, and 30 years for securities issued in 1980 or later.

The restrictions imply that the resulting yield curve is off-the-run. The liquidity or trading intensity of the included Treasury securities for constructing the daily yield curve is relatively uniform across the term structure. In other words, there is no significantly different liquidity risk premium with respect to the time to maturity along the yield curve. This is an important characteristic of the GSW dataset.

Though the GSW dataset dates back to 1961, the 10-year maturity yields are available only from August 16, 1971. To obtain the longest history, yield curves of only 1-year to 10-year maturities are selected for analysis. The yield curve at the bottom in Figure 4.1 comprises a 10-year yield of 1.4607% per annum observed on July 25, 2012, the historical low in the GSW dataset. It is even twice lower than the 1-year yield of the yield curve on top in Figure 4.1. Historically, this yield curve of October 7, 1992, is the steepest ever, with the difference between the 10-year and 1-year yields being 3.8234%.

4.3.3 *Downward-sloping yield curve*

The U.S. Treasury yield curve is dependent on the monetary policy of the Federal Reserve, which sets the target for the federal funds rate in order to strike a balance between economic growth and price stability. The federal funds rate is the interbank interest rate on overnight loans of bank reserves from one bank to another. It is the interest rate that the Federal Reserve tries to influence directly through its monetary policy and open market operation — effectively a form of central bank intervention in the fixed income markets. The Federal Reserve buys and sells short-term Treasury securities in the open market so that the market's federal funds rate stays close to the monetary policy's target federal funds rate.

When the target rate is adjusted,[1] short-term securities such as 1-month and 3-month Treasury bills will be impacted directly because the federal funds rate is a short-term interest rate. In other words, short-term Treasury securities are subject to monetary policy risk.

Just how large is the monetary policy risk? The minimum quantum by which the federal funds rate target is adjusted is 25 basis points. In the fixed income market, a stepwise change or jump of 25 basis points is huge, for the daily market prices of U.S. Treasury securities typically change by less than 10 basis points. In particular, the short-term securities such as 1-month T-bills and 3-month T-bills usually vary by less than 5 basis points day-to-day. Therefore, a change of 25 basis points is a discontinuous change, and the monetary risk may be considered as the jump risk in the fixed income market.

To further illustrate, recall that the present value (PV) is the price investors pay to obtain the future value:

$$\text{PV} = \frac{\text{FV}}{(1+r)^T} \approx \text{FV} \times (1 - rT). \tag{4.5}$$

When r increases, the price of the fixed income security becomes cheaper, and vice versa. Consider, for example, the 1-month T-bill. Before the policy change, suppose the interest rate is 1%. So for every one million dollars, the interest payable is, using the convention of 360 days per year in (4.5),

$$\text{FV} - \text{PV} \approx \text{FV} \times rT = \$1{,}000{,}000 \times \frac{0.01 \times 30}{360} = \$833.33.$$

Suppose an increment of 25 basis points is imposed after the monetary policy announcement. The interest payable becomes

$$\$1{,}000{,}000 \times \frac{0.0125 \times 30}{360} = \$1{,}041.67.$$

---

[1]When inflation is expected to increase, the Federal Reserve is likely to increase the target federal funds rate to fend off excess inflation. Conversely, when inflation rate is expected to remain within an "acceptable" band, the Federal Reserve can afford to be more accommodative by either not changing the target rate, or lowering the target rate to induce economic growth.

The difference of \$208.34 may not seem much. But in the money market, trade size is of the order of hundreds of million. The additional 25 basis points become fairly sizable, especially from the short-term reinvestment or refinancing point of view.

Since the 1990's, the Federal Reserve releases the monetary policy statements on a regular basis. Each statement contains not only the target federal funds rate, but also the likely direction of the target federal funds rate for the next policy statement. In addition, the Federal Reserve takes great pain to craft and debate over the choice of words in its monetary policy statement,[2] in order to make its policy stance as predictable as possible. The precise, measured, and systematic manner by which the monetary policy message is communicated to the market has an eye on reducing the uncertainty surrounding the monetary policy change.

Even so, the market may *perceive* that the monetary policy risk has increased substantially, especially when the overall level of the yield curve has elevated. The market forecasts of the federal funds rate target may become divided, some anticipating the Federal Reserve to cut the target rate, while others expecting the Federal Reserve to leave the target rate untouched. In this scenario, which is unusual, the short-term default-free yields may become larger than the long-term interest rates, resulting in a downward sloping yield curve such as Figure 4.2.

In summary, the slope of the yield curve is influenced by two risks: long-term opportunity plus uncertainty risks, and short-term reinvestment plus monetary policy risks. Intuitively, if we define the term risk differential as

Term Risk Differential := Long-term risks − Short-term risks,

then it is quite natural to think that the slope is steeper if the term risk differential is higher, i.e., the overall gradient of the yield curve

---

[2]The monetary policy statement is one of the most important macroeconomic news in the financial market. All experienced traders know that the scheduled release of the monetary policy statement at 2 p.m. Eastern Time will generate temporarily high volatility in not only the fixed income markets, but also the forex markets, stock markets, commodity markets, futures markets, and the list goes on.

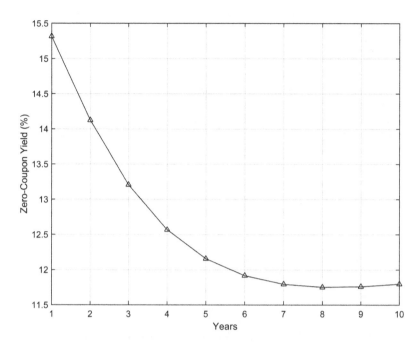

Fig. 4.2   Yield curve of December 12, 1980.
Source: Dataset created and maintained by Gurkaynak *et al.* [GSW06].

is an increasing function of the term risk differential. But when the short-term risks are a lot riskier, then the yield curve may become downward sloping, which means that the term structure of interest rates is inverted.

4.3.4   *U-shape and hump-shape yield curves*

Figure 4.3 provides two examples of U-shape yield curves. The mid-term yields in these curves are lower than the yields of the 1-year and 10-year maturities. This situation arises when the monetary policy risks have risen substantially in anticipation of probable changes to the federal funds target rate. From the upward sloping shape, the yields of short-term maturities increase much more than the rest of the yield curve. Conversely, from the downward sloping shape, the mid-term yields may decrease by a larger amount than usual when the short-term risks — perhaps driven by markets' expectation that

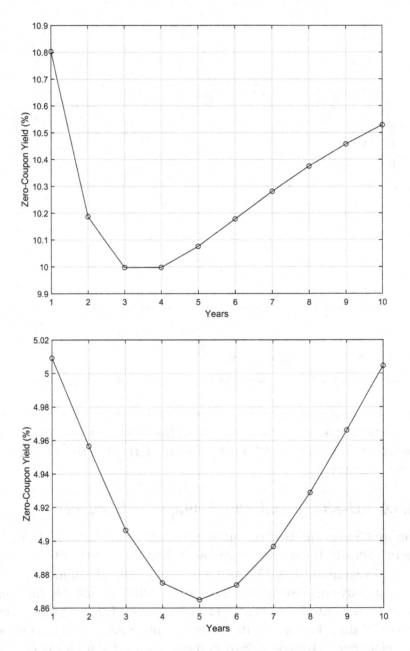

Fig. 4.3   Yield curves of April 29, 1980 (top) and of June 5, 2007.

Source: Dataset created and maintained by Gurkaynak *et al.* [GSW06].

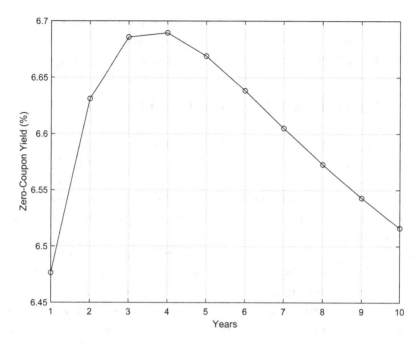

Fig. 4.4   Yield curve of March 5, 1973.

Source: Dataset created and maintained by Gurkaynak *et al.* [GSW06].

the Federal Reserve would lower the federal funds rate target in the future — become a major concern going forward. The net effect is that the 4- to 6-year maturities have relatively lower yields compared to the long-term and short-term maturities.

Another possible shape is the hump-shape term structure shown in Figure 4.4. The hump-shape yield curves, like the U-shape curves, may be thought of as comprising two segments. The short-term segment is upward sloping whereas the mid- to long-term segment is downward sloping. A possible cause for the hump-shape curve could be that the Federal Reserve is about to lower the target federal funds rate. The short-end segment responds quicker than the long-end segment, and thus the hump-shape curve appears.

Note that in contrast to the upward and downward sloping curves, the U- and hump-shape curves are relatively "flat," as the range of variations is tight. In Figures 4.3 and 4.4, the range is less than 0.8% over the 10 maturities. Historical evidence suggests that these two unusual shapes usually occur when the yield curve transitions to and fro between upward and downward sloping shapes.

4.4 Interest Rate Risk and Bond Return

You have seen in the previous sections that the risk-free rate fluctuates in response to changes in the supply and demand of risk-free assets. This section provides a generic description of the return from holding a risk-free asset with respect to the interest rate risk.

At any given time t, the bond price is a function of maturity T, which is denoted as $P(T,t)$. Consider an investor who buys the bond at the price of $P(T,t)$. Instead of holding the bond to maturity, the investor sells it at a later time $t + \epsilon$. The time to maturity of the bond is no longer T but $T - \epsilon$, and the selling price becomes $P(T - \epsilon, t + \epsilon)$. From the perspective of investment and trading, the bond pricing function $P(T,t)$ reflects the fact that you sell a bond that has a shorter maturity $T - \epsilon$ than you bought earlier at time t.

Therefore, if no coupon is received during the holding period ϵ, the return R for holding the bond over a period of ϵ is

$$R = \frac{P(T - \epsilon, t + \epsilon) - P(T,t)}{P(T,t)}.$$

Inserting $0 = -P(T, t + \epsilon) + P(T, t + \epsilon)$ into the numerator gives rise to

$$R = \frac{\left(P(T - \epsilon, t + \epsilon) - P(T, t + \epsilon)\right) + \left(P(T, t + \epsilon) - P(T,t)\right)}{P(T,t)}$$

$$= \frac{P(T - \epsilon, t + \epsilon) - P(T, t + \epsilon)}{P(T,t)} + \frac{P(T, t + \epsilon) - P(T,t)}{P(T,t)}. \tag{4.6}$$

The first term is the return due to the passage of time ϵ in the bond's maturity. The second term captures the return arising from capital appreciation or depreciation of the bond. When the interest rate remains constant, everything else bing equal, Treasury bonds of maturity T should sell at the same price, whether at time t or at time $t + \epsilon$. However, if over the period ϵ, interest rates have changed, then $P(T, t + \epsilon)$ will no long equal $P(T, t)$. This return is thus attributable to the premium for the exposure to the interest rate risk or the price risk alluded to in Section 4.3.

4.4.1 *Return from the passage of time*

The return from the passage of time, denoted by R_d and written as

$$R_d := \frac{P(T - \epsilon, t + \epsilon) - P(T, t + \epsilon)}{P(T, t)} \tag{4.7}$$

is the return earned from lending out the money for a period of ϵ. In the numerator, the Taylor expansion with respect to maturity T results in[3]

$$R_d = \frac{1}{P} \left(-\frac{\partial P}{\partial T}\epsilon + \frac{1}{2!}\frac{\partial^2 P}{\partial T^2}\epsilon^2 - \frac{1}{3!}\frac{\partial^3 P}{\partial T^3}\epsilon^3 \right.$$
$$\left. + \cdots + (-1)^n \frac{1}{n!}\frac{\partial^n P}{\partial T^n}\epsilon^n + \cdots \right). \tag{4.8}$$

In the following, we show that R_d is the return alluded to in the first principle of Quantitative Finance, which suggests that the value of a risk-free asset increases with time, and thus R_d must be positive.

Recall that a zero-coupon bond pays \$1 at maturity and the price to pay today is $P = 1/(1 + r)^T$, as in (4.2). If the zero-coupon bond

---

[3]Recall that the Taylor expansion of function $f(x)$ with respect to a constant c is

$$f(x) = f(c) + \frac{df}{dx}\Big|_{x=c}(x - c) + \frac{1}{2!}\frac{d^2f}{dx^2}\Big|_{x=c}(x - c)^2 + \cdots.$$

In this case, we let $x = T - \epsilon$, differentiate $P(T - \epsilon, t + \epsilon)$ with respect to x, and perform the Taylor expansion with respect to T. The first term in the Taylor's expansion, $P(T, t + \epsilon)$, cancels the term in the numerator of (4.7). Note that $x - T = -\epsilon$ and the first-order term is thus given by $\frac{\partial P}{\partial x}(T, t + \epsilon)\Big|_{x=T}(-\epsilon)$. Next, we note that $\epsilon = T - x$, and hence $t + \epsilon = t + T - x$. Consequently, with $x = T$ and ϵ being a constant, and noting that $\frac{\partial P}{\partial x} = \frac{\partial P}{\partial T}$, we obtain $\frac{\partial P}{\partial x}(T, t + \epsilon)\Big|_{x=T}(-\epsilon) = \frac{\partial P}{\partial T}(T, t)(-\epsilon)$. The same line of arguments is applicable in general for higher-order differentials, which allows us to write (4.8) with P being an abbreviation for $P(T, t)$.

is held to maturity, the (simple) return is, according to (2.1),

$$R(T) = \frac{1 - \dfrac{1}{(1+r)^T}}{\dfrac{1}{(1+r)^T}} = (1+r)^T - 1. \tag{4.9}$$

Given that the bond price is explicitly given by $P = 1/(1+r)^T = \exp(-T \ln(1+r))$, we compute the differentials to obtain

$$\frac{1}{P}\frac{\partial^n P}{\partial T^n} = (-1)^n \ln(1+r)^n, \quad \text{for } n = 1, 2, \dots, \infty.$$

Substituting these differentials into (4.8), we obtain the return on the discount bond as follows:

$$R_d = \sum_{n=1}^{\infty} \frac{\left(\ln(1+r)\epsilon\right)^n}{n!} = \sum_{n=0}^{\infty} \frac{\left(\ln(1+r)\epsilon\right)^n}{n!} - 1.$$

Hence,

$$R_d = \exp\left(\ln(1+r)\epsilon\right) - 1 = (1+r)^\epsilon - 1, \tag{4.10}$$

which is indeed the return $R(T)$ of a discount bond maturing in $\epsilon = T$ years as in (4.9).

4.4.2　*Return due to the change in interest rate*

It goes without saying that the second return in (4.6) does not remain constant, as r may and does vary over time. We define

$$R_s := \frac{P(T, t+\epsilon) - P(T, t)}{P(T, t)} = \frac{dP}{P}.$$

Holding the maturity constant, this return allows us to examine the return in relation to a change in the interest rate.

To gain further insight, we first define the fluctuation (risk) in interest rate in percentages as follows:

$$\Delta r := \frac{(1+r+\delta r) - (1+r)}{1+r} = \frac{\delta r}{1+r}. \tag{4.11}$$

The change in interest rate is denoted by δr in this definition. Next, we consider the first-order price change with respect to r:

$$dP = \frac{\partial P}{\partial r}\delta r.$$

For the discount bond, the price is $P = 1/(1+r)^T$ as before, and we get

$$\frac{\partial P}{\partial r} = -T\frac{1}{(1+r)^{T+1}} = -T\frac{1}{1+r}P.$$

Consequently, the return due to a change in interest rate (yield curve shift) is, up to the first order,

$$R_s = \frac{dP}{P} = -T\frac{\delta r}{1+r} = -T\triangle r.$$

The negative sign in this result is a reflection of the fact that the bond price moves in the opposite direction of the interest rate. From this result, it is evident that the longer the time to maturity is, the larger is the price risk arising from $\triangle r$.

It is interesting to note that the return is proportional to the risk captured by $\triangle r$, which is consistent with the second principle of Quantitative Finance. As an example, suppose the discount bond has 10 years to maturity, and the interest rate decreases from 2.25% to 2%. The return is

$$R_s = -10 \times \frac{-0.0025}{1+0.0225} = 0.02445.$$

If $|\delta r|$ is larger, then the return R_s will be larger.

For 1-year bond, the return due to the same interest rate change is 10 times smaller than the 10-year bond. In other words, the longer is the duration D of the passage of time, the greater is the sensitivity to the interest rate fluctuation. For this reason, we write generically the price risk as

$$R_s = -D\triangle r. \tag{4.12}$$

Now, up to the second order of the change in interest rate δr, the bond price $P(r + \delta r)$ is given by

$$P(r + \delta r) = P(r) + \frac{\partial P}{\partial r}\delta r + \frac{1}{2}\frac{\partial^2 P}{\partial r^2}(\delta r)^2.$$

Accordingly, as a result of interest rate change δr, a more accurate estimate for the bond return is

$$R_s = \frac{P(r + \delta r) - P(r)}{P(r)} = \frac{1}{P(r)} \left(\frac{\partial P}{\partial r} \delta r + \frac{1}{2} \frac{\partial^2 P}{\partial r^2} (\delta r)^2 \right).$$

The percentage price change R_s can thus be written as

$$R_s = -D_m \delta r + \frac{1}{2} C_m (\delta r)^2.$$

In view of (4.12) and the definition of $\triangle r$, (4.11), we define what is known as the modified duration:

$$D_m := \frac{D}{1 + r}.$$

The modified convexity C_m is defined analogously as

$$C_m := \frac{1}{P} \frac{\partial^2 P}{\partial r^2}.$$

As a summary, in terms of the percentage change in the interest rate, $\triangle r$, the return corresponding to the interest rate risk is

$$R_s = -D \triangle r + \frac{1}{2} C (\triangle r)^2, \tag{4.13}$$

where the convexity C is

$$C := (1 + r)^2 C_m.$$

Again we see in (4.13) that the price risk or interest rate risk is captured in a way that is consistent with the second principle of Quantitative Finance. The larger the interest rate risk (i.e., $|\triangle r|$) is, the larger will be the absolute value $|R_s|$ of the return.

For zero-coupon bonds or discount bonds, the duration is the time to maturity T, so $D = T$. It is also straightforward to derive the result that the convexity is $C = T(T + 1)$ (see Q6). For the straight bond holders, the convexity always acts in their favor, as it always contributes a positive return in (4.13).

4.5   Interest Rate Risk and the Yield Curve Shape

In this section, we apply the results obtained in Section 4.4, which are consistent with the principles of Quantitative Finance, to the problem of modeling the yield curve shape from the perspectives of the long-term and short-term risks discussed earlier.

4.5.1 A model of long-term risks

Recall (4.6) for the bond return. It has two components, one due to the passage of time, and the other due to the fluctuation in interest rate. As discussed in the previous subsections, the bond return is,

$$R = R_d + R_s = (1+r)^\epsilon - 1 - D\triangle r + \frac{1}{2}C(\triangle r)^2,$$

which is the sum of the two constituents, (4.10) and (4.13). For zero-coupon bonds, $D = T, C = T(T+1)$, and we have

$$R = (1+r)^\epsilon - 1 - T\triangle r + \frac{1}{2}T(T+1)(\triangle r)^2. \qquad (4.14)$$

Thus, the return on a zero-coupon bond is dependent on its time to maturity T.

By setting $\epsilon = 1$, the expected annual yield R is,

$$\mathbb{E}(R) = r - (T-1)\mathbb{E}(\triangle r) + \frac{1}{2}(T-1)T\mathbb{E}((\triangle r)^2), \quad \text{for } T \geq 1.$$

This is the marked-to-market yield of a zero-coupon bond with original T years to maturity after a year has passed. Sure enough, if the 1-year Treasury security is held to maturity when $T = 0$, from (4.14), the return is r, which is none other than the yield to maturity at the time of purchase a year ago.

Therefore, the second component $-T\triangle r + T(T+1)(\triangle r)^2/2$ in (4.14) is the potential risk that the investor is exposed to, or the potential return that the investor might gain if the investor decides to sell when $\triangle r < 0$ and the zero-coupon bond price rises. Put differently, the potential gain is the risk premium or compensation for the exposure to interest rate risk $\triangle r$.

From the perspective of the term structure of zero-coupon yields, it is appropriate to regard r as the level. Next, consider the case where $\triangle r > 0$. This scenario is detrimental to the bondholder. When an urgent need arises and the bond can no longer be held to maturity as previously planned, the asset might have to be liquidated at an unfavorable price. To compensate for this uncertainty risk, it is appropriate to consider the absolute value $|\triangle r|$ instead. Then, $T\mathbb{E}(|\triangle r|) + T(T+1)\mathbb{E}((\triangle r)^2)/2$ might be regarded as the risk premium for bearing not only this uncertainty risk, but also the opportunity cost risk, which is the risk of missing the opportunity to profit from selling the security at a higher price when the interest rate drops before maturity.

For these reasons, the zero-coupon yields on the yield curve with opportunity cost risk and uncertainty risk taken into consideration can be expressed as

$$Y_T^{(\ell)} = r + T\mathbb{E}(|\triangle r|) + \frac{1}{2}T(T+1)\mathbb{E}((\triangle r)^2). \qquad (4.15)$$

In this model, we have assumed that the reinvestment risk and the monetary policy risk are absent for the time being. From this expression, it is evident that the yield $Y_T^{(\ell)}$ on the yield curve is larger than the level r. Also, when $T = 0$, we have $Y_0^{(\ell)} = r$ as required. The level r is the baseline return that the investor earns for holding the risk-free asset to maturity, in accordance to the first principle of Quantitative Finance. The additional terms in (4.15) are the risk premiums expected by investors for bearing the opportunity cost risk and the uncertainty risk.

For the 1-year yield,

$$Y_1^{(\ell)} = r + \mathbb{E}(|\triangle r|) + \mathbb{E}((\triangle r)^2).$$

Similarly, for 10-year maturity, the annual yield is obtained as follows:

$$Y_{10}^{(\ell)} = r + 10\mathbb{E}(|\triangle r|) + 55\mathbb{E}((\triangle r)^2).$$

We see that $Y_{10}^{(\ell)}$ has a larger opportunity cost risk premium, which is $10\mathbb{E}(|\triangle r|) + 55\mathbb{E}((\triangle r)^2)$. Clearly, the spread between 10-year and 1-year yields is

$$Y_{10}^{(\ell)} - Y_1^{(\ell)} = 9\mathbb{E}(|\triangle r|) + 54\mathbb{E}((\triangle r)^2),$$

which is necessarily positive under normal conditions when the opportunity cost risk and the uncertainty risk are dominant.

With $Y_{10}^{(\ell)} \geq Y_1^{(\ell)}$, we have thus demonstrated that the 10-year yield on the yield curve is greater than the 1-year yield, which means that the long-term risk is mainly responsible for the yield curve to slope upward, under the assumption that $\triangle r$ is not too large in magnitude.

We define a gross slope s of the yield curve from the spread between the 10-year and 1-year yields as follows:

$$s = \frac{Y_{10}^{(\ell)} - Y_1^{(\ell)}}{10 - 1} = \mathbb{E}(|\triangle r|) + 6\mathbb{E}((\triangle r)^2). \qquad (4.16)$$

Since $(\triangle r)^2 = |\triangle r|^2$, the gross slope s is rewritten as

$$s = \mathbb{E}(|\triangle r| + 6|\triangle r|^2).$$

The gross slope s can be estimated from the observed yield curve. Therefore, we write

$$\mathbb{E}(6|\triangle r|^2 + |\triangle r| - s) = 0.$$

In this form, an implied absolute percentage change in the interest rate is obtainable as

$$|\triangle r|_* = \frac{-1 + \sqrt{1 + 24s}}{12} \approx s. \qquad (4.17)$$

The implied $|\triangle r|_*$ is interpretable as a measure to estimate the gross average interest rate risk across the 1-year to 10-year maturities. As a numerical example, consider the largest ever spread $Y_{10}^{(\ell)} - Y_1^{(\ell)}$ of 3.8234% in Figure 4.1. The slope is 0.4248% per year. The implied $|\triangle r|_*$ works out to be 0.4145% per year, which provides an estimate for the interest rate risk on average across the 1- to 10-year maturities.

Another interesting observation is that $1 + 24s$ in (4.17) must be positive. Hence, the gross slope of the yield curve must satisfy

$$s > -\frac{1}{24} = -4.1667\%.$$

This result provides a criterion to examine the application limit of the model. More specifically, the slope of an inverted yield curve cannot be steeper than $1/24$.

Finally, we note from (4.17) that if the term structure is flat, i.e., $s = 0$, then $|\triangle r|_* = 0$, which suggests that the bond market has little interest rate risk. This is probably an understatement as the reinvestment risk and in particular, monetary policy risk, are not accounted for.

4.5.2 *A model of short-term risks*

In the previous subsection, we have provided a model of long-term risk and how the model can be used to account for the positive slope s under normal market conditions. The model assumes that the zero-coupon assets under consideration are default-free, and that they have the same level of trading activity or liquidity. The model uses only the notion of holding-period return, and a straightforward mathematical decomposition into two parts. With an additional caveat that the expected value of the percentage interest rate fluctuation $|\triangle r|$ is not too large, the model obtained is in principle robust against the model risk because only the Taylor expansion is involved.

Holding the reinvestment risk constant, the model of long-term opportunity cost risk always gives rise to a monotonically upward sloping yield curve. This is because the change of slope with respect to T is always positive. Indeed, from (4.15), we find

$$\frac{\partial^2 Y_T^{(\ell)}}{\partial T^2} = \mathbb{E}\left((\triangle r)^2\right) > 0.$$

However, to account for the typically concave shape of the yield curve, we need to incorporate the reinvestment risk. In contrast to the opportunity cost risk, the reinvestment risk is the risk of facing a potentially lower interest rate at maturity. From the reinvestment perspective, the lower interest rate means a lower yield. To compensate for this risk, the current interest rate must be *lower* so that come maturity, having collected the par value of 1, the interest rate might be *higher* for reinvestment.

As mentioned previously, short-term security such as 1-year issue has to grapple with reinvestment risk every year, while a 10-year bond once every 10 years. In other words, the reinvestment risk is negatively related to the time to maturity T. Inspired by Nelson and Siegel [NS87], we postulate that the reinvestment risk is captured by the following function of T:

$$R_r(T) = \frac{1 - e^{-T/\tau}}{\frac{T}{\tau}} - e^{-T/\tau},$$

where τ is a positive parameter that severs as a scale of time. The function $R_r(T)$ can be written as

$$R_r(T) = \frac{e^{-T/\tau}\left(e^{T/\tau} - 1 - T/\tau\right)}{\frac{T}{\tau}}$$

$$= \frac{e^{-T/\tau}\left(\frac{1}{2}(T/\tau)^2 + \frac{1}{6}(T/\tau)^3 + \cdots\right)}{\frac{T}{\tau}},$$

which is strictly positive, i.e., $R_r(T) > 0$ for all $T \geq 0$.

The function $R_r(T)$ has a maximum at approximately $T = 1.25\tau$ for $\tau < 1$. Hence, when τ is smaller than 0.795905, which corresponds to $T \geq 1$, the function $R_r(T)$ decreases monotonically as T increases. In this range of T, the larger T is, the smaller is the value of the reinvestment risk premium. Moreover, when T becomes larger and larger, $R_r(T)$ will start to converge toward 0. This property of $R_r(T)$ fits our earlier discussion of reinvestment risk, where short-term securities are generally more exposed to reinvestment risk than long-term bonds are.

In the yield curve setting, since the yield must be lower as discussed earlier to account for the reinvestment risk, we write

$$Y_T^{(s)} = r - \beta_s \left(\frac{1 - e^{-T/\tau}}{\frac{T}{\tau}} - e^{-T/\tau}\right).$$

In this model, the long-term risks (opportunity cost risk and uncertainty risk) are assumed to be absent for the time being. The parameter β_s acts as the short-term risk premium. It is noteworthy that this model satisfies the important condition that $Y_0 = r$ by applying the l'Hôpital's Rule as follows:

$$\lim_{T \to 0} \frac{1 - e^{-T/\tau}}{\frac{T}{\tau}} = 1.$$

Consequently, $\lim_{T \to 0} Y_T^{(s)} = r$, the level of the yield curve.

4.5.3 Summary of a tale of long- and short-term risks

In sum, using the symbol Y_T for the T-year zero-coupon yield, we write

$$Y_T = r + \beta^{(\ell)} \left(aT + \frac{b}{2} T(T+1) \right) - \beta^{(s)} \left(\frac{1 - e^{-T/\tau}}{\frac{T}{\tau}} - e^{-T/\tau} \right),$$

where $a = \mathbb{E}(|\triangle r|)$ and $b = \mathbb{E}((\triangle r)^2)$. This yield curve model Y_T may be regarded as a reduced model of zero-coupon yields. It is motivated by the results obtained from analyzing the holding-period return and the insights articulated by Nelson and Siegel [NS87].

The six parameters are r, τ, $\beta^{(\ell)}$, $\beta^{(s)}$, a, and b. If the higher-order term $\mathbb{E}((\triangle r)^2)$ in (4.15) can be ignored, the parameter space reduces to four dimensions, as $\beta^{(\ell)} \times a$ collapses into one parameter $\beta^{(l)}$. Accordingly, we obtain a parsimonious model with only four parameters.

$$Y_T = r + \beta^{(l)} T - \beta^{(s)} \left(\frac{1 - e^{-T/\tau}}{\frac{T}{\tau}} - e^{-T/\tau} \right). \qquad (4.18)$$

As before, r is the level of the yield curve. It is the risk-free yield in the absence of any risk. The second parameter is $\beta^{(l)}$, which is the aggregate premium for the long-term risks of opportunity cost and uncertainty. The long-term risks are directly proportional to T, and contribute toward the slope of the yield curve only. The nonlinear term in the model contributes toward not only the slope but also the curvature. The parameter τ provides a scale of the time T for the short-term risk modeling, which is weighted by the short-term risk premium $\beta^{(s)}$.

Using the parsimonious version of Y_T, (4.18), we simulate or fit the two yield curves of Figure 4.1. The first yield curve on top in Figure 4.5 is given by

$$r = 6.17\%; \quad \beta^{(l)} = 0.00132; \quad \beta^{(s)} = 0.105; \quad \tau = 0.4.$$

The yield curve at the bottom is given by

$$r = -0.35\%; \quad \beta^{(l)} = 0.00174; \quad \beta^{(s)} = -0.015; \quad \tau = 0.3.$$

Visual inspection[4] shows that they bear strong resemblance to the respective curves in Figure 4.1. For the first set of parameters, every estimate is, as anticipated, positive. For the second set of parameters, both the level r and $\beta^{(s)}$ are negative. The "wrong" sign[5] for the short-term risks may be attributed to the Federal Reserve pursuing the unprecedented experiment on ultra accommodative quantitative easing. Having set the target federal funds rate close to 0%, the Federal Reserve has to resort to "Operation Twist." Interestingly, it seems that quantitative easing is characterized by a negative interest rate level.

It is noteworthy that downward-sloping curves can be generated by having a negative $\beta^{(s)}$. The negativity of $\beta^{(s)}$ suggests that reinvestment is not a concern, for the short-term interest rates are typically expected to rise higher when the yield curve is being inverted from the upward-sloping shape. The U-shape curve is simulated by the short-term weight $\beta^{(s)}$ having a negative value too. On the other hand, the hump-shape curve is generated by the long-term weight $\beta^{(l)}$ instead taking a negative value. All in all, these abnormal shapes entail either $\beta^{(s)}$ or $\beta^{(l)}$ to be negative.

---

[4]Nonlinear least squares curve fitting with constraints can be performed to fit the model with the GSW data [GSW06] for 1- to 10-year maturities.

[5]Note that the first principle of Quantitative Finance does not exclude the possibility of a negative risk-free rate.

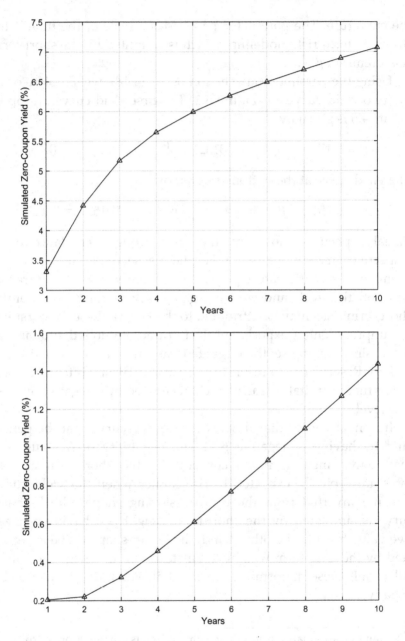

Fig. 4.5   Simulated yield curves corresponding to Figure 4.1.

4.6 Liquidity Risk

The notion of liquidity[6] intuitively attempts to capture how smooth does a financial transaction flow through the market. Intuitive as it may seem, it is hard to quantify liquidity. As explained in Section 2.3 and also in Section 3.9, a measure of liquidity is the difference between the prevailing best bid and ask prices. The bid-ask spread is a gauge of liquidity risk in trading. Suppose you as a trader have purchased an asset at the higher ask or offer price and suppose you regret and immediately sell the asset at the lower bid price. The resulting loss is captured by the bid-ask spread. The wider the bid-ask spread is, the larger will the loss be.

In the market of Treasury securities, investors prefer on-the-run bonds than off-the-run securities. On-the-run Treasury issues are the most recently auctioned bonds and are attractive to many investors and traders. Because of the stronger preference and thus a higher demand, on-the-run securities typically trade at a premium to off-the-run Treasuries, as investors are willing to pay a higher price for the greater tradability offered by these securities. So usually, off-the-run securities offer a higher yield (and thus priced lower) than on-the-run securities, everything else being equal.

Having fitted a smoothed Treasury yield curve, Gurkaynak *et al.* construct a "synthetic" off-the-run Treasury security with any maturity date and coupon rate desired [GSW06]. They compare the yield of the synthetic Treasury security with the yield of on-the-run security of equivalent maturity and coupon payments. Their empirical analysis shows that the liquidity premium is about 10 basis points when the market is tranquil. More specifically,

Yield of off-the-run 10-year issue − Yield of 10-year on-the-run issue
$$\approx 10 \text{ basis points.}$$

---

[6]The term "liquidity" in the context of credit and funding is a totally different concept altogether. In this section, our discussion of liquidity is anchored upon the degree of ease with which a security is converted into cash and vice versa by way of transaction.

Significantly, Gurkaynak *et al.* [GSW06] note that this liquidity premium appears to move up during periods of financial turmoil, including the stock market crash of 1987 and the seizing up of markets in the fall of 1998. Moreover, the premium remained relatively high from 2000 to 2002, a period during which the supply of on-the-run issues was curtailed.

4.7   Credit Risk

So far, we have considered only non-defaultable or risk-free securities. From the U.S.-centric viewpoint, all other bonds are considered to be defaultable, including those issued by Germany, the U.K., Japan, and a handful of smaller developed economies whose sovereign debts are rated as triple A. Corporate bonds, in particular, will default on their debt obligations when corporations are hit with severe cash flow problems to pay the coupons and/or principals.

By the second principle of Quantitative Finance, bonds with default risk should provide a yield higher than the risk-free bonds. The higher the credit risk is, the greater is the yield from the risky asset.

It is a common practice to compare the yield of a defaultable bond with that of a risk-free bond having the same time to maturity. In other words, holding the time to maturity constant, the spread between the interest rates on bonds with default risk and default-free bonds indicates how much additional yield is needed to entice investors to buy the risky bonds of identical maturity, coupon rate, trading liquidity, etc.

An example of this additional yield, commonly known as the Treasury-Eurodollar spread, or the TED spread, is the difference between the 3-month LIBOR and the 3-month U.S. Treasury bill. LIBOR stands for "London InterBank Offered Rate." It is the average interest rate at which banks could potentially borrow large amounts of money from each other in London. The British Banking Association on each London business day conducts a survey, asking major banks in London to base their LIBOR rate submission for each of the 10 major currencies with 15 maturities quoted for each — ranging from overnight to 12 months — on the following question:

> At what rate could you borrow funds, were you to do so by asking for and then accepting interbank offers in a reasonable market size just prior to 11 am?

In other words, LIBOR serves as an indicative benchmark of the average rate at which a LIBOR contributor bank might be able to obtain unsecured funding in the London interbank market for a given period, in a given currency. It is neither the risk free rate, nor the actual interest rate transacted in the interbank market. LIBOR reflects the aggregate average of the participating banks' credit ratings.

The Treasury-Eurodollar (TED) spread is therefore the difference between the interest rate at which the U.S. Treasury is able to borrow on a three-month period via T-bills, and the three-month LIBOR at which major banks in London could obtain funding in U.S. dollars without posting collateral. Since the risk of a major bank defaulting is more likely than the U.S. government defaulting, the TED spread is the additional return needed to compensate creditors for bearing the credit risk. The TED spread measures the overall credit risk on average that banks in London pose on each other. The higher the perceived risk that one or several banks may have liquidity or solvency problems, the higher the rate a bank will ask of its loans to other banks compared to its loans to the government. Consequently, the TED spread is an indicator of the systemic interbank credit risk. It provides a gauge to diagnose the health of the entire banking system.

Figure 4.6 plots the TED spread from January 1986 through end of March 2015. The average TED spread is 60 basis points for this sample period. Although the standard deviation is only 45 basis points, it is evident that there are extreme movements in the time series, when the TED spread can be approximately a hundred times larger, reaching as high as 458 basis points at the peak of the 2007–2008 credit crisis.

More generically, the spread with reference to the U.S. Treasury rate — also called the risk premium — comprises not only the credit

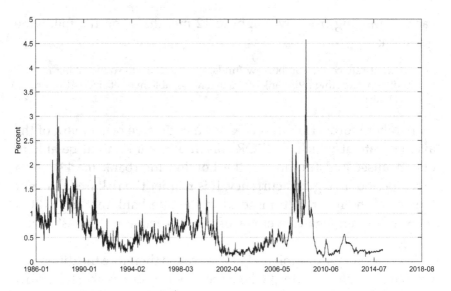

Fig. 4.6   TED spread.

Source: Federal Reserve Bank of St. Louis, TED Spread [TEDRATE].

risk but also the liquidity risk discussed in the previous section. This is because risk-free Treasury bonds are more liquidly traded compared to non-government bonds such as U.S. corporate bonds. In other words, for a given maturity, the spread's composition may be illustrated as follows:

$$\text{Yield spread} = \text{Credit spread} + \text{Liquidity risk.}$$

Suppose the credit spread can be isolated from the overall yield spread, and applying the second principle of Quantitative Finance, higher credit risk implies larger credit spread. Any models of credit risk must satisfy this qualitative feature.

4.8   Exercises

Q1. This is the First Illustration in one of the earliest books on financial mathematics by Moore [Moo29]: The Marshall National Bank pays 4% on time deposits. What is the annual interest payment on a time deposit of $250,000?

Q2. The effective annual rate (EAR) is a useful concept to compare the yields of money market securities, which mature in less than a year. Suppose Bank U offers a structured product consisting of two time deposits with equal weight:

(A) A 1-year time deposit at 2.68%.
(B) A half-year time deposit of 3.00% followed by another half year at 2.50%.

    (a) What is the overall EAR of the second deposit (B)?
    (b) What is the overall EAR of this structured product?
    (c) A simple time deposit offered by Bank V yields 2.50% for 1 year tenor. For a principal sum of $50,000, how much more interest does Bank U pay in comparison to Bank V?

Q3. Annuity is a stream of regular cash flows, either in the form of payment or receipt. Suppose you save an amount c every year, up to n years from time 0. The interest rate is y. Let $x := 1 + y$.

    (a) Show that the cash flow of this annuity at maturity amounts to

$$\frac{cx\left(x^{n-1} - 1\right)}{x - 1}.$$

    (b) Suppose you save $100 every half year for 20 years. How much will the annuity amount to if the interest rate is 4%?

Q4. The prevailing interest rate is 10% per annum for the tenor of 20 years. Suppose a bond pays 7% per annum and the frequency of coupon payment is semiannual. This bond is traded at $74.26 per $100 par value.

    (a) If $74.26 is invested as a time deposit at the prevailing interest rate of 10% for 20 years with semiannual compounding. What is the cash flow from this time deposit at maturity?
    (b) Verify that the yield to maturity of the bond is indeed 10%.
    (c) What is the total cash flow from the bond?

(d) Suppose every coupon received can be immediately reinvested as a time deposit earning 10% per annum with semi-annual compounding, and the maturity date of the time deposit matches that of the bond.

    i. What is the total cash flow from these reinvestments at maturity?

    ii. What is the total cash flow of the bond plus reinvestments?

    iii. Why must the total cash flow of the bond plus reinvestments equal that of the time deposit in Q4(a)?

    iv. What is the total interest earned from reinvesting?

    v. What will happen if the coupons cannot be reinvested at the same rate of 10% per annum?

Q5. The total cash flow of the bond plus reinvestments should equal the time deposit of the same tenor and compounding scheme. Suppose p is the bond price in percent. Also denote the per period coupon rate by c and the bond yield per period by y. The number of periods is n.

(a) Derive the compact bond pricing formula below based on this insight and show that:

$$(1+y)^n = \frac{c-y}{c-py}. \qquad (4.19)$$

(b) Show that an approximate solution of the compact bond pricing formula (4.19) for the yield to maturity y is

$$y \approx \frac{nc - (p-1)}{np - \dfrac{(p-1)^2}{2c}}.$$

(c) Use the bond information in Q4 to check the approximate solution.

(d) Show that the approximation becomes more exact as $p \longrightarrow 1$.

Q6. The definition of convexity requires a second derivative of the bond price with respect to the interest rate r. Show that the convexity of the zero-coupon bond is indeed $T(T+1)$, where T is the time to maturity.

Chapter 5

Derivatives with Linear Payoffs

5.1 Introduction

In the previous chapter, we have discussed risk-free securities and the term structure of risk-free yields in detail. The takeaway is that the interest rate risks, which reflect the fluctuation in the supply and demand of fixed income securities, cause the risk-free bond price to be dependent on the time to maturity. By pricing the maturities of bonds issued by the same U.S. Treasury differently, the term structure of risk-free interest rates becomes anything but a flat line. We then applied the principles of Quantitative Finance to model the shapes of the yield curve by the introductions of long-term and short-term risks.

This chapter provides more applications of the three principles, with a bent toward pricing the derivatives: Financial contracts that derive their values on the basis of their underlying assets and payoff conditions. We start the chapter by first introducing the basic features of derivatives. Thereafter, we apply the principles of Quantitative Finance to price financial derivatives with linear payoff.

Traded exclusively OTC, the financial derivatives discussed in this chapter are frequently used by financial institutions and corporations to manage their interest rate and forex risks, and also their assets and liabilities. According to a 2014 report[1] by the Bank of International Settlements, the daily average turnover of outright FX forward was \$680 billion in April 2013. In a separate BIS report,[2] 2013 April daily turnover of forward rate agreements was \$754 billion. More impressively, turnover of interest rate swaps was \$1,415 billion. The sheer daily sizes of these FX and interest rate derivative markets suggest the importance of these instruments to the financial institutions.

5.1.1 *Linear payoffs*

The forward contract discussed in Section 3.5 is a typical derivative whose payoff is a linear function of the underlying asset price. At the initiation of the forward contract, neither payment is made nor is the delivery of the underlying asset. Only the price for future transaction is agreed upon. Effectively, the forward contract is a price agreement for transaction at the maturity date.

The market convention has it that the party paying the fixed or pre-determined cash flow F_0 and receiving the uncertain or floating cash flow S_T is the buyer. Based on this convention, the net cash flow to the buyer at maturity T is expressed as follows:

$$\text{Cash flow to the buyer} = S_T - F_0.$$

At time 0, the underlying asset's value S_T to be realized at maturity T is uncertain, and therefore called floating. The fixed price F_0 in the forward contract is certain, as it is determined at the time of contract initiation and held constant throughout until maturity.

As evident in Figure 5.1, the forward buyer will have a positive payoff if at maturity $S_T > F_0$. The forward buyer pays the forward seller F_0 for the underlying asset and immediately sell it in the open market at a higher price of S_T, thus realizing the payoff $S_T - F_0$. On the other hand, the forward buyer's payoff will be negative if $S_T < F_0$. Despite the market price being lower, the forward buyer

---

[1]See the "Triennial Central Bank Survey: Global foreign exchange market turnover in 2013."

[2]See the "Triennial Central Bank Survey: OTC interest rate derivatives turnover in April 2013."

is contractually obligated to buy the underlying asset at the higher price of F_0.

Moreover, whether positive or negative, the payoff function is linear with respect to S_T. On the other hand, it is noteworthy that in theory, the payoff can be infinitely large as the underlying price S_T is not bounded from above. The worst downside, on the other hand, is when $S_T = 0$ and therefore limited.

5.1.2   Nonlinear payoffs

Though the downside is limited to $-F_0$, it may still be unbearable for the risk-averse forward buyer. Is it possible to cap the down-side risk to 0? A positive answer lies in the modification of the pay-off function. As shown in Figure 5.2, the buyer does not have any downside but only the upside. Stated differently, the buyer has the "right" to benefit from the upside gain but no obligation whatsoever when S_T disfavors the long forward position.

The payoff function in Figure 5.2 is nonlinear, because of the "kink" at $S_T = F_0$ where the gradient of the line changes. Mathematically, the payoff is expressed as

$$\max\left(S_T - F_0, 0\right) \geq 0.$$

The nonlinear payoff function is totally unfavorable to the seller, who has zero upside and only the downside. No seller will want to enter into an agreement that has absolutely no possibility of a gain. Therefore, unlike the forward contract for which no cash

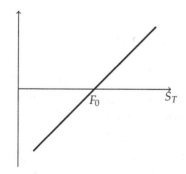

Fig. 5.1   The payoff of the forward buyer at maturity T.

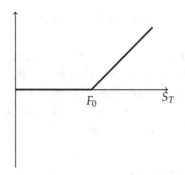

Fig. 5.2   The payoff of the option buyer at maturity T.

flow exchange occurs at the contract initiation, sellers of this payoff function will demand a premium to be paid upfront by the buyers to compensate them for this asymmetric payoff arrangement.

Financial contracts of nonlinear payoffs, known as options, are more general. In fact, the forward contract discussed earlier in Section 5.1.1 is just a special case where the payoff function becomes linear, which obliges the buyer to pay the seller when $S_T - F_0$ is negative. Void of any optionality, the "option" premium must be zero at contract initiation.

In this chapter, we discuss only derivatives with linear payoff for which both parties have contractual obligation. The chapter applies the three principles of Quantitative Finance to price these linear derivative products, which have become the indispensable tools for commercial banks to deal with the market risks. For options and derivatives with nonlinear payoffs, we leave it to the subsequent chapters.

5.2   Forward Forex Rate

In Chapter 3, we have provided an example of how the principles of Quantitative Finance are useful in pricing a forward contract on stock. The forward price F_0 is shown to be

$$F_0 = (1 + r_0)^T S_0. \tag{5.1}$$

This formula provides the theoretical value of the forward contract at time 0, given the underlying price S_0, the risk-free rate r_0, and the time to maturity T. The key idea in obtaining (5.1) is to create a self-financing and assured future cash flow.

In this section, we consider the forward contract on exchange rate. The OTC market for forward FX rates is almost as large as the spot market. A simple reason is that both traders, investors, as well as merchants and firms in the real economy need to hedge their currency exposures.

5.2.1 *Interest rate parity*

Suppose the spot exchange rate is denoted by S_0 and the to-be-determined forward exchange rate is denoted by f_0. These rates are in terms of the quote currency to exchange for one unit of the base currency. Let the interest rate for the quote currency be r_q and the interest rate for the base currency be r_b. Moreover, these interest rates are quoted at time 0 for tenor T, which is the same as the time to maturity for the forward contract.

At time 0, the forward exchange rate seller:

- Sells a forward contract with an agreed exchange rate f_0 for 1 unit of base currency at maturity;
- Borrows quote currency of notional amount $\frac{S_0}{(1+r_b)^T}$ at the rate of r_q;
- Exchanges the borrowed cash for $\frac{1}{(1+r_b)^T}$ units of base currency at the spot exchange rate of S_0; and
- Uses the exchanged base currency to buy a risk-free zero-coupon bond of amount $\frac{1}{(1+r_b)^T}$ in the base currency.

Notice that at time 0, the net cash flow is zero for the forward seller.

At maturity, time T, the zero-coupon bond matures and 1 unit of cash in the base currency is obtained from the bond issuer. The forward seller will have to:

- Sell the obtained 1 unit of base currency at the pre-determined price of f_0;
- Pay the loan of an amount

$$\frac{S_0}{(1+r_b)^T} \times (1+r_q)^T.$$

The net cash flow at time T is therefore

$$f_0 - \frac{S_0}{(1+r_b)^T} \times (1+r_q)^T.$$

As evident in Figure 5.3, the self-financing position at time 0 is established by the forward seller as the net cash flow is 0. The first principle of Quantitative Finance states that the risk-free asset whose value is zero remains zero. Therefore, the net cash flow at time T must also be zero, leading to what is known as the interest rate parity.

$$f_0 = \frac{(1+r_q)^T}{(1+r_b)^T} S_0. \tag{5.2}$$

At maturity when the spot rate S_T is observed, the payoff to the forward buyer is $S_T - f_0$.

This result is similar to the forward price of stock. Indeed, r_q is the earlier risk-free rate r_0, for stocks are transacted in the quote currency. The novelty here is the "discount factor" $1/(1+r_b)^T$. In other words, the forward exchange rate f_0 can be written as

$$f_0 = \frac{F_0}{(1+r_b)^T},$$

where F_0 is expressed in (5.1) with $r_0 = r_q$.

Intuitively, it makes sense to have F_0 reduced in value by $1/(1+r_b)^T$. For stock, the forward seller possesses the shares from time 0 to T. Meanwhile, the seller does not benefit from owning the stock as it is not paying dividend. By contrast, the base currency purchased by the forward seller can be invested in the risk-free bond issued in the base currency to earn interest.

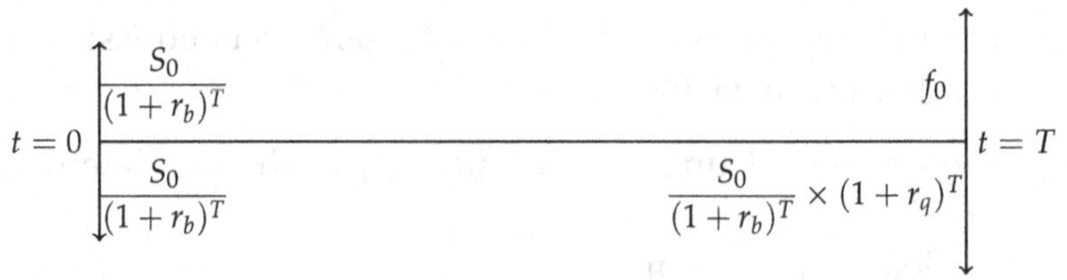

Fig. 5.3   The cash flows of forward forex seller.

Rightfully, the cash flow from the interest payment belongs to the forward buyer. This is because if you, the forward buyer, were to purchase the base currency now, you would invest in the risk-free bond denominated in the base currency as well. In a way, forward seller is merely the care-taker of the underlying asset. Any cash flow resulting from possessing the asset belongs to the forward buyer. In this light, if a stock pays dividend before the forward contract expires, the forward price F_0 must be made smaller by the dividend.

Conversely, it is costly for the forward seller to hold the asset on behalf of the forward buyer. If the forward seller sells the asset at the spot price of S_0 and invests the proceeds at the risk-free rate of r_0, by time T, the value will be $(1 + r_0)^T S_0$. That is the reason why F_0 is larger than S_0 when the underlying asset attracts no cash flow. In general, the costs incurred for holding the asset will be factored into the forward price by increasing it, and the benefits for possessing the asset will decrease the theoretical value of the forward price.

5.2.2 Forward FX rates in practice

In practice, the rate for a forward FX deal is generally expressed as the amount by which the forward rate diverges from the spot rate.

$$f_0 - S_0 = \frac{(1 + r_q)^T - (1 + r_b)^T}{(1 + r_b)^T} S_0.$$

This difference is called the forward margin, also known as the swap point. If the swap point is negative, the base (foreign) currency is said to be trading at a forward discount to the quote (domestic) currency. From the perspective of the investor whose country of domicile's currency is the base currency, the current spot rate S_0 is cheap, because one unit of base currency now can exchange for more units of quote currency than the forward FX rate f_0 can in the future. Conversely, if this difference is positive, it is known as the forward premium.

As a percentage per annum, we write

$$\frac{f_0 - S_0}{S_0} = \frac{(1 + r_q)^T - (1 + r_b)^T}{(1 + r_b)^T} \approx (r_q - r_b)T.$$

In this form, the forward FX deal is really a trade on the difference or the spread between the two interest rates r_b and r_q of tenor T. These two rates are the yields of debt securities issued by the governments of the base and quote currencies, respectively.

Interestingly, the forward margin in percent offers a comparison of the two yield curves populated by, respectively, r_q and r_b. With the U.S. dollar being the base currency, and given the quadruple-A rating given by Buffett, $r_q > r_b$ will be the case across the term structure for the vast majority of the quote currencies. This credit-driven argument suggests that most of the currencies will be traded at the premium in relation to the Greenback.

5.2.3 *Non-Deliverable Forward (NDF)*

Thus far, we have assumed that the forward contract binds the two counterparties to a physical exchange of funds at maturity. By contrast, NDF is an outright forward contract in which counterparties settle the difference between the contracted forward rate and the prevailing spot price rate on an agreed notional amount. In other words, there is no physically delivery or electronic wiring of the currencies involved. Because an NDF is a cash-settled instrument, the notional amount *per se* is never exchanged. What is exchanged, however, is the dollar amount computed by first taking the difference between the NDF rate and the spot market rate prevailing at the so-called fixing date, and then multiplying the resulting difference by the notional amount. Most NDFs are cash-settled in U.S. dollars.

Many emerging markets such as China, Indonesia, India, South Korea, Taiwan, South Africa and so on exercise capital controls over the tradability of their currencies. Under this form of market friction, non-residents may not have full access to the onshore credit, giving rise to the NDF price f_0^* of

$$f_0^* = \frac{(1 + r_i)^T}{(1 + r_b)^T} S_0.$$

Here, r_i is the NDF-implied yield on the capital-controlled currency offshore. The implied yield r_i in general does not equal the onshore r_q.

We can easily solve for r_i as follows:

$$r_i = (1 + r_b) \left(\frac{f_0^*}{S_0} \right)^{\frac{1}{T}} - 1.$$

A wide spread between the onshore interest rate and the offshore NDF-implied yield would indicate an effective segmentation of onshore and offshore FX markets.

5.3 Implied Forward Interest Rate

This section discusses yet another simple forward contract. This time round, instead of asset prices, the quantity of concern — especially to the banks and their clients — is the interest rate.

Suppose an investor wants to borrow money, not now (time t_0) but at a future time t_1 instead for a period of $t_2 - t_1$. At time t_0, the investor wants to lock in the interest rate for future borrowing. What should be the value of f_0 for both the borrower and lender to reach an agreement that it is a fair deal? To answer this question, it is important to look at two zero rates y_a and y_b on the yield curve.

From Figure 5.4, we see that y_a is of a shorter maturity compared to y_b. The interest rate f_0 is called the forward interest rate. Over the time period from t_0 to t_2, the return from the lender's perspective is y_b. At t_0, for each dollar invested, the amount that is guaranteed to be received is

$$(1 + y_b)^{t_2 - t_0}.$$

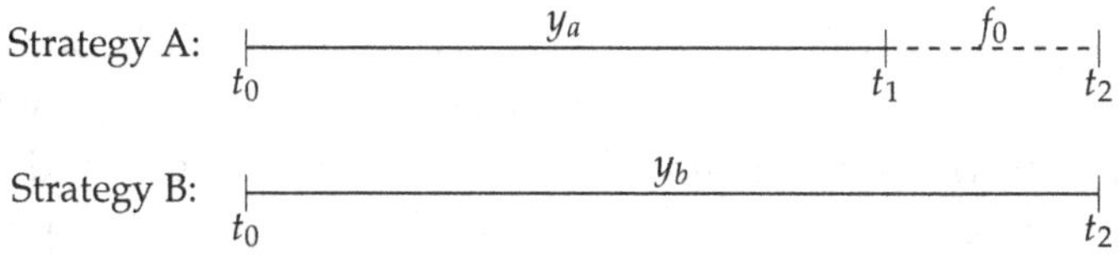

Fig. 5.4 Two strategies that give rise to the same forward value.

It is worth emphasizing that y_b is observed at time t_0 and therefore this guaranteed cash flow is exactly known for Strategy B.

If the forward interest rate f_0 applicable from time t_1 to t_2 is determined at time t_0, then the guaranteed cash flow should also be known for Strategy A as well. Moreover, both Strategies A and B should have the same cash flow. This is because y_a is also a risk-free rate and the forward rate f_0 is determined at t_0. Since there is no uncertainty and thus no risk, by the first and third principles of Quantitative Finance, the future cash flow of Strategy A must equal that for Strategy B. In other words, we must have

$$(1 + y_a)^{t_1 - t_0} \times (1 + f_0)^{t_2 - t_1} = (1 + y_b)^{t_2 - t_0} \qquad (5.3)$$

to prevent risk-free arbitrage.

Solving for f_0, we obtain

$$f_0 = \left(\frac{(1 + y_b)^{T_2}}{(1 + y_a)^{T_1}} \right)^{\frac{1}{T_2 - T_1}} - 1.$$

For notational convenience, we have let $T_1 := t_1 - t_0$ and $T_2 := t_2 - t_0$. The theoretical value f_0 obtained by the principles of Quantitative Finance is called the implied forward rate.

When the compounding scheme is continuous, instead of (5.3), we have

$$e^{r_a T_1} e^{f_0 (T_2 - T_1)} = e^{r_b T_2}.$$

So, under continuous compounding, the implied forward rate is obtained as follows:

$$f_0 = \frac{r_b T_2 - r_a T_1}{T_2 - T_1}.$$

5.4   Forward Rate Agreement

The International Swaps and Derivatives Association (ISDA) defines a forward rate agreement (FRA) as a forward contact on a short-term interest rate, usually LIBOR, in which cash flow obligations at maturity are calculated on a notional amount and the net cash flow is based on the difference between a predetermined forward rate and the market rate prevailing on that date. In a typical

FRA, one of the counterparties (A) agrees to pay the other counterparty (B) LIBOR settling t years from now applied to a certain notional amount (say, \$500 million). In return, counterparty B pays counterparty A a pre-agreed interest rate (say, 1.05%) applied to the same notional. The contract matures on day T (say, 3 months) from the settlement date, and interest is computed on an actual/360 day count basis.

By this industry definition, two counterparties that have entered into an FRA are obligated to exchange cash flow in the future based on a predetermined strike rate K and a forward spot rate R, which becomes observable at forward time. In practice, the strike rate K is referred to as the FRA rate, and the future spot rate R as the fixing rate. There is no cash flow at the current time t_0 when the FRA is dealt. The counterparties, among other things, agree upon the strike rate K that is "fair" to both parties.

For FRAs of short-term maturities, the fair value K is given by the following relationship:

$$(1 + \tau_1 r_1)(1 + \tau_k K) = 1 + (\tau_1 + \tau_k) r_2, \qquad (5.4)$$

where

- r_1 is the spot rate with a shorter maturity.
- τ_1 is the maturity for the spot rate r_1, expressed as a fraction of a year under a day count convention specified in the FRA contract.
- τ_k is the maturity for the FRA, expressed as a fraction of a year under a day count convention specified in the FRA contract.
- r_2 is the spot rate with maturity $\tau_1 + \tau_k$.

The relationship expressed by (5.4) indeed is similar in nature to (5.3). The left side of (5.4) corresponds to Strategy A and the right side is Strategy B in Figure 5.4. The only difference is the compounding scheme.

In a nutshell, the FRA rate is the (implied) forward rate that compounds the shorter maturity loan earning a rate of r_1 in such a way that the overall interest earned is equal to that of a longer maturity loan with interest rate r_2. Since the interest earned over a period of $\tau_1 + \tau_k$ is equal for these two types of loans, the rate K is then the fair value rate for the FRA. It follows from (5.4) that the FRA rate is given by

$$K = \frac{1}{\tau_k} \left(\frac{1 + (\tau_1 + \tau_k)r_2}{1 + \tau_1 r_1} - 1 \right). \tag{5.5}$$

Given r_1 and r_2 along with τ_1 and τ_k, the strike rate has to be the K of (5.5). Otherwise, there will be arbitrage opportunities. Thus, we see that the concept of implied forward rate derived from the principles of Quantitative Finance is applied in an FRA for computing the FRA rate K.

At this juncture, it is beneficial to introduce the concept of discount factor. As the name suggests, the discount factor is a quantity used for discounting the future cash flow as a function of time to maturity and an interest rate. Each future cash flow C_i ($i = 1, 2, \ldots, n$) is receivable at time τ_i with respect to today (time 0). The present value for the stream of cash flows is then obtained as follows:

$$PV = \sum_{i=1}^{n} DF_i \times C_i.$$

The discount factor DF_i is a function of the time to maturity t_i. So for the coupon-bearing bond (4.4), the specific form of the discount factor is

$$DF_i = \frac{1}{\left(1 + \frac{z_i}{2}\right)^i}, \tag{5.6}$$

for $i = 1, 2, \ldots, 2n - 1, 2n$.

Given the term structure of short-term interest rates r ranging from overnight to one year, the discount factor that corresponds to the compounding scheme of (5.4) is, as anticipated,

$$DF_\tau = \frac{1}{1 + \tau r}. \tag{5.7}$$

Corresponding to the two short-term maturities τ_1 and $\tau_1 + \tau_k$, the discount factors are, respectively,

$$DF_1 = \frac{1}{1 + \tau_1 r_1} \quad \text{and} \quad DF_k = \frac{1}{1 + (\tau_1 + \tau_k)r_2}.$$

Thus, (5.5) may be written in terms of the discount factors as

$$K = \frac{1}{\tau_k}\left(\frac{DF_1}{DF_k} - 1\right). \tag{5.8}$$

At time τ_1 when the FRA expires, the LIBOR rate R of tenor τ_k is observed. The cash flow to the buyer is then given by

$$\text{Notional amount} \times (R - K)\tau_k \left(\frac{1}{1 + R\tau_k}\right).$$

It is evident that this payoff function is linear. The gain of one party is at the expense of the counterparty. The cash flow generated by the interest rate differential is discounted by the discount factor $\frac{1}{1+R\tau_k}$. This is because instead of entering into the "physical" borrowing over the tenor of τ_k starting from τ_1, the anticipated cash flow at $\tau_1 + \tau_k$, namely, notional amount $\times (R - K)\tau_k$, is settled at τ_1 by discounting it back from $\tau_1 + \tau_k$ to τ_1.

To obtain intuition on how the shape of the yield curve affects the pricing of K, (5.4) is re-written as

$$\frac{(1 + r_1\tau_1)K - r_2}{\tau_1} = \frac{r_2 - r_1}{\tau_k}.$$

The right side of this equation is the linearized slope of the yield curve in the region between τ_1 and $\tau_1 + \tau_k$. Accordingly, if the yield curve is downward sloping or flat, then K will surely be less than r_2. On the other hand, when the yield curve slopes upward, K is not necessarily larger than r_2.

For tenor longer than a year, the spot rates on the relevant yield curve are quoted on the bond equivalent basis with semi-annual compounding. In this case, the following relationship applies:

$$\left(1 + \frac{r_1}{2}\right)^m \left(1 + \frac{K}{2}\right)^n = \left(1 + \frac{r_2}{2}\right)^{m+n}. \tag{5.9}$$

Here, m is the number of half years for spot rate r_1, and n is the number of half years for the FRA rate K. From (5.9), the FRA rate is obtained as follows:

$$\frac{K}{2} = \left(\frac{\left(1 + \frac{r_2}{2}\right)^{m+n}}{\left(1 + \frac{r_1}{2}\right)^{m}} \right)^{\frac{1}{n}} - 1.$$

Applying logarithm on both sides of (5.9) and using the approximation that $\ln(1 + x) \approx x$, we obtain

$$\frac{K - r_2}{m} \approx \frac{r_2 - r_1}{n}.$$

Again, we see that the slope of the yield curve, $(r_2 - r_1)/n$, provides a clue to the size of K relative to r_2.

5.5 Interest Rate Swap

Instead of exchanging only one cash flow, why not have more than one exchange on a regular basis? The natural extension of FRA is the interest rate swap (IRS). According to the definition by ISDA, IRS is an agreement to exchange interest rate cash flows, calculated on a notional principal amount, at specified intervals (payment dates) during the life of the agreement. Each party's payment obligation is computed using a different interest rate. In an IRS, the notional principal is never exchanged. Although there are no standardized contracts for interest rate swaps, a plain vanilla IRS typically refers to a generic IRS in which one party pays a fixed rate and the other party pays the floating rate, typically based on LIBOR.

By this industry definition, two counterparties that have entered into an IRS are obligated to exchange a series of cash flows on predetermined dates in the future based on the terms agreed upon on the trade date.

The legal terms of a plain vanilla IRS at deal initiation are set in such a way that the present value of the stream of payments to be paid is equal to the present value of the stream of payments to be received. In other words, the net present value is 0 at time 0. The basic premise of an IRS is that the counterparty choosing to pay the fixed rate and the counterparty choosing to pay the floating rate each assumes they will gain some advantage in doing so. Their

Fig. 5.5   The cash flows of interest rate swap buyer over eight quarters since deal date.

assumptions will be based on their needs and their estimates of the level and other changes in the interest rates during the life of the swap contract.

Because an interest rate swap may be deemed as a series of cash flows occurring at *known* future dates, it can be valued by simply summing the present value of each of these cash flows. In order to calculate the present value of each cash flow, it is necessary to first obtain the correct discount factor for each period when a cash flow exchange occurs, as shown in Figure 5.5.

The discount factor is intimately related to the concept of par bond and par yield. Recall that when a coupon-bearing bond is freshly issued, it is typically selling at par, meaning that the present value of the sum of all discounted future cash flows is equal to 1 or 100%. Mathematically, the par bond is expressed as

$$1 = \sum_{i=1}^{n} \mathrm{DF}_i \times C_i.$$

In this expression, DF_i is the discount factor for the cash flow C_i, which is to be received at a future time t_i. If the stream of cash flows comprises n (constant) coupons at the rate c plus the principal of 100%, then we may write

$$1 = c \sum_{i=1}^{n} \mathrm{DF}_i + \mathrm{DF}_n \times 1. \tag{5.10}$$

In light of the discount factor (5.6), this equation is effective the same as (4.4) after a re-labeling of time periods and setting $p = 1$ because the bond is selling at par.

Also, recall that the yield to maturity of a par bond, in short the par yield, is none other than the coupon rate. Thus, by looking at the coupon rate c of a par bond maturing at time T, we obtain the par yield c. Moreover, par bonds of different maturities will give rise to different par yields. It follows that the term structure of these par yields can be constructed. The resulting curve is called the par yield curve.

Now, the fixed rate K for the fixed leg of the IRS is determined as if a bond is issued at par value of 1 as follows:

$$1 = K \sum_{i=1}^{n} \mathrm{DF}_i + \mathrm{DF}_n. \tag{5.11}$$

This expression is equivalent to a bond selling at par with n coupons at a fixed coupon rate of K. The last term DF_n is the present value of the face value of future cash flow of 1, as in (5.10). The subscript i denotes the ith period cash flow.

From the practical standpoint, a better way to conceptualize an IRS is in terms of NPV. For the IRS buyer, who receives floating and pays fixed, the net present value of the IRS at time 0 is

$$\mathrm{NPV}_0 = \left(\sum_{j=1}^{n} \mathrm{DF}_j \times \text{Floating CF}_j + \mathrm{DF}_n \times 1 \right)$$
$$- \left(\sum_{i=1}^{n} \mathrm{DF}_i \times \text{Fixed CF}_i + \mathrm{DF}_n \times 1 \right).$$

In this form, IRS is effectively a long-short strategy on two bonds. The IRS buyer is effectively betting on a position that is long in the floating rate security and short in the fixed rate bond. At time 0, since both bonds are issued at par, by the third law of Quantitative Finance, we must have $\mathrm{NPV}_0 = 0$. Accordingly, we set the floating bond to its par value to obtain

$$0 = 1 - \sum_{i=1}^{n} \mathrm{DF}_i \times \text{Fixed CF}_i - \mathrm{DF}_n \times 1.$$

When all the discount factors are calculated from the relevant term structure, the theoretical value of the fixed cash flow, $K = $ Fixed CF$_i$ for $i = 1, 2, \ldots, n$, as in (5.11), is then obtained as

$$K = \frac{1 - \mathrm{DF}_n}{\sum_{i=1}^{n} \mathrm{DF}_i}. \tag{5.12}$$

It is interesting to note from (5.12) that the fixed rate K is dependent only on the term structure of discount factors.

5.6 Cross-Currency Interest Rate Swap (CIRS)

We show in this section that CIRS may be regarded as a generalized version of an IRS.

Given the spot FX rate S_0, which is the units of quote currency needed to exchange for one unit of base current, the net present value for the CIRS buyer is

$$\text{NPV}_0 = S_0 \left(\sum_{j=1}^{n} \text{DF}_j \times \text{Floating CF}_j + \text{DF}_n \times 1 \right)$$
$$- \left(\sum_{i=1}^{n} \text{DF}_i \times \text{Fixed CF}_i + \text{DF}_n \times 1 \right).$$

In this example, the fixed cash flows are denominated in the quote currency, but the floating cash flows are in the base currency. To convert it to the quote currency, the spot forex rate S_0 is applied. Again, this is a long-short strategy. The CIRS buyer is long a floating bond denominated in the base currency and short in a fixed rate bond in the quote currency.

This time round, what is the value of NPV_0 at time 0? The answer is $S_0 - 1$, not 0 anymore. Why? The reason is quite simple. From the long-short viewpoint, the CIRS buyer sells the fixed rate bond at par and obtains one unit of quote currency. The CIRS buyer uses the proceeds to fund the purchase of a unit of floating bond, which is S_0 in the quote currency. Since the bonds are valued at par of 100% for the respective currencies, therefore, $\text{NPV}_0 = S_0 - 1$.

For this reason, we have

$$S_0 - 1 = S_0 - \left(\sum_{i=1}^{n} \text{DF}_i \times \text{Fixed CF}_i + \text{DF}_n \times 1 \right).$$

Solving for K, we find that the fixed rate is still given by the same formula: (5.12)!

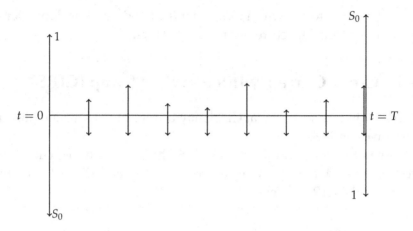

Fig. 5.6   The cash flows of cross-currency interest rate swap buyer over eight quarters since deal date.

Now, it is operationally possible to make NPV_0 equal to zero at time 0. Simply, both parties exchange the principal sum at time 0. The buyer receives the base currency in exchange for the quote currency at the spot rate S_0. This cash flow, which is $1 - S_0$, will offset the non-zero net present value NPV_0. The cash flow diagram in Figure 5.6 illustrates the cash flows of a CIRS buyer.

Therefore, CIRS is a general form of IRS. When both the fixed bond and the floating rate bond are issued in the same currency, i.e., $S_0 = 1$, then there is no need to exchange the principal at time $t = 0$ and $t = T$. Consequently, Figure 5.6 reduces to Figure 5.5.

5.7   Discount Factors in Practice

Earlier, we have briefly touched on the discount factors. This section provides more details. In the industry, the common practice is to make the deal date (DD) effective two days after the deal is initiated. It turns out that this arrangement, which is motivated by internal control and bookkeeping, has a far reaching effect in creating a gap between theory and practice.

First, the discount factors corresponding to overnight (O/N) and tomorrow next (T/N) on the par yield curve are calculated as follows:

$$DF_{(O/N)} = \frac{1}{1 + \text{Overnight Rate} \times \tau_0}. \tag{5.13}$$

$$DF_{(T/N)} = \frac{DF_{(O/N)}}{1 + \text{Tomorrow Next Rate} \times \tau_1}. \tag{5.14}$$

Here, τ_0 and τ_1 are the year fractions for overnight and tomorrow next, respectively. Both O/N and T/N rates are taken from the par yield curve.

To compute the discount factors for maturities from DD up to 1 year with money market par rates, the formula is

$$DF_\tau = \frac{DF_{\text{spot}}}{1 + r\tau}, \tag{5.15}$$

where the discount factor DF_{spot} is the spot discount factor. As the settlement is $T + 2$, the spot discount factor is given by $DF_{(T/N)}$, which is

$$DF_{\text{spot}} = DF_{(T/N)}.$$

The par rate r is the rate on the par yield curve for maturity τ. Notice that the numerator in (5.15) is not the usual textbook value of 1 as in (5.7).

The maturity expressed as year fraction τ is the number of calendar days from DD date to the maturity date divided by the number of days per year under a certain day-count basis for money market. For USD, both the money market basis and the swap basis are 360, and those for GBP and SGD are both 365. For JPY, the money market basis is 360 but the swap basis is 365. An application example of these formulas are tabulated in Table 5.1.

Next, we consider maturities equal to and longer than a year. The gap between theory and practice is even wider. Commercial software computes year fractions very differently. For example, the year fraction for 3 and a half years computed by Kondor+ suit is 0.49863, which is counter-intuitive as you would expect the number to be close to 3.5 (see Figure 5.7 and Table 5.2).

Table 5.1　Short-term discount factors for IRS swaps in US$ for August 13, 2009.

Tenor	Days	Par rate (%)	DF
O/N	1	2.17750	0.9999395175
T/N	1	2.24500	0.9998771641
DD	3	2.39875	0.9996773328
1　Week	7	2.39875	0.9994110152
1　Month	31	2.46375	0.9977603531
2 Months	61	2.67375	0.9953676303
3 Months	94	2.80438	0.9926087392
4 Months	122	2.90188	0.9901399801
5 Months	153	3.00875	0.9872529752
6 Months	186	3.10313	0.9840992598
7 Months	213	3.12563	0.9817218763
8 Months	243	3.15188	0.9790477375
9 Months	273	3.18000	0.9763328963
10 Months	304	3.20938	0.9734940813
11 Months	334	3.24000	0.9706979827
1　Year	367	3.27063	0.9676147070

Source: Reuters.

The crux of the matter is that Kondor+ uses the relative day difference from the previous 6 months to compute the year fraction rather than the absolute number of days from the Begin Date in Table 5.2. The "Days (Diff)" column for tenor of 1 year and longer in Table 5.2 is the difference between the current number of days from and the number of days for the previous 6 months. For example, the Days (Diff) of 184 for 2Y tenor is obtained from taking the difference between 730 and 546. With ACT/365 being the day count convention in this SGD-Swap example, the year fraction is calculated as 0.50410958904. Observe that this year fraction is about 0.5 even when the maturity is longer than a year.

The discount factors for long-term maturities are listed under the heading "$DF_{Today}(\cdot)$." They are computed via a bootstrapping method. The starting point is the O/N tenor, which is the same for both DF_{Today} (O/N) and DF_{Spot} (O/N). Notice that the tenor for O/N is 3 days (more precisely 3 nights) because there are three days

SGD-SWAP SGD SWAP (19/09/2008)

Config Curve Rates

Spot Date: 23/09/2008

Par Rate:

Tenor	Begin Date	Maturity Date	Cal. Days in Period	Par Rate	Zero Cpn. ACT/365	Discount Factor	Forward 3M ACT/360
O/N	19/09/2008	22/09/2008	3	1.383470	1.3930044849	0.9998863031	1.4182901186
T/N	22/09/2008	23/09/2008	1	1.437500	1.4067138333	0.9998469255	1.4214180822
DD	23/09/2008	24/09/2008	1	2.531620	1.6370914538	0.9997775815	1.4117442352
1 Week	23/09/2008	30/09/2008	7	2.531620	2.1412095657	0.9993617193	1.3547221814
1 Month	23/09/2008	23/10/2008	30	1.024180	1.0733703383	0.9990059705	1.6446944615
2 Months	23/09/2008	24/11/2008	62	1.346240	1.3569918994	0.9975657283	1.7128888494
3 Months	23/09/2008	23/12/2008	91	1.441160	1.4471946898	0.9962673082	1.8135976635
4 Months	23/09/2008	23/01/2009	122	1.510393	1.5144651173	0.9948246152	2.0348596289
5 Months	23/09/2008	23/02/2009	153	1.579627	1.5822850492	0.9932700389	2.2849360601
6 Months	23/09/2008	23/03/2009	181	1.642160	1.6437136249	0.9917706259	2.5310743488
7 Months	23/09/2008	23/04/2009	212	1.749464	1.7493956948	0.9897894089	2.3024435557
8 Months	23/09/2008	25/05/2009	244	1.860229	1.8585293515	0.9875660444	1.9577181987
9 Months	23/09/2008	23/06/2009	273	1.960610	1.9573487804	0.9853967828	1.5746007820
10 Months	23/09/2008	23/07/2009	303	1.932268	1.9285195496	0.9840621028	1.7342299786
11 Months	23/09/2008	24/08/2009	335	1.902037	1.8976400193	0.9826920179	1.9407725785
1 Year	23/09/2008	23/09/2009	365	1.865000	1.8696428235	0.9814474581	2.1636076217
1Y 6M	23/09/2008	23/03/2010	546	1.996411	2.0040877430	0.9705426193	2.4267594420
2 Years	23/09/2008	23/09/2010	730	2.130000	2.1411269408	0.9582920398	2.7178112885
2Y 6M	23/09/2008	23/03/2011	911	2.266370	2.2818175680	0.9450108506	2.9958214054
3 Years	23/09/2008	23/09/2011	1 095	2.405000	2.4257154425	0.9303768813	3.1259739068
3Y 6M	23/09/2008	23/03/2012	1 277	2.519060	2.5448317812	0.9155817510	3.3650117529
4 Years	23/09/2008	24/09/2012	1 462	2.635000	2.6668138187	0.8996876753	3.0578168610
4Y 6M	23/09/2008	25/03/2013	1 644	2.687500	2.7216041504	0.8858214780	3.1687671976
5 Years	23/09/2008	23/09/2013	1 826	2.740000	2.7769038834	0.8716846426	3.2506129640
5Y 6M	23/09/2008	24/03/2014	2 008	2.789863	2.8298083636	0.8574246047	3.3582691288
6 Years	23/09/2008	23/09/2014	2 191	2.840000	2.8834673021	0.8428636601	3.4673225363
6Y 6M	23/09/2008	23/03/2015	2 372	2.889589	2.9370335302	0.8282543680	3.5769179461
7 Years	23/09/2008	23/09/2015	2 556	2.940000	2.9919429775	0.8132083956	3.3151230601
7Y 6M	23/09/2008	23/03/2016	2 738	2.966545	3.0201645157	0.7996940995	3.3745139751
8 Years	23/09/2008	23/09/2016	2 922	2.993382	3.0490120159	0.7860223991	3.4352762950

KONDOR+ © REUTERS Ltd. Load done.

Fig. 5.7 SGD–SWAP curve with the begin date of September 19, 2008 and spot date of September 23, 2008.

Table 5.2 Illustration of how the year fraction denoted as YF is defined and applied in Figure 5.7.

Tenor	Par rate (%)	Days	Days (Diff)	YF	DF_{Spot} (Tenor)	DF_{Today} (Tenor)
O/N	1.383470	3			0.9998863031	0.9998863031
T/N	1.437500	1			0.9999606180	0.9998469255
6M	1.642160	181	181	0.49589041096	0.9919224639	0.9917706259
1Y	1.865000	365	184	0.50410958904	0.9816914544	0.9814474581
1Y6M	1.996411	546	181	0.49589041096		0.9705426193
2Y	2.130000	730	184	0.50410958904		0.9582920398
2Y6M	2.266370	911	181	0.49589041096		0.9450108474
3Y	2.405000	1095	184	0.50410958904		0.9303768813
3Y6M	2.519060	1277	182	0.49863013699		0.9155817492

from the begin date, which is a Friday in this example, to the following business day on Monday.

The next tenor of T/N for $DF_{Today}(T/N)$ is obtained as follows:

$$DF_{Today}(T/N) = DF_{Today}(O/N) \times DF_{Spot}(T/N).$$

Similarly, the 6-month tenor is obtained as

$$DF_{Today}(6M) = DF_{Today}(T/N) \times DF_{Spot}(6M).$$

Having obtained the 6-month discount factor, the bootstrapping formula for tenors 1-year and above is

$$DF_i = \frac{DF_{Today}(T/N) - R_i \sum_{h=0.5}^{i-0.5} t_h DF_h}{1 + t_i R_i}, \qquad (5.16)$$

where R_i is the par rate and t_i is the year fraction. In contrast to the short-term maturities, Kondor+ uses the discount factor $DF_{Today}(T/N)$ here. As an example, the DF for 1 year maturity is calculated as

$$\begin{aligned} DF_1 &= \frac{DF_{Today}(T/N) - R_1 t_{0.5} DF_{0.5}}{1 + t_1 R_1} \\ &= \frac{0.9998469255 - 0.01865 \times 0.49589041096 \times 0.9917706259}{1 + 0.01865 \times 0.50410958904} \\ &= 0.9814474581. \end{aligned}$$

At this juncture, you may wonder whether these practices are purely discretionary and void of any principle. To address this concern, we emphasize that (5.16) is the analogue of (4.4), i.e.,

$$\begin{aligned} DF_{Today}(T/N) = R_i t_{\frac{1}{2}} \times DF_{\frac{1}{2}} + R_i t_1 \times DF_1 + R_i t_{\frac{3}{2}} \\ \times DF_{\frac{3}{2}} + \cdots + R_i t_i \times DF_i + 1 \times DF_i. \end{aligned}$$

In this bootstrapping form, the discount factors $DF_h, h = 0.5, 1.0, 1.5, \ldots, i-1$ have already been determined, and it allows DF_i to be ascertained. The cash flow is $R_i t_h$. It corresponds to the fixed coupon $c \times 0.5$ of a coupon-bearing bond paying interest on the half-yearly basis at the annual rate of c. The year fraction t_h is more precise because it takes into account the fact that the *actual* number of days in each half of the year is not equal to 0.5 exactly.

Moreover, it is easy to recognize that $DF_{Today}(T/N)$ is the present value of the stream of discounted future cash flows. When this coupon-bearing bond is issued at par, the present value should be 1. But to account for the days required to settle and clear the deal, the resulting present value becomes $DF_{Today}(T/N) < 1$ instead of $p = 1$ in (5.11).

5.8 Exercises

Q1. A popular trading strategy among currency traders is called the carry trade. It is a no-brainer. Borrow the currency that charges a low interest rate, exchange it into a currency that pays a higher interest rate. In other words, buy the currency that pays a higher interest rate by selling the borrowed currency.

(a) Suppose the Japanese money market charges 0.4% per annum while the U.S. money market takes in deposit and offers to pay 5% per annum. An investor borrows ¥10 billion when the spot exchange rate is 120 yens per dollar. A year later, the investor unwinds the carry trade position. Suppose the exchange rate remains unchanged a year later.

    i. What is the P&L in Japanese yens?

    ii. What is the return on U.S. dollar terms?

    iii. If the exchange rate becomes 114.74 yens to a dollar. What is the P&L in Japanese yens?

(b) What is the fair forward FX rate for the data in Q1a?

(c) In an unexpected move, on October 31, 2014, 1:44 pm Japan Standard Time, the policy board of the Bank of Japan announced that it would expand the pace of its quantitative easing to ¥80 trillion[3] (an addition of about 10 to 20

---

[3]See the announcement at https://www.boj.or.jp/en/announcements/release_2014/k141031a.pdf by the Bank of Japan.

trillion yens compared to the past). Is this a good news or bad news for the yen carry traders? Explain.

Q2. The day count convention for SGD swap par rate is 365 days per year. Based on the bootstrapping approach adopted by the financial industry, and with reference to Table 5.2,

(a) Verify that the discount factor for O/N is indeed 0.9998863031.

(b) Verify that the discount factor for T/N is 0.9998469255.

(c) Verify that the discount factor for DD is 0.9997775815.

Chapter 6

Derivatives with Nonlinear Payoffs

6.1 Introduction

In Section 5.1.2, we have briefly touched on the simplest nonlinear derivative known as option. Historians have traced the first nonlinear derivative to circa 1792 to 1750 BC when Hammurabi reigned in Mesopotamia as the king of Babylon. Remarkably, this derivative is about 200 years earlier than the forward contract between Laban and Jacob (see Section 3.5). In the Code of Hammurabi, it is written,

> If any one owe a debt for a loan, and a storm prostrates the grain, or the harvest fail, or the grain does not grow for lack of water; in that year he need not give his creditor any grain, he washes his debt-tablet in water and pays no rent for this year.

This 48th Code spells out the payoff of the creditor who has given a loan to the farmer. The underlying asset is the grain, which will be received after harvest. But if the weather conditions are averse, the creditor receives nothing. This law of Hammurabi effectively renders the payoff to the creditor nonlinear, being contingent on how the vagary of nature plays out.

Options in modern days began trading in 1973 when the Chicago Board of Options Exchange (CBOE) was founded and became the first marketplace for trading *listed* options. Intriguingly, this historical milestone coincides with the publication of the ground breaking paper by Black and Scholes [BS73]. As mentioned in Section 1.1, the publication of an option-pricing equation marks the watershed of Quantitative Finance's emergence from Finance.

In the U.S., the growth of option trading is exponential. According to the Options Clearing Corporation, in 1973, 1.1 million option contracts on 32 equity issues were traded. By 2014, the annual volume of equity and index options had grown to 3.8 billion contracts; meanwhile, the number of listed security issues increased to 4,278.

According to a joint survey report [NP14] by the World Federation of Exchanges (WFE) and the International Options Market Association (IOMA), the exchange-traded equity option volume in 2013 was about 8 billion contracts worldwide. Of this amount of volume, about 46% were traded on the U.S. option exchanges. Non-equity options have also grown substantially. The takeaway here is that exchange-traded options have become standard products for traders and investors.

Following the historical preamble and statistics, we introduce plain vanilla options. The adjective "plain vanilla" comprises two nonce words to emphasize that the option payoff is of the simplest possible nonlinear function in the space of continuous functions. Namely, the payoff function comprises two lines with different slopes joined at a point, which is a triangle with one side missing.

In terms of how the options expire or mature, European options are the simplest, as they can only be exercised exclusively at maturity. With an add-on option for the buyer to exercise before maturity, American options are also discussed in this chapter. This deceptively benign and straightforward provision for the option buyer to exercise the option early at the buyer's discretion turns out to be momentous in transforming the European option into something that is challenging from the pricing perspective.

We apply the principles of Quantitative Finance to derive three no-arbitrage properties of the price of an European option as a function of the strike price K. The crux of this chapter is not about the absolute value of the option but the relationships that must hold under the framework of relative valuation discussed in Section 3.4. We then proceed to derive the bounds of European call premium, and likewise for the European put premium. Put–call parity and box spread parity are also shown to be obtainable from the three principles of Quantitative Finance.

6.2 European and American Puts and Calls

A simple or plain vanilla call option is characterized by the following payoff function of the underlying asset's spot price S_T at a future date T:

$$f(S_T) := \max (S_T - K, 0).$$

In this function, K is called the strike price, which is fixed and known at time 0 called today. Associated to this payoff function is an option named the plain vanilla call option. It is a financial contract that gives the holder (the buyer) the right, but not the obligation, to buy a given financial asset (stock, currency, or a bond) at the pre-agreed strike price K in the future. When the holder exercises the call option to buy the underlying asset at the price K and immediately sell the asset at S_T, the payoff will be $f(S_T)$. Obviously, call option holder will not exercise the option whenever $S_T \leq K$.

At any time t before or at maturity, i.e., $t \leq T$, if $S_t - K > 0$, the call option is said to be in the money. More generally, the option is in the money when the payoff function is non-zero, and the option is said to have intrinsic value. Otherwise, if $S_t - K < 0$, the call option is out of the money. Near the money is the term used for describing the situation where $S_t \approx K$. Finally, at the money is when $S_t = K$.

Indeed, Hammurabi's Code 48 is effectively a kind of call option sold by the farmer to the loan creditor. If harvest materializes, this call option will be in the money and the farmer is obligated to deliver grain to the creditor. But if the harvest is not forthcoming, the call option is out of the money and the creditor loses the rent, which is the call option premium.

Consider another nonlinear payoff function defined as

$$g(S_T) := \max (K - S_T, 0).$$

It is a mirror image of $f(S_T)$ with respect to the strike price K in the vertical direction (see the plot on the right in Figure 6.1). Options

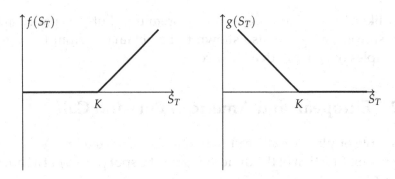

Fig. 6.1 The payoffs of plain vanilla call (left) and put (right) options buyer at maturity.

of this payoff function for the buyers are known as put options. Each put option allows the option buyer to sell the underlying asset to the put option seller at the pre-determined strike price K in the future. If the underlying asset's price S_T is higher than the strike price, the put option holder is under no obligation to sell. So the downside is capped at 0. The upside gain is when S_T is lower than K. In this case, the option holder can buy from the spot market at the price of S_T and sell the just acquired asset to the option seller immediately at the strike price K, gaining the amount of $K - S_T$ in the process.

From the perspective of sellers, call and put options have the respective payoffs of $-f(S_T)$ and $-g(S_T)$. Their payoff diagrams are depicted in Figure 6.2.

As can be seen from Figures 6.1 and 6.2, the payoff of a short call is the mirror image of a long call with respect to the horizontal axis of strike price. Similarly, long put and short put are mirror image of each other. Notice that options sellers have no upside at all. Since option sellers, also called the option writers, have zero up side, justifiably, they demand to get paid a price called the option premium or option price for bearing the downside risk.

If options can only be exercised on the option expiry date, then this type of exercise is known as European style. Another type of exercise method is more flexible in giving the option holders the possibility to exercise the option any time before and on the expiry

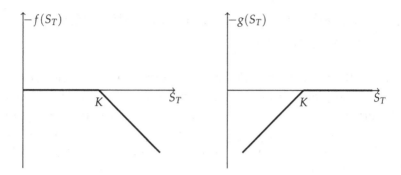

Fig. 6.2   The payoffs of plain vanilla call (left) and put (right) options seller at maturity.

date. The more flexible exercise style is called the American style. Everything else being equal, American options cost more than European options for the buyers because the option to exercise at buyers' demand anytime is an additional option. Using the lower case alphabets to denote European option prices and upper case alphabets to denote American option prices, we write

$$c \leq C, \qquad p \leq P.$$

The flexibility accorded to American option buyers to exercise the options anytime before or on expiration prompts sellers to demand an "early exercise" premium. Conceptually, we may decompose the plain vanilla American call and put options as

$$C = c + \text{early exercise premium}, \qquad P = p + \text{early exercise premium}. \tag{6.1}$$

In this decomposition, the European options c and p are on the same underlying asset, of the same strike price and expiration date as C and P, respectively. However, they are not observable because the market does not trade the early exercise premium. Rather, the American option is traded as it is, without any demarcation. In this regard, the decomposition in (6.1) is purely synthetic.

6.3   Overall Shape of European Call Option Price Function

We apply the principles of Quantitative Finance to shed light on the shape of the plain vanilla option price curve as a function of the strike price. Throughout our discussion in this section, the options are on the same underlying asset and expire on the same future date T. Moreover, one option contract is to one unit of the underlying asset when exercised.[1]

We first demonstrate that a call with a low strike is at least as valuable as an otherwise identical call of a higher strike price. This statement suggests that the call option price is non-increasing, i.e., by and large a monotonically decreasing function of the strike price.

6.3.1   *Monotonous with respect to the strike price*

Consider two strike prices K_1 and K_2 with $K_1 < K_2$, and also the following two portfolios:

- Portfolio 1
  A European call option $c_0(K_1)$ of strike K_1.
- Portfolio 2
  A European call option $c_0(K_2)$ of strike K_2.

At expiration, the value of Portfolio 1 (denoted by $V_1(T)$) is by definition $\max(S_T - K_1, 0)$, whereas Portfolio 2's value (denoted by $V_2(T)$) is $\max(S_T - K_2, 0)$. With respect to these two strike prices, and the underlying asset price at time T, denoted by S_T, three mutually exclusive scenarios are exhaustive:

1. $S_T < K_1$,
2. $K_1 \leq S_T \leq K_2$,
3. $S_T > K_2$.

---

[1]In practice, however, one option contract is usually on more than one unit of the underlying asset. For example, in the U.S., one equity option contract allows the option holder to buy or sell 100 shares when exercised.

In the first scenario of $S_T < K_1$, both are worthless, and $V_2(T) = V_1(T) = 0$. In the second scenario where $K_1 \leq S_T \leq K_2$, the value of Portfolio 1 is $S_T - K_1$ but the value of Portfolio 2 is still zero. So, $V_2(T) < V_1(T)$ in the second scenario. In the third scenario, both options are in the money, $V_1(T) = S_T - K_1$ and $V_2(T) = S_T - K_2$. Since $K_1 < K_2$, it it clear that $S_T - K_2 < S_T - K_1$, which implies that $V_2(T) < V_1(T)$ in the third scenario as well.

Accordingly, it is established that $V_2(T) \leq V_1(T)$ at time T. By the third principle of Quantitative Finance as in (3.7), it must be that at time 0, the call option price $c_0(K_2)$ of a higher strike is less than or equal to the call option price $c_0(K_1)$ of a lower strike, i.e.,

$$c_0(K_2) \leq c_0(K_1).$$

Hence, we have established that the price level of a European call option will be higher or equal when the strike price is lower, and vice versa. The implication is that the gradient of the call option price curve $c_0(K)$ is non-positive, because $c_0(K_2) - c_0(K_1) \leq 0$.

6.3.2 *Lower and upper bounds for the slope*

Next, we examine the lower bound for the slope of the call option price curve $c_0(K)$. For this purpose, let us construct two portfolios as follows:

- Portfolio 3
  A long position in call option $c_0(K_1)$ of strike price K_1 and a short position in call option $c_0(K_2)$ of strike price K_2.
- Portfolio 4
  A risk-free time deposit of amount $(K_2 - K_1)e^{-rT}$, tenor T, and interest rate r.

The marked-to-market value of Portfolio 3 at time 0 is $V_3(0) = c_0(K_1) - c_0(K_2)$, which is non-negative as proven earlier.

Portfolio 3 is more commonly known as the bull call spread.[2] The spread generally is profitable if the stock price moves higher — just

---

[2]The Options Industry Council is an excellent open resource on the subject of standard options trading strategies.

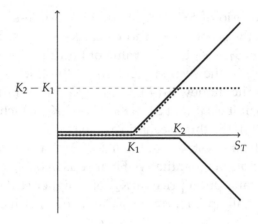

Fig. 6.3   The payoff function (dotted lines) of a bull call spread for the buyer at maturity. Bull call spread consists of a long call struck at K_1 and a short call at a larger strike K_2.

as a regular long call strategy would — up to the point where the short call caps further gain. This portfolio requires a smaller cash outlay, as the short call helps pay for the long call's upfront cost.

At maturity, the value or payoff of the portfolio is shown in Figure 6.3. The three mutually exclusive scenarios discussed above and the respective payoffs are captured in the plot.

At expiration, it is evident from Figure 6.3 that the payoff of the bull call spread is less than or equal to $K_2 - K_1$, which coincides with the value of Portfolio 4. Since $V_3(T) \leq V_4(T)$ at time T, their prices at time 0, according to the first and third principles of Quantitative Finance, must observe the same inequality:

$$c_0(K_1) - c_0(K_2) \leq (K_2 - K_1)e^{-rT} \leq K_2 - K_1.$$

In conjunction with the earlier upper bound result that $c_0(K_2) - c_0(K_1) \leq 0$, these inequalities provide an upper bound and a lower bound for the gradient of the call price curve $c_0(K)$ as follows:

$$-1 \leq \frac{c_0(K_2) - c_0(K_1)}{K_2 - K_1} \leq 0.$$

In summary, $c_0(K)$ is a downward sloping curve with respect to K.

6.3.3 *Convexity*

Finally, we examine the curvature or convexity of the call option price curve. For this purpose, we consider three strike prices sorted by magnitude as $K_1 < K_2 < K_3$. Moreover, we define a positive ratio as follows:

$$\lambda := \frac{K_3 - K_2}{K_3 - K_1} < 1. \tag{6.2}$$

This ratio is smaller than one and thereby allows us to express K_2 as a linear combination of K_1 and K_3:

$$K_2 = \lambda K_1 + (1 - \lambda)K_3.$$

The portfolios relevant to the curvature or convexity analysis are

- Portfolio 5
  A long position in one contract of call option struck at K_2.
- Portfolio 6
  A long position in λ contracts of call option struck at K_1 and another long position in $1 - \lambda$ contracts of call option of strike price K_3.

Now that we have one more strike price K_3, we need to consider one additional scenario, namely $K_2 < S_T \leq K_3$ at maturity date T. In Table 6.1, we tabulate the payoffs of these two portfolios, scenario by scenario.

It is noteworthy that a simple computation suggests that

$$\lambda(S_T - K_1) + (1 - \lambda)(S_T - K_3) = S_T - K_2. \tag{6.3}$$

If follows that in the first scenario where $S_T < K_1$ and the last scenario where $S_T > K_3$, both Portfolios 5 and 6 will have equal values at time T of 0, and $S_T - K_2$ because of (6.3), respectively.

In the second scenario where $K_1 \leq S_T \leq K_2$, the non-zero value of Portfolio 6 is larger than the value of Portfolio 5, which is 0 since it is out of the money.

What about the third scenario where $K_2 < S_T \leq K_3$? To answer this question, we need to recognize that the payoff of Portfolio 5 is the right side of (6.3) when the call option is in the money. Since (6.3) holds as a mathematical identity, we can further analyze $S_T - K_2$

Table 6.1   Payoffs of two portfolios of call options with strike prices $K_1 < K_2 < K_3$ at maturity T for the buyer.

Scenario	$S_T < K_1$	$K_1 \leq S_T \leq K_2$	$K_2 < S_T \leq K_3$	$S_T > K_3$
Portfolio 5				
Long 1 contract of call struck at K_2	0	0	$S_T - K_2$	$S_T - K_2$
Portfolio 6				
Long λ contracts of call struck at K_1	0	$\lambda(S_T - K_1)$	$\lambda(S_T - K_1)$	$\lambda(S_T - K_1)$
Long $1 - \lambda$ contracts of call struck at K_3	0	0	0	$(1 - \lambda)(S_T - K_3)$
Aggregate of Portfolio 6	0	$\lambda(S_T - K_1)$	$\lambda(S_T - K_1)$	$S_T - K_2$

by the left side of (6.3). The first term on the left side of (6.3), i.e., $\lambda(S_T - K_1)$, is positive. However, the second term $(1 - \lambda)(S_T - K_3)$ is negative. This is because $S_T \leq K_3$ in this scenario. Accordingly, after taking out the negative term, it must be that $\lambda(S_T - K_1) \geq S_T - K_2$. So even in this scenario, $V_5(T) \leq V_6(T)$ holds.

Thus we see that in all scenarios, $V_5(T) \leq V_6(T)$. Again, the third principle of Quantitative Finance (3.7) requires the prices of these two portfolios at time 0 to be

$$c_0(K_2) \leq \lambda c_0(K_1) + (1 - \lambda)c_0(K_3).$$

Substituting in the explicit form of λ, i.e., (6.2) into this inequality, we arrive at

$$(K_3 - K_1)c_0(K_2) \leq (K_3 - K_2)c_0(K_1) + (K_2 - K_1)c_0(K_3).$$

We write the left side of the inequality as $(K_3 - K_2)c_0(K_2) + (K_2 - K_1)c_0(K_2)$, and then rearrange the inequality into

$$(K_3 - K_2)\big(c_0(K_2) - c_0(K_1)\big) \leq (K_2 - K_1)\big(c_0(K_3) - c_0(K_2)\big).$$

Next, we divide both sides by $(K_3 - K_2)(K_2 - K_1)$ to obtain

$$\frac{c_0(K_2) - c_0(K_1)}{K_2 - K_1} \leq \frac{c_0(K_3) - c_0(K_2)}{K_3 - K_2}.$$

To gain further insight, we define the gradients

$$G_{K_2} := \frac{c_0(K_2) - c_0(K_1)}{K_2 - K_1}; \quad G_{K_3} := \frac{c_0(K_3) - c_0(K_2)}{K_3 - K_2},$$

and express the inequality as

$$G_{K_3} - G_{K_2} \geq 0,$$

or

$$\frac{G_{K_3} - G_{K_2}}{K_3 - K_2} \geq 0.$$

This result shows that the curvature of the call option price function is non-negative, implying that it is convex for a monotonically non-increasing function. As K increases from near 0 to a larger and larger K, the gradient increases from near -1 to become less negative, which eventually flattens out.

In summary, the overall shape of the call option price declines monotonically from a high price (in the money) with negative gradient. The call option price curve $c(K)$ tapers off in a convex fashion as K becomes (deep out of the money) a very larger number.

6.4 Overall Shape of European Put Option Price Function

This section performs a similar analysis to gain insights on the put option price curve $p_0(K)$ at time 0, as a function of the strike price K.

6.4.1 *Put option monotonicity and slope*

First and foremost, the non-decreasing monotonicity of $p_0(K)$ is easily shown when given two strike prices K_1 and K_2 such that $K_2 > K_1$ as before. We examine at maturity T the value $V_{1'}(T)$ of Portfolio 1' comprising $p_0(K_1)$ relative to the value $V_{2'}(T)$ of Portfolio 2' consisting of $p_0(K_2)$. By definition of the put option, we have $V_{1'}(T) = \max(K_1 - S_T, 0)$ and $V_{2'}(T) = \max(K_2 - S_T, 0)$. When $S_T > K_2$, the two put options are out of the money and worthless, which implies that $V_{1'}(T) = V_{2'}(T)$. Otherwise, when either

$S_T < K_1$ or $K_1 \leq S_T \leq K_2$, which are the two remaining possibilities that S_T can be, then $K_2 - S_T > K_1 - S_T$ by assumption of $K_2 > K_1$. Consequently, $V_{1'}(T) \leq V_{2'}(T)$ in all three scenarios and the third principle (3.7) suggests that at time 0, it must be that $p_0(K_1) \leq p_0(K_2)$.

Next, for studying the slope of a put option, in parallel to the previous section, we construct the following two portfolios:

- Portfolio 3'
  A long position in put option $p_0(K_2)$ of strike price K_2 and a short position in put option $p_0(K_1)$ of strike price K_1.
- Portfolio 4
  A risk-free time deposit of amount $(K_2 - K_1)e^{-rT}$, tenor T, and interest rate r.

The marked-to-market value of Portfolio 3' at time 0 is $V_{3'}(0) = p_0(K_2) - p_0(K_1)$, which is non-negative as proven earlier. Portfolio 4 is the very same one used in the previous section.

In the option market, Portfolio 3' is known as the bear put spread. It is a strategy consisting of buying one put hoping to profit from a decline in the underlying asset, and writing another put with the same expiration, but of a lower strike price, as a way to offset some of the cost. The value of this bear put spread strategy at time 0 is $p_0(K_2) - p_0(K_1)$, which is none other than $V_{3'}(0)$.

The payoff diagram at maturity of a long position in the bear put spread is shown in Figure 6.4.

As the asset price S_T moves down toward the lower strike price, the bear put spread works a lot like its long put component would as a stand-alone strategy. However, in contrast to the stand-alone long put, the possibility of a greater payoff stops at K_1. This is the tradeoff. The short put price $p_0(K_1)$ mitigates the cost of $p_0(K_2)$ but also sets a ceiling of $K_2 - K_1$ on the payoff.

At maturity T, from Figure 6.4, Portfolio 4 will be valued at the sure value of $V_4(T) = K_2 - K_1$, regardless of where S_T fluctuates toward. Now, Portfolio 3' will be of the largest value when $S_T < K_1$ as both put options in this portfolio are in the money. In this case, $V_{3'}(T) = (K_2 - S_T) - (K_1 - S_T) = K_2 - K_1 = V_4(T)$. Otherwise,

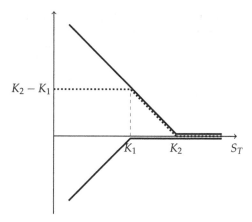

Fig. 6.4 The payoff function of a bear put spread (dotted lines) for the buyer at maturity T. Bear put spread consists of a long put struck at K_2 and a short put at a smaller strike K_1.

$V_{3'}(T) < V_4(T)$ as shown in Figure 6.4. Applying the first and third principles of Quantitative Finance, it must follow at time 0 that

$$p_0(K_2) - p_0(K_1) \le (K_2 - K_1)e^{-rT} \le K_2 - K_1, \quad \text{or}$$
$$\frac{p_0(K_2) - p_0(K_1)}{K_2 - K_1} \le 1.$$

In conjunction with the lower bound $0 \le p_0(K_2) - p_0(K_1)$ due to the non-decreasing nature of the put option price, we obtain

$$0 \le \frac{p_0(K_2) - p_0(K_1)}{K_2 - K_1} \le 1.$$

This result shows that the gradient of a put option curve is non-negative and it increases to the largest possible value of 1 when the strike price K increases toward a very large value.

6.4.2 *Put option convexity*

In an analogous fashion, the convexity of the put option price curve is established by analyzing the following two portfolios:

- Portfolio 5′
  A long position in one contract of put option struck at K_2.

Table 6.2   Payoffs of two portfolios of put options at maturity T for the buyer.

Scenario	$S_T < K_1$	$K_1 \leq S_T \leq K_2$	$K_2 < S_T \leq K_3$	$S_T > K_3$
Portfolio 5′				
Long 1 contract of put struck at K_2	$K_2 - S_T$	$K_2 - S_T$	0	0
Portfolio 6′				
Long λ contracts of put struck at K_1	$\lambda(K_1 - S_T)$	0	0	0
Long $1 - \lambda$ contracts of put struck at K_3	$(1 - \lambda)(K_3 - S_T)$	$(1 - \lambda)(K_3 - S_T)$	$(1 - \lambda)(K_3 - S_T)$	0
Aggregate of Portfolio 6′	$K_2 - S_T$	$(1 - \lambda)(K_3 - S_T)$	$(1 - \lambda)(K_3 - S_T)$	0

- Portfolio 6′

  A long position in λ contracts of put option struck at K_1 and another long position in $1 - \lambda$ contracts of put option of strike price K_3.

The ratio λ has already been defined in (6.2). Also note the important property $K_2 = \lambda K_1 + (1 - \lambda)K_3$ for the three strike prices arranged in the ascending order, i.e., $K_1 < K_2 < K_3$.

Table 6.2 presents the different payoffs for four exhaustive and mutually exclusive scenarios of S_T with respect to the three strike prices.

By construction $\lambda K_1 + (1 - \lambda)K_3 = K_2$, hence $\lambda(K_1 - S_T) + (1 - \lambda)(K_3 - S_T) = K_2 - S_T$. Replacing $c_0(K)$ by $p_0(K)$, the same train of thought concerning the convexity in the previous section applies. In particular,

$$K_2 - S_T < (1 - \lambda)(K_3 - S_T).$$

The reason is because $K_1 - S_T < 0$ in the second scenario of Table 6.2. Accordingly, after taking out this negative term, and in view of (6.3), it must be that $(1 - \lambda)(K_3 - S_T) > K_2 - S_T$.

From Table 6.2, it is evident that at time T,

$$V_{5'}(T) \leq V_{6'}(T).$$

It follows that at time 0,

$$p_0(K_2) \leq \lambda p_0(K_1) + (1 - \lambda)p_0(K_3),$$

in accordance to the third principle (3.7). Substituting in the explicit form of λ, i.e., (6.2) into this inequality, we arrive at

$$(K_3 - K_1)p_0(K_2) \leq (K_3 - K_2)p_0(K_1) + (K_2 - K_1)p_0(K_3).$$

Further, writing the left side of the inequality as $(K_3 - K_2)p_0(K_2) + (K_2 - K_1)p_0(K_2)$, and rearranging, we obtain

$$\frac{p_0(K_2) - p_0(K_1)}{K_2 - K_1} \leq \frac{p_0(K_3) - p_0(K_2)}{K_3 - K_2}.$$

Thus, we arrive at the conclusion that the curvature of the put option price curve is also positive and hence convex. In short, the put option price curve $p_0(K)$ is non-decreasing and the positive gradient that begins at almost zero increases until it reaches one as the strike price increases.

6.4.3 *Summary*

As a summary, the results we have derived for plain vanilla European puts in this section and calls in the previous section are as follows. For any three strike prices K_1, K_2, and K_3 for which $K_1 < K_2 < K_3$, we have:

1. Monotonicity in the price level

$$c_0(K_2) \leq c_0(K_1); \qquad p_0(K_1) \leq p_0(K_2).$$

2. Boundedness in the gradient

$$-1 \leq \frac{c_0(K_2) - c_0(K_1)}{K_2 - K_1} \leq 0; \qquad 0 \leq \frac{p_0(K_2) - p_0(K_1)}{K_2 - K_1} \leq 1.$$

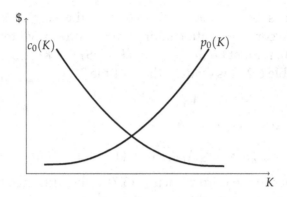

Fig. 6.5   The price curves of put $(p_0(K))$ and call $(c_0(K))$ options as functions of the strike price K.

3. Convexity

$$\frac{c_0(K_2) - c_0(K_1)}{K_2 - K_1} \leq \frac{c_0(K_3) - c_0(K_2)}{K_3 - K_2};$$

$$\frac{p_0(K_2) - p_0(K_1)}{K_2 - K_1} \leq \frac{p_0(K_3) - p_0(K_2)}{K_3 - K_2}.$$

These three properties based on the general principle allow us to depict the price curves as functions $c_0(K)$ and $p_0(K)$ of the strike price K qualitatively in Figure 6.5.

It is important to recognize that the three features of monotonicity, gradient boundedness, and convexity are model-free in the following sense:

- Models for the stochastic dynamics of the underlying asset are not needed.
- Models to price the options are not needed.

In fact, the three model-free properties must be satisfied by any models and formulas for pricing options. Britten-Jones and Neuberger [BJN00] even go so far as to suggest that, quite the reverse, given a complete set of option prices, it is possible to extract as much information as possible about the dynamics of the underlying asset, particularly the volatility of the asset return.

6.5 Bounds of European Option Price

The third principle of Quantitative Finance is particularly useful to derive the bounds of call and put prices.

6.5.1 *Bounds on call prices*

Consider two portfolios at time 0.

- Portfolio A
  A call contract c_0 to buy the underlying asset at the strike price K on expiration date T.
- Portfolio B
  A share or unit of the underlying asset priced at S_0 per unit.

At time T, the value of portfolio A is worth $S_T - K$ or 0, i.e., $V_A(T) = \max(S_T - K, 0)$, while portfolio B's value is $V_B(T) = S_T$. Since $S_T - K \leq S_T$ for $K \in \mathfrak{R}_+$ at time T, we know at time 0 that the equality $V_A(T) \leq V_B(T)$ will hold true in the future. Applying the third principle (3.7) of Quantitative Finance, it must be that at time 0, the prices must fulfil the following inequality:

$$c_0 \leq S_0.$$

Therefore, we see that the call option price c_0 cannot exceed the underlying asset price S_0. In other words, S_0 is the upper bound of the call option price.

To find the lower bound, we consider

- Portfolio C
  A call contract c_0 to buy the underlying asset at the strike price K on expiration date T, and a risk-free time deposit of amount Ke^{-rT} of tenor T and interest rate r.
- Portfolio B
  A share or unit of the underlying asset priced at S_0 per unit.

At time T, the value of the time deposit will be K. For the call option, there are only two possibilities: Either in the money and the call option is worth $S_T - K$, or out of money and the call option is worthless. Therefore, if the call option is in the money, the value of Portfolio C will be $S_T - K + K = S_T > K$. Effectively, the cash K is used to buy the underlying asset at the cheaper strike price K. The simple reason for exercising the option is that the asset is traded at S_T yet it can be bought at a lower price of K, i.e., $K \leq S_T$. If the call option expires worthless, then the value of Portfolio C is K. These two possible values can be summarized succinctly as $V_C(T) = \max(S_T, K)$.

At time T, it must be that $S_T = V_B(T) \leq V_C(T) = \max(S_T, K)$. Applying the third principle à la relative valuation, the price or value of the two portfolios at time 0 must satisfy

$$S_0 \leq c_0 + Ke^{-rT},$$

which is rewritten as

$$S_0 - Ke^{-rT} \leq c_0.$$

In this way, the lower bound of the European call option is found.

As a summary, the third principle (3.7) establishes the bounds for the call options as follows:

$$S_0 - Ke^{-rT} \leq c_0 \leq S_0. \tag{6.4}$$

It is noteworthy that these inequalities are very generic. They are model-free in the sense that no option pricing models are needed. Moreover, regardless of the kind of stochastic process driving the underlying asset fluctuation, the call option price c_0 must be bounded by (6.4). Any breaches of these bounds present risk-free arbitrage opportunities.

6.5.2   *Bounds on put prices*

Using the same approach, we set out to find the upper bound of put option price p_0. Consider the following two portfolios:

- Portfolio D
  A put option of price p_0 to sell one share of the underlying asset at the strike price of K at time T.

- Portfolio E

  A risk-free time deposit of amount Ke^{-rT} of tenor T and interest rate r.

At the expiration date T, Portfolio D's value is $V_D(T) = \max(K - S_T, 0)$, and Portfolio E's value is $V_E(T) = K$. Since $V_D(T) \leq V_E(T)$ for any $K \in \mathfrak{R}_+$, the third principle (3.7) requires the prices at time $t = 0$ to abide by

$$p_0 \leq Ke^{-rT}. \tag{6.5}$$

Having found the upper bound for p_0, the lower bound requires the following portfolios for establishing it:

- Portfolio F

  A put option of price p_0 to sell one share of the underlying asset at the strike price of K at time T, as well as one unit of the underlying asset.

- Portfolio E

  A risk-free time deposit of amount Ke^{-rT} of tenor T and interest rate r.

At maturity, Portfolio F's value is $\max(K - S_T, 0) + S_T$. If the put option is out of the money when $K < S_T$, then the value of Portfolio F will be the underlying asset valued at S_T in the market. But if the put option is in the money, the put option is exercised by selling the one share at hand at the higher strike price K. Therefore, $V_F(T) = \max(K, S_T)$, which is equal to or larger than Portfolio E's value of K.

Applying the third principle of Quantitative Finance (3.7), since $V_E(T) \leq V_F(T)$, it must be that at time 0,

$$Ke^{-rT} \leq p_0 + S_0.$$

After a rearrangement of terms, and in conjunction with the upper bound (6.5), we conclude that

$$Ke^{-rT} - S_0 \leq p_0 \leq Ke^{-rT}. \tag{6.6}$$

It is interesting to note that when $S_0 \to 0$, the put option premium $p_0 \to Ke^{-rT}$. The intrinsic value of the put option is defined as $K - S_0$. So at this $S_0 \to 0$ limit when the put option is deep in the money, the option premium $p_0 \approx Ke^{-rT}$ can become smaller than the intrinsic value $K - S_0 \approx K$. On the other hand, when $K \to 0$ or deep out of the money, the put option premium p_0 must approach zero too.

6.5.3 *Summary*

In Section 6.3, the overall shape of the call and put options as a function of the strike price K is derived. Using again primarily the third principle of Quantitative Finance, we demonstrate in this section that the European option price is bounded within a certain range. With respect to the underlying price S_0 and the discounted strike price Ke^{-rT}, the call and put options are bounded. Since option prices can never be negative, we rewrite the two inequalities (6.4) and (6.6) as follows:

$$\text{Call}: \quad \max\left(0, S_0 - Ke^{-rT}\right) \leq c_0 \leq S_0, \tag{6.7}$$

$$\text{Put}: \quad \max\left(0, Ke^{-rT} - S_0\right) \leq p_0 \leq Ke^{-rT}. \tag{6.8}$$

Note that the lower bounds are the discounted version of the payoff function. Indeed, if the option was to expire today ($t = 0$; $T = 0$), the lower bound would be the option value. It is worth emphasizing again that these inequalities are derived without assuming any underling price process, nor any option pricing model. Similar to the derivation for the overall shape of the option price function, the inequalities are model free.

6.6 Put–Call Parity

Put–call parity is a very important equation. To derive it, let the European plain vanilla call option price be c_0 and that for the put option price be p_0. Both the call and put options have identical underlying with price S_0 at time 0, maturity date T, and strike price K. As assumed in the previous sections, suppose one option contract allows the holder to buy or sell one unit of the underlying asset when exercised.

Consider now a position at time 0 comprising a long position in put and a share of the underlying, and a short position in call. The long position costs $p_0 + S_0$ and the short position brings in a cash amount of c_0, which is the premium received from the option buyer. The net cash flow is therefore $c_0 - p_0 - S_0$, and the value of this portfolio at time 0 is $S_0 + p_0 - c_0$.

Interestingly, this portfolio will generate a 100% certain cash flow of K at time T, regardless of how the price of the underlying asset turns out to be. If $S_T - K > 0$, the put option will be worthless and the call option will be exercised and we simply sell the underlying asset to the call option holder. If $S_T - K < 0$, this time round the call option is worthless but the put option will allow us to sell the underlying asset at the price of K. Of course, if $S_T = K$, the underlying asset will be sold at the price of K. So whatever the value of S_T is, the cash flow from selling the underlying asset is K. This combination of cash flows, which results in a constant payoff at maturity, is illustrated in Figure 6.6.

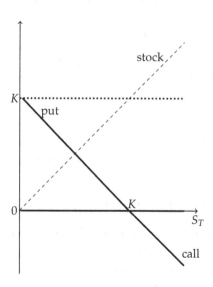

Fig. 6.6 The total payoff (horizontal dotted line) at maturity T for a position long in the underlying asset S_T (dashed line), long in a European put option struck at K, and short in the corresponding European call option also struck at K.

When $S_T < K$, the underlying asset and the put combine to make the payoff equal K in Figure 6.6. In fact, $S_T + (K - S_T) = K$. When $S_T \geq K$, however, any gain in the underlying is canceled by the loss in the short option position, resulting in $S_T - (S_T - K) = K$.

Since the cash flow K is guaranteed and certain, there is no risk whatsoever and the first principle of Quantitative Finance suggests that the present value of the position at time 0 ought to be Ke^{-rT}. In other words,

$$\text{PV of the portfolio} = Ke^{-rT}.$$

The third principle of Quantitative Finance rules out risk-free arbitrage opportunity, hence this present value of the portfolio is none other than the portfolio value at time 0 because the portfolio is worth K at time T as discussed earlier. Buyer and seller of this portfolio will not trade other than this present value. Therefore, we have

$$S_0 + p_0 - c_0 = Ke^{-rT},$$

and this put–call parity is more commonly written as

$$c_0 - p_0 = S_0 - Ke^{-rT}.$$

At any time $t \leq T$, with $T - t$ being the remaining time to maturity, the put–call parity is

$$c_t - p_t = S_t - Ke^{-r(T-t)}. \tag{6.9}$$

This interesting relationship between the call, put, the underlying asset, and the discounted strike price has many applications.

6.6.1 *Implied forward price*

As a simple application of the put–call parity, we consider the scenario where there is a continuum of strike prices. By construction, the put and call option prices are functions of the strike price. Holding other quantities constant, there is a strike price K^* such that $c(K^*) = p(K^*)$, which corresponds to the situation where the two price curves in Figure 6.5 crosses.

With respect to the intersection point, the put–call parity (6.9) becomes

$$0 = S_t - K^* e^{-r(T-t)},$$

and it is re-written as

$$K^* = S_t\, e^{r(T-t)}.$$

This result shows that the strike price K^* at which the call option price equals the put option price is none other than the forward price of the underlying asset at time t.

Since this forward price is inferred from the option prices, it is appropriate to name it the implied forward price. An interesting aspect of this forward price is that neither the knowledge of the underlying asset price S nor the risk-free interest rate r is needed. By simply examining the strike price K^* where the two put and call price curves interest, the implied forward price is obtained.

6.6.2   *Early exercise of American option*

By subtracting and adding the strike price K, the put–call parity (6.9) at time t can be re-written as

$$c_t = S_t - K + p_t + K\big(1 - e^{-r(T-t)}\big). \tag{6.10}$$

The first term $S_t - K$ is simply the value that would be obtained if the call option was exercised immediately at time t. The last term $K\big(1 - e^{-r(T-t)}\big)$ is intuitively interpretable as the interest amount payable at time t of a continuously compounding loan K. This interest amount becomes lesser and lesser as t approaches maturity T, which is a characteristic of an amortizing loan. Now, since the put option and the interest payable are positive numbers, it must be that

$$c_t > S_t - K.$$

Another application of the put–call parity in the form of Equation (6.10) concerns the early exercise of an American call option. In Section 6.1, it is mentioned that an option that can be exercised anytime prior to or at the expiration date T is an American-style option. Given the early exercise premium, the American call option C_t on a non-dividend-paying stock[3] costs more then an otherwise identical European call option. It follows that early exercise of an American call option is not optimal whenever the option premium is higher than $S_t - K$, i.e.,

$$C_t \geq c_t > S_t - K.$$

Intuitively, (6.10) shows that early exercise not only accelerates the payment for the underlying stock but also foregoes, as it were, the implicit put protection in case the stock price later moves below the strike price. Hence, an American-style call option on a non-dividend-paying stock should never be exercised prior to expiration (see Chapter 10 in Hull [Hul12] and refer also to McDonald [McD13]).

Instead of exercising early, the American call option holder is better off to liquidate it in the option market when the call becomes profitable. Hence, the American call option is not distinguishable from the European call option, and it follows that $C_t = c_t$ for $t \leq T$.

On the other hand, it makes economic sense for the American put option to be exercised early when the underlying stock does not pay dividend. Since the benefit of holding the stock is not forthcoming, everything else being equal, it is better to exercise the put option early so as to receive cash K by selling the underlying stock. The cash is then kept at the money market account to earn interest.

But there again, under what condition does an American put option become *not* optimal to exercise early? To answer this question, we apply the put–call parity, and having added and subtracted K, the European put option is expressed as

$$p_t = K - S_t + c_t - K(1 - e^{-r(T-t)}).$$

If the stock does not pay dividend, then $c_t = C_t$, the above equation is re-written as

$$p_t - (K - S_t) = C_t - K(1 - e^{-r(T-t)}).$$

The term $K - S_t$ is none other than the value or the payoff that the put option holder would get if it was exercised at time t.

---

[3]Throughout this chapter, we have implicitly assumed that the stock does not pay dividends.

When $C_t > K(1 - e^{-r(T-t)})$, it must be that $p_t > K - S_t$. Since $P_t \geq p_t$, it follows that

$$P_t \geq p_t > K - S_t,$$

which is to say, the American put option is more valuable than if it were to be exercised immediately to receive the payoff $K - S_t$. Stated differently, it is not optimal to exercise the American put option if its price is higher than the payoff $K - S_t$ under the condition that $C_t > K(1 - e^{-r(T-t)})$. The put option holder is better off to sell the American option at the price of P_t in the market than to exercise it.

This analysis suggests that when the underlying stock pays no dividend, the early exercise policy for the American put option is, intriguingly, determined by the call option price, i.e., whether C_t is or is not higher than an amortizing interest payment $K(1 - e^{-r(T-t)})$.

6.6.3 *The Modigliani–Miller Proposition I*

As discussed in Section 2.2, the shareholders of a company, as co-owners, have no liability if the company goes bankrupt. Also in Section 2.5, corporations may also raise funds from the bond market to finance their business and investment opportunities. The composition of equity and bond by which a corporation finances its assets is called the capital structure. A firm that has zero debt is said to be unlevered, whereas a firm that also issues corporate bond in addition to equity is said to be levered.

For simplicity, suppose a levered firm has outstanding only a zero-coupon bond with face value K maturing at time T. Next, we denote the market value of an unlevered but otherwise identical firm by S_t. When $S_T < K$, i.e., when the market value S at maturity T turns out to be less than K, shareholders of the levered firm will invoke limited liability by accepting zero market value of their shares. In other words, the equity of the shareholders at time T is $\max(S_T - K, 0)$. This is equivalent to the payoff of the European-style call option c_0 struck at K. Therefore, the market value of the levered firm's equity is essentially the call option "premium" $c_0(K)$

whose exercise price K is the firm's liability K that matures at time T. It follows that c_0 at time 0 is interpretable as the market value of the shares in the levered firm.

Now, the put–call parity (6.9) can also be expressed as, at time 0,

$$S_0 = c_0 + Ke^{-rT} - p_0. \tag{6.11}$$

In this expression, Ke^{-rT} corresponds to the present value or market value of the zero-coupon bond at time 0 if the levered firm is risk-free. But of course, the levered firm is far from risk-free since it may default on its liability. For this reason, the actual market value of the debt need to be discounted so that it is worth only $Ke^{-rT} - p_0$. The put premium p_0 may be interpreted as the insurance premium required by the bondholders against default by the levered firm. From the perspective of the levered firm, p_0 is interpretable as a bankruptcy cost of debt. If we define a return $\hat{r}$ by

$$Ke^{-\hat{r}T} := Ke^{-rT} - p_0,$$

then clearly the return $\hat{r}$ required by the investors is larger than the risk-free rate r. The implication is that the actual amount of capital $Ke^{-\hat{r}T}$ raised by the zero-coupon bond is less than Ke^{-rT} because of the cost of bankruptcy.

By construction, the call option c_0 is dependent on K, the face value of the zero-coupon bond. Hence, the market value of the levered firm's debt, $Ke^{-rT} - p_0$, and that of its equity, c_0, are respectively, functions of the firm's debt K. But the put–call parity in the form of (6.11) says that the total value of a levered firm is equal to the value of the unlevered firm S_0, and thereby independent of K. In other words, the combined pieces of the capital structure add up to S_0, the market value of the unlevered but otherwise identical firm. This result is the well-known Modigliani–Miller Proposition I [MM58], which states that the value of a levered firm and the value of a firm composed only of equity S_0 are equal. Put differently, the capital structure of a firm, i.e., whether levered or unlevered, is irrelevant to the market valuation of a firm.

It is intriguing that the put–call parity is applicable as a mathematical representation of the Modigliani–Miller proposition I [Mil88]. That said, a deeper look at the root of the Modigliani–Miller

Proposition I finds that both are grounded on the third principle of Quantitative Finance. If a firm's market value could be changed by changing the proportion of stocks and bonds they issue, then arbitrageurs could also repackage the existing stocks and bonds to make a sure profit. Hence, the value of the firm should depend only on the sum of the values of its stocks and bonds, not on whether the firm's capital is weighted more heavily on debt or on equity (see Varian [Var87]).

6.7 Box Spread Parity

Another application of the principles of Quantitative Finance is to derive a parity known as the box spread parity.

As in Q1, it is possible to create a synthetic long position payoff of the forward contract from European options by a long call and a short put with identical strike price and maturity. Conversely, a short position in the forward payoff can be synthesized from a pair of European short call and long put. If a synthetic long forward is created with "forward price" K_1 in conjunction with a synthetic short forward of "forward price" K_2, then the payoff function plotted in Figure 6.7 is obtained.

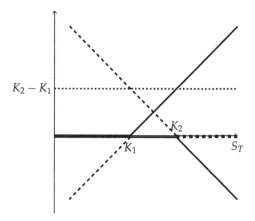

Fig. 6.7   The payoff function of a box spread strategy (horizontal dotted lines) for the buyer at maturity T. A box spread strategy comprises a bull call spread (solid lines) and a bear put spread (dashed lines).

Table 6.3 Analysis of the payoff of two long positions in bull call spread and bear put spread.

Asset price range	Payoff from bull call spread	Payoff from bear put spread	Total payoff
$S_T < K_1$	0	$K_2 - K_1$	$K_2 - K_1$
$K_1 \leq S_T \leq K_2$	$S_T - K_1$	$K_2 - S_T$	$K_2 - K_1$
$S_T > K_2$	$K_2 - K_1$	0	$K_2 - K_1$

In Figure 6.3, the payoff function of a bull call spread is depicted. It consists of a long call struck at the lower strike price of K_1 and a short call struck at the higher K_2. In Figure 6.4, the pairing of a long put struck at the higher K_2 and a short put struck at the lower K_1 is illustrated. This strategy is known as the bear put spread in the option market. By combining the bull call spread with a bear put spread, a pair of synthetic long and short forward positions is obtained, giving rise to the same payoff function plotted in Figure 6.7. Interestingly, the total payoff from a box spread comprising four options turns out to be a constant $K_2 - K_1$ for the buyer, as demonstrated in Table 6.3.

In other words, at time T when all the four options mature, the payoff of $K_2 - K_1$ is a guaranteed certainty, regardless of which direction the asset price S_T is fluctuating toward. This situation fits the type governed by the first principle of Quantitative Finance. When the future cash flow is known today, the price for that cash flow is simply to discount it with a relevant risk-free interest rate r. Therefore the price of going long on a box spread is simply

$$(K_2 - K_1)e^{-rT}.$$

Accordingly, we have

$$c_0(K_1) - c_0(K_2) + p_0(K_2) - p_0(K_1) = (K_2 - K_1)e^{-rT}. \qquad (6.12)$$

The term $c_0(K_1) - c_0(K_2)$ is the cost of longing a bull call spread, and $p_0(K_2) - p_0(K_1)$ is the price of a bear put spread. Equation (6.12) is known as the box spread parity.

If we re-group the left side of the box spread parity, and subtract and add S_0, the result is

$$\big(c_0(K_1) - p_0(K_1) - S_T\big) - \big(c_0(K_2) - p_0(K_2) - S_T\big).$$

The put–call parity (6.9) can then be applied for strike K_1 and K_2 separably. It is easily verifiable that the applications of put–call parity on these two re-grouped terms result in $K_2 - K_1$ discounted by the factor e^{-rT}, which is the term on the right side of (6.12).

Assuming that options and bonds are liquidly traded, if the box spread parity is violated, then the following risk-free arbitrage opportunities will arise.

1. If the left side of (6.12) is more valuable than the right side, an arbitrage profit can be made by shorting the box spread in the option market, which is effectively a synthetic discount bond. Part of the proceeds will be used to buy a *de facto* risk-free zero-coupon bond, and the remainder is the arbitrage profit.
2. Conversely, if the left side of the box spread parity is less valuable than the right side, borrow money and use part of the proceeds to long a box spread, and the balance is the risk-free arbitrage profit.

But this risk-free arbitrage strategy is not as easy as it seems on paper. Beyond making the assumption that options and bonds are liquidly traded, which they are not, it is necessary in the first scenario to ensure that the maturity of the risk-free discount bond exactly matches the expiration date of the four European options. Also in borrowing money for the second scenario, it is imperative to make sure that the creditor cannot contractually demand the early withdrawal of the borrowed amount before the box spread expires.

Another important aspect concerns the details and procedures by which the expired contracts are settled. This point is seldom discussed but is really important. There are two main ways in which options are settled in options trading:

- Physical Settlement
  Transfer of the actual underlying asset between the holder and the writer.

- Cash Settlement

  Settling the P&L in cash only between the option holder and the writer without the actual transfer of any asset.

  Physical settlement is the most common type of settlement method for equity options. In fact, all stock options that are publicly traded in the U.S. are settled by "physical delivery." Holders get to buy the stock for exercising the call option, and get to sell shares for exercising the put option. However, for the risk-free trading strategy to work, cash settlement is preferred.

  Since the options involved in constructing a box spread must be European, equity options are not suitable as they are American. Fortunately, index options such as the options on S&P 500 index are European. Moreover, index options are settled in cash when exercised.

  Another crucial part of the settlement is collateral posting and actual payment date (and time). In the case of exchange-traded options, margin has to be posted prior to trading. One important point to note is that when you sell or write options, you cannot withdraw the sales proceeds because you must not only deposit or maintain the sales proceeds but also to top up 10 to 15% of the aggregate contract value, which is the current index level times the price multiplier. In the case of S&P 500 index option, the price multiplier is $100. Since the box spread has two short positions, it is not possible to use the proceeds to buy the zero-coupon bond. So the arbitrage strategy cannot proceed.

  For U.S. Treasury securities, payment is made on the day of purchase, and sufficient funds must be deposited in a bank account *before* the bond issue date. When the U.S. Treasury bond matures, payment is deposited into your bank account on day T. But when options are exercised, actual payment occurs on the business day following expiration, which could be $T + 3$. These details are especially important in examining the feasibility of an apparently risk-free arbitrage strategy.

6.8 Put–Call Inequalities for American Options

The put–call parity (6.9) are valid only for options that are strictly exercisable on expiration date. When the early exercise feature is added, things become more complicated. Nevertheless, the third principle of Quantitative Finance still permits similar analysis to derive insights regarding a pair of American put and call options on the same underlying, of identical strike and expiration date.

First, we consider two portfolios G and H constructed as follows:

- Portfolio G
  A European call struck at K and expiring on day T, plus cash K invested in a risk-free security yielding r.
- Portfolio H
  An American put option struck at K and expiring on day T, plus one share of stock.

First, we examine the value of Portfolio G. At time 0, its value is $c_0 + K$. At expiration time T, Portfolio G is worth

$$\max(S_T - K, 0) + Ke^{rT} = \max(S_T, K) + K(e^{rT} - 1).$$

The right side of the above expression is obtained when the following two scenarios are incorporated.

(1) The European call option is at or in the money since $S_T \geq K$. Then the value of Portfolio G is $S_T - K + Ke^{-rT}$, which is $S_T + K(e^{rT} - 1)$.
(2) The European call option is out of the money because $S_T < K$. Then the value of Portfolio G is $0 + Ke^{-rT}$, which is $K + K(e^{rT} - 1)$.

The term common to these two mutually exclusive scenarios is $K(e^{rT} - 1)$, i.e., the interest earned from time 0 to time T for an initial principal sum of K. In the first scenario, the uncommon term is S_T, which is larger than or equal to K. For the second scenario, the uncommon term is K, which is larger than S_T. If we write the uncommon term as $\max(S_T, K)$, these two scenarios are thus taken care of correctly and nicely.

If the put option is not exercised early and held until time T, then portfolio H's value will become $\max(S_T, K)$ at time T. This is because when $S_T \geq K$, the put option expires worthless and the Portfolio H consist of the share, which is valued as S_T. But when $S_T < K$, the put option is exercised and the value become K. Hence, $V_H(T) = \max(S_T, K)$ if the put option is held to maturity. It is clear that

$$\max(S_T, K) = V_H(T) \leq V_G(T) = \max(S_T, K) + K(e^{rT} - 1).$$

The two portfolios' values are equal only in the special case where the time to maturity is zero ($T = 0$).

If the put option is exercised early at time t_e by selling the one share at the strike price, the value of Portfolio H will become K. The marked-to-market value of Portfolio G is $c_{t_e} + Ke^{rt_e}$. Also evidently, since $K < Ke^{rt_e}$, it follows that

$$K = V_H(t_e) < V_G(t_e) = c_{t_e} + Ke^{rt_e}.$$

Notice that $t_e < T$ is a random time depending on K, S_t, r, and T, among others. Being random, it is impossible to have the cash amount Ke^{-rt_e} in place of K in Portfolio G at time 0 so as to make the bound tighter.

In any case, regardless of whether the American put option is exercised or not, V_H is smaller than V_G at time T and at any early exercise time $t_e < T$. By the third principle (3.7), the value of Portfolio H must also be smaller than Portfolio G at time 0. Since $c_0 \leq C_0$, the value $V_G(0)$ of Portfolio G, which is $c_0 + K$, will be smaller or equal to $C_0 + K$. It follows that

$$P_0 + S_0 \leq C_0 + K.$$

In this fashion, we have obtained the lower bound for the synthetic long forward $C_0 - P_0$ as follows:

$$S_0 - K \leq C_0 - P_0. \tag{6.13}$$

As mentioned earlier, the equality occurs in the trivial case when the the options expire ($T = 0$).

In deriving the upper bound, we need to consider the following portfolios:

- Portfolio I
  An American call struck at K and maturing at time T, plus an amount Ke^{-rT} invested in a risk-free security paying the rate of r.
- Portfolio J
  A European put option with the same strike price and expiration, plus one share of the underlying stock.

If the American call is held to maturity, the value of Portfolio I will become

$$V_I(T) = \max(S_T - K, 0) + K = \max(S_T, K).$$

On the other hand, Portfolio J's value will also be $V_J(T) = \max(K - S_T, 0) + S_T = \max(S_T, K)$. These results follow from the same lines of thought earlier for Portfolios G and H. Therefore, in the case where the American call option is not exercised early, we have $V_I(T) = V_J(T)$.

But if the call option is exercised early at any time t_e before T, the value $V_I(t_e)$ of Portfolio I becomes

$$S_{t_e} - K + Ke^{-r(T-t_e)} = S_{t_e} - K\left(1 - e^{-r(T-t_e)}\right),$$

which is less than S_{t_e}. Portfolio J's value when marked to market at time t_e will be $p_{t_e} + S_{t_e}$, which is larger than S_{t_e} and hence also larger than $V_I(t_e)$. Therefore, this analysis suggests that $V_I(T) = V_J(T)$ at time T, and $V_I(t_e) < V_J(t_e)$ for any $t_e < T$.

Because Portfolio J is worth at least as much as Portfolio I in all circumstances, by the third principle of Quantitative Finance, (3.7), at time 0, it must be that

$$V_I(0) = C_0 + Ke^{-rT} \le p_0 + S_0 = V_J(0).$$

Since the European put p_0 is less than or equal to the American put P_0, it follows that

$$C_0 + Ke^{-rT} \le P_0 + S_0,$$

and hence

$$C_0 - P_0 \le S_0 - Ke^{-rT}.$$

Notice that if both options were European, this result would be the put–call parity (6.9). In conjunction with the lower bound result (6.13) obtained earlier for the American options, the put–call inequalities are written as

$$S_0 - K \le C_0 - P_0 \le S_0 - Ke^{-rT}. \tag{6.14}$$

As a corollary of these inequalities, we have

$$-K\left(1 - e^{-rT}\right) < e_{c_0} - e_{p_0} \le 0,$$

equivalently,

$$0 \le e_{p_0} - e_{c_0} < K\left(1 - e^{-rT}\right),$$

where e_{c_0} and e_{p_0} denote the early exercise premium of, respectively, the American call C_0 and the American put P_0. This corollary is readily obtained when we write

$$C_0 = c_0 + e_{c_0}, \qquad P_0 = p_0 + e_{p_0},$$

and apply the put–call parity (6.9) on the European option components. A key insight from this corollary is that, everything else being equal, the early exercise premium of an American put option is larger and no less than that of a corresponding American call option. Moreover, the early exercise difference $e_{c_0} - e_{p_0}$ is bounded from above by $K\left(1 - e^{-rT}\right)$, which is the interest a zero-coupon bond issuer pays to the bond holder who bought K amount of it at the price of e^{-rT} for every dollar to be received at time T.

6.9 Exercises

Q1. In Section 3.5, as an application of the three principles of Quantitative Finance, the fair price for the forward contract is obtained. The payoff function is $S_T - F_0$ for the buyer at maturity.

(a) Show that the forward's payoff function can be synthetically replicated by a pair of European put and call options on the same underlying, with identical strike price $K = F_0$ and maturity T as follows:

$$c_T - p_T.$$

(b) Plot the payoff diagram of the forward contract replicated by $c_T - p_T$.

(c) Show that the marked-to-market value F_t of the outright forward before maturity $(t < T)$ is
$$F_t = S_t - Ke^{-r(T-t)}.$$

(d) In the context of this question, apply the principles of Quantitative Finance to prove the put–call parity (6.9).

Q2. A long straddle is an option strategy established by buying a call and a put on the same strike price written on the same underlying asset and with identical expiration date.

(a) Plot the payoff function at maturity.

(b) What is the view of the option trader long in a straddle?

Q3. A long strap is a variation of straddle. Instead of one call and one put, the strap has two calls and one put.

(a) Plot the payoff function at maturity.

(b) What is the view of the option trader long in a strap?

Q4. A long strip is another variation of straddle. It has one call and two puts.

(a) Plot the payoff function at maturity.

(b) What is the view of the option trader long in a strip?

Q5. A long strangle is an option strategy that involves the simultaneous buying of a slightly out-of-the-money put and a slightly out-of-the-money call of the same underlying asset and expiration date.

(a) Plot the payoff function at maturity.

(b) What is the view of the option trader long in a strangle?

(c) Compare the premiums of strangle and straddle.

Q6. The butterfly spread is an option strategy that involves three different strike prices: $K_1 < K_2 < K_3$. The exercise price K_2 is at the money, and usually, K_1 and K_3 are chosen such that
$$K_2 = \frac{K_1 + K_3}{2}.$$
A long position in the butterfly spread with calls is to buy two at-the-money calls $c(K_2)$ and sell an in-the-money call $c(K_1)$ and an out-of-the-money call $c(K_3)$.

(a) Applying the convexity property of options, show that the net cash flow required to establish a long position in the butterfly spread is positive:

$$c(K_1) + c(K_3) - 2c(K_2) \geq 0.$$

(b) Draw the payoff function of the butterfly spread at maturity.

(c) The long position in the put butterfly spread is established by buying the puts $p(K_1)$ and $p(K_3)$ and selling two at-the-money puts $p(K_2)$. Is the net cash flow positive or negative?

(d) The long position in an iron butterfly is established by buying the out-of-the-money put $p(K_1)$ and call $c(K_3)$ and selling the at-the-money put $p(K_2)$ and call $c(K_2)$. Is the net cash flow positive or negative?

Chapter 7

Binomial Models

7.1 Introduction

In the previous chapters, random time series such as the spot gold prices (Figure 2.1), South Sea company stock prices (Figure 3.3), and the TED spreads (Figure 4.6) are plotted. Also, the concept of random variable is applied contextually without a formal definition. We have relied on the daily usage of "random" as an adjective to describe a phenomenon that is lacking any regular order or purpose.

A useful perspective to illustrate randomness is to consider non-randomness instead. A non-random event is one for which the outcome is 100% certain. An example of a non-random event is to drop two objects of different masses from a height at the same time. For this experiment, three mutually exclusive possibilities are, in principle, possible. First, the heavier object hits the leveled ground first. Second, the heavier object hits the leveled ground last. Third, both objects hit the ground at the same time. Governed by the laws of physics in a vacuum, only the third possibility will happen, as the same acceleration by gravity known as the g force applies equally to both objects. Therefore, prior to the experiment, the third possibility is 100% certain to happen, leaving no room for randomness and statistical forecasting.

By contrast, a random event is the complete opposite of a non-random event. In particular, it is inherently impossible to forecast which of the plausible outcomes will happen with 100% certainty.

As an illustration, consider two identical blank coins without any insignia etched on either sides. At one side of each coin, there is a blue dot at the center, and the flip side has a red dot. The focus of the experiment is to observe which side of the coin will turn up. Even though both coins will hit the ground at the same time in the vacuum, it is not possible to forecast whether the side with the blue dot would turn up for sure. Two possible outcomes are conceivable: (A) Both coins have the same color turning up; (B) Both coins have different colors turning up. Intriguingly, despite the fact that the motions are subject to the laws of physics, a tiny little difference in the angle at which the coin hits the ground and bounces will introduce a great amount of uncertainty in how it finally lays on the ground. As both sides of the coin are of the same make except for the colored dots, outcome (A) is as equally likely to happen as outcome (B).

Since antiquity, the concept of randomness was intertwined with cleromancy for divine guidance. Intuitively, it was understood that if the casting of lots cannot be directed by human will, then the outcome of cleromancy must be a sign from some supernatural beings. For example, in Chapter 16 of the *Book of Proverbs*, we read in Verse 33 that

> The lot is cast into the lap; but the whole disposing thereof is of the Lord.

Indeed, in circa 1300 BC, Aaron, the first Israelite high priest, was to cast lots upon the two goats as a ritual to determine which was acceptable to the Lord as a sin offering for the Israelites.

Another civilization with long history also regards the random event as a heavenly oracle. By the time of Western Zhou dynasty, circa 1200 BC, ancient Chinese had assembled a book called the *Scripture of Changes* (*I Ching*). It contains a distilled sophistication of past symbologies and numerologies of divination since the beginning of Chinese civilization when Fuxi emerged as the tribal leader. The pre-historic, mythological Fuxi is widely attributed to have invented a system of eight different guàs or trigrams for auguries known as the Bāguà, four of which can be found in the flag of South Korea. The atomic building block of a guà is either ying or yang.

So, it appears that binary system had already been invented thousands of years ago. Moreover, the binary system had been applied in the context of dealing with uncertainties and forecasting. The uncertainty arises because of randomness. Against the backdrop of randomness, we discuss in this chapter a binomial model invented by Cox, Ross, and Rubinstein to price options [CRR79]. Their iterative method based on the binary system is very powerful and general. It allows different specifications of nodes, which represent the points in time, during the period spanning between the valuation date and the option's expiration date.

7.2   Random Walk

Randomness is of crucial importance in Quantitative Finance, not because it has got anything to do with demons or gods. Rather, it is the raison d'être of probability and statistics.

The simplest form of randomness in a stochastic process is random walk, a term first coined by the statistician Karl Pearson in 1905 [Pea05]. It goes as follows:

> A man starts from a point O and walks *l* yards in a straight line; he then turns through any angle whatever and walks another *l* yards in a second straight line. He repeats this process *n* times.

The "any angle whatever" is the randomness in the direction that the man is walking in. Pearson ascribes this randomness to the drunken stupor that has completely overpowered him.

A simplified version of the two-dimensional random walk is the random walk on a line. Starting from point 0, the drunken man can either move upward one step, or move downward one step, with equal odds. To simulate this 50–50 chance, we toss the blue–red coin of Section 7.1. If blue turns up, move upward one step, else move downward. This up–down movement is binary in nature.

What are the possible outcomes after 3 periods? This question is equivalent to tossing the binary blue–red coin thrice. Denote the upward movement by U_t and the downward movement by D_t, where $t = 1, 2$ and 3. There are $2^3 = 8$ possibilities, and they are

$$U_1U_2U_3, \quad U_1U_2D_3, \quad U_1D_2U_3, \quad U_1D_2D_3,$$
$$D_1U_2U_3, \quad D_1U_2D_3, \quad D_1D_2U_3, \quad D_1D_2D_3.$$

These eight possible outcomes are anything but Fuxi's Bāguà. In this regard, the binary system of coding information (knowledge and wisdom), the basic language of a computer processor, had been discovered and applied thousands of years before Gottfried Leibniz published the *Explication de l'Arithmétique Binaire*.

Each of these eight possible outcomes occurs with a probability of 1/8. The first outcomes $U_1\ U_2\ U_3$ results in three steps above the origin. Three outcomes, $U_1\ U_2\ D_3$, $U_1\ D_2\ U_3$, and $D_1\ U_2\ U_3$ will find the drunken man at one step above the origin. Conversely, for $U_1\ D_2\ D_3$, $D_1\ U_2\ D_3$, and $D_1\ D_2\ U_3$, the resulting position is one step below the origin. Finally, $D_1\ D_2\ D_3$ leads to 3 steps below the origin. These eight paths and the final numbers of steps above or below the origin are depicted in Figure 7.1.

In the classic *I Ching*, each of these eight possible paths is assigned a triagram and a meaning. For example, the combination $U_1\ U_2\ U_3$ represents "heaven," and $D_1\ D_2\ D_3$ symbolizes "earth." In Quantitative Finance, however, Figure 7.1 is called the binomial tree of three time periods. In general, a binomial tree can have many time periods. Interestingly, the double-layered guà in the *I Ching*

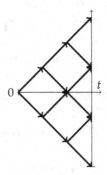

Fig. 7.1 Eight paths of binary upward or downward movement and their final distance from the origin after three periods.

corresponds to the binomial tree of 6 time periods, hence there are altogether $2^6 = 8 \times 8 = 64$ guà's.

A more generic description of a random walk $\widetilde{S}_t$ with a binary random variable $\widetilde{C}_t$ as the source of randomness is

$$\widetilde{S}_t = S_{t-1} + \widetilde{C}_t, \qquad \text{where } t = 0, 2, \ldots, T. \tag{7.1}$$

To highlight that a variable is a random variable, a tilde is put on top of it. The random variable $\widetilde{C}_t$ has two possible values of ± 1 with equal probability of happening.

Every possible path up to time t is produced by starting from the origin S_0 and the addition of the binary random variable $\widetilde{C}_i$, i.e.,

$$\widetilde{S}_t = S_0 + \sum_{i=1}^{t} \widetilde{C}_i.$$

We have assumed in Figure 7.1 that $\widetilde{C}_i = 1$ if the color is blue and $\widetilde{C}_i = -1$ if red. Therefore, for each i, $\mathbb{E}(\widetilde{C}_i) = 0$, and $\mathbb{V}(\widetilde{C}_i) = 1/2(1-0)^2 + 1/2(-1-0)^2 = 1$. By design, each toss of the blue–red coin is independent of the other toss. Consequently, the unconditional mean and variance are, respectively,

$$\mathbb{E}(\widetilde{S}_t) = S_0, \qquad \mathbb{V}(\widetilde{S}_t) = t.$$

The expected value of the binary random walk is the constant S_0. By contrast, the variance increases with time t. Intuitively, we see this increment from the binomial tree that its branches spread further from the origin as the number of periods increases.

Now, suppose S_{t-1} is known and given, then the expectation of $\widetilde{S}_t$ conditional on this information is, from (7.1),

$$\mathbb{E}(\widetilde{S}_t | S_{t-1}) = S_{t-1}. \tag{7.2}$$

This property of the conditional expectation is referred to as martingale. Also, we find that the conditional variance is

$$\mathbb{V}(\widetilde{S}_t | S_{t-1}) = 1. \tag{7.3}$$

This time round, the conditional mean changes with S_{t-1} while the conditional variance is a constant. What (7.2) suggests is that the best forecast of the next position is the current position S_{t-1}. Moreover, (7.3) indicates that $S_{t-1} \pm 1$ is one standard deviation from S_{t-1}, which is intuitive indeed.

7.3 One-Period Option Pricing

The random walk and in particular the binomial tree is useful to price options. First, we modify the random walk slightly as we want to ensure that the price of the underlying asset is positive. Instead of addition, we consider multiplication by a positive random variable $\widetilde{\Lambda}_t$, which can either be $u > 1$ or $d < 1$. We call the value u the up factor, and d the down factor. The multiplicative random walk is defined as

$$\widetilde{S}_t = S_{t-1}\widetilde{\Lambda}_t.$$

Up to time t from time 0, the price of the asset is obtained as

$$\widetilde{S}_t = S_0 \prod_{i=1}^{t} \widetilde{\Lambda}_i. \tag{7.4}$$

The binomial tree is recombinant, i.e., the resulting price is the same as the starting price after two movements of opposite direction. Whether the price moves up first then down, or down first then up, the resulting price and the starting price are equal. In other words, the order of movement does not matter:

$$\widetilde{S}_t = ud\widetilde{S}_{t-2} = du\widetilde{S}_{t-2} = \widetilde{S}_{t-2}.$$

To make the tree recombinant, we must have

$$d = \frac{1}{u}.$$

This recombinant property is crucial to the practical usefulness of the binomial tree. Otherwise, if $ud \neq 1$, tossing the blue-red coin n times will give rise to 2^n end nodes. A not-so-big number of say $n = 100$ periods will have $2^{100} \approx 10^{30}$ end nodes. The floating-point calculations alone for this enormous number will take more than one million years to complete on the world's fastest supercomputer.[1]

---

[1]According to Top 500 The List (http://www.top500.org/), as of June 2014, Tianhe-2, a supercomputer developed by China's National University of Defense Technology, is the fastest computing machine in the world with a performance of 33.86 Pflop/s (quadrillions of calculations per second).

7.3.1 *Pricing*

We now consider the one-period case. At time 0, the underlying price is S_0. At time 1, the underlying price S_1 can either be uS_0 with probability p, or dS_0 with probability $1 - p$. The values of u and d are constant. But at time 0, we do not know which of the two outcomes will pan out at time 1.

We construct a portfolio consisting of a long position in the underlying asset at the price of S_0, plus a short position in its call option c_0 with a strike price K that matures at time 1. For a start, the call option's strike price K is chosen in such a way that it will be in the money if the underlying price goes up. Also, the call option will be worthless if the underlying price moves down.

At time 0, suppose we buy x_0 units of the risky asset. The value of the portfolio at time 0 is $V_0 = x_0 S_0 - c_0$. The portfolio value V_1 at time 1 is unknown at time 0 because we do no know which of the two outcomes will materialize. But is there a way to make the portfolio value V_1 to be known at time 0? The answer is yes. You buy x_0 shares in such a way that the portfolio value V_1 is the same for both outcomes.

- $S_1^+ = uS_0$

  In this case, the option holder will exercise the call option and the portfolio value V_1^+ at time 1 in dollars is

$$V_1^+ = x_0 uS_0 - (uS_0 - K).$$

- $S_1^- = dS_0$

  In this case, the option is worthless and the portfolio value is simply

$$V_1^- = x_0 dS_0.$$

In Figure 7.2, we illustrate the portfolio value V_0 at time 0, and the two possible values V_1^+ and V_1^- at time 1.

The key idea is that if you let $V_1^+ = V_1^-$, then there will be no more uncertainty. This can be achieved by solving the equal-value equation $V_1^+ = V_1^-$ for x_0:

$$x_0 uS_0 - (uS_0 - K) = x_0 dS_0.$$

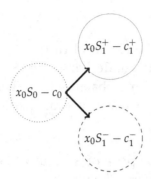

$$x_0 S_1^+ - c_1^+$$

$$x_0 S_0 - c_0$$

$$x_0 S_1^- - c_1^-$$

Fig. 7.2   One-period binomial pricing of a call option c_0.

The number of shares to buy is easily obtained as

$$x_0 = \frac{uS_0 - K}{(u - d)S_0}.$$ (7.5)

Notice that x_0 is a function of the known quantity S_0 at time 0.

Therefore, the portfolio value at time 1 is also known at time 0, and we have

$$V_1 = V_1^+ = V_1^- = \frac{d(uS_0 - K)}{u - d} = \frac{S_0 - dK}{u - d}.$$

Since there is no uncertainty, by the first principle of Quantitative Finance, the present value of the portfolio at time 0 must be discounted by the risk-free rate r as follows:

$$V_0 = e^{-r}V_1 = \frac{e^{-r}d(uS_0 - K)}{u - d}.$$

We shall call e^{-r} the risk-free discount factor. But the portfolio value at time 0 is $V_0 = x_0 S_0 - c_0$. Therefore,

$$\frac{e^{-r}d(uS_0 - K)}{u - d} = x_0 S_0 - c_0.$$

Substituting in x_0 from (7.5), we find that the value c_0 of the call option should be

$$c_0 = x_0 S_0 - \frac{e^{-r}d(uS_0 - K)}{u - d} = \frac{1 - e^{-r}d}{u - d}(uS_0 - K).$$ (7.6)

The slope of this call option is

$$\frac{\partial c_0}{\partial K} = -\frac{1 - e^{-r}d}{u - d}.$$

From Section 6.4.3, we know that the gradient is bounded from below by -1. Therefore, we conclude that

$$\frac{1 - e^{-r}d}{u - d} \leq 1.$$

Applying this result to the one-period pricing formula for call options, we obtain an upper bound:

$$c_0 \leq uS_0 - K.$$

This upper bound is different from S_0 (see (6.7)). Since the upper bound S_0 for the call option is derived under the model-free condition, it must be that

$$uS_0 - K \leq S_0.$$

This requirement imposes a consistency condition on u:

$$u \leq \frac{S_0 + K}{S_0}.$$

From the put–call parity, it is readily shown that the one-period put option price is

$$p_0 = \frac{ue^{-r} - 1}{u - d}(K - dS_0). \tag{7.7}$$

Also, the bound on put's gradient requires that

$$\frac{\partial p_0}{\partial K} = \frac{ue^{-r} - 1}{u - d} \leq 1.$$

In turn, it imposes an upper bound on the put option price as follows:

$$p_0 \leq K - dS_0.$$

This upper bound must be smaller or equal to the upper bound of (6.8). Therefore, a consistency condition must be met:

$$K - dS_0 \leq Ke^{-r},$$

leading to

$$d \geq \frac{K(1 - e^{-r})}{S_0}.$$

7.3.2   *Risk-neutral probability*

When pricing the call option in the one-period binomial setting, the probability p of upward movement by the underlying is not needed. This is because we have made the portfolio (underlying asset and call option) indifferent to either outcomes. Whether up or down, the portfolio value is the same. Since there is no uncertainty, probability is redundant.

By definition, the risk-free rate r is also indifferent to the up-or-down outcome. If the dollar value corresponding to the risky asset S_0 is invested in the risk-free bond, according to the first principle of Quantitative Finance, the value of this bond will become $e^r S_0$ at time 1 for sure. On the other hand, with probability p, the upward outcome is $u S_0$, whereas the downward outcome $d S_0$ occurs with a probability of $1 - p$. Thus, we have an equation,

$$u S_0 \times p + d S_0 \times (1 - p) = e^r S_0. \tag{7.8}$$

It is equivalent to saying that the up and down outcomes combine to produce a single value of $e^r S_0$. This idea requires the probability p to weigh the respective contributions of $u S_0$ and $d S_0$. The left side of (7.8) is $\mathbb{E}_0(\widetilde{S}_1)$. Hence, the first principle of Quantitative Finance in the binomial world can be expressed as

$$S_0 = e^{-r} \mathbb{E}_0(\widetilde{S}_1). \tag{7.9}$$

In words, under the probability p, today's asset price is the expected value of its future price discounted by the risk-free rate.

From (7.8), we obtain the probability p of upward movement:

$$p = \frac{e^r - d}{u - d}. \tag{7.10}$$

The probability p is called the risk-neutral probability. It is risk neutral in the sense that, although by definition probability implies uncertainty and hence risk, yet the combined outcome is neutral to either the upward outcome $u S_0$ or the downward outcome $d S_0$.

Using the risk-neutral probability p, two distinct outcomes are combined into one entity S_0 after discounted by the risk-free rate.[2]

Furthermore, since the probability is positive, it must be that

$$e^r > d.$$

The same analysis based on

$$1 - p = \frac{u - e^r}{u - d},$$

suggests that $u > e^r$. We summarize these relationships as follows

$$d < e^r < u. \tag{7.11}$$

The risk-neutral probability (7.10) is also embodied in the pricing formulas for call and put options, (7.6) and (7.7), respectively. To see it, we rewrite these pricing formulas as

$$c_0 = \frac{e^r - d}{u - d} e^{-r}(uS_0 - K), \qquad p_0 = \frac{u - e^r}{u - d} e^{-r}(K - dS_0).$$

It is easy to find that

$$\frac{e^r - d}{u - d} + \frac{u - e^r}{u - d} = 1.$$

In the light of the risk-neutral probability (7.10), we write

$$c_0 = e^{-r}(p \times (uS_0 - K) + (1 - p) \times 0);$$
$$p_0 = e^{-r}(p \times 0 + (1 - p) \times (K - dS_0)).$$

We denote the value of the call option at time 1 as $c_1^+ = uS_0 - K$ for the up state, and that for the down state as $c_1^- = 0$. In general, c_1^- may not be zero when the options are deep in the money. With the risk-neutral probability p, we invoke the notion of expected future value of c_1, which is denoted by $\mathbb{E}_0(c_1)$, and we write

$$c_0 = e^{-r}(pc_1^+ + (1 - p)c_1^-) = e^{-r}\mathbb{E}_0(c_1). \tag{7.12}$$

By the same argument, for the put option p_0, we also obtain

$$p_0 = e^{-r}(pp_1^+ + (1 - p)p_1^-) = e^{-r}\mathbb{E}_0(p_1). \tag{7.13}$$

---

[2]Intriguingly, the concept of two opposite outcomes becoming one entity is a foundational tenet of *I Ching*.

These equations suggest that under the risk-neutral probability, the fair price of option today is the expected value of its future payoff discounted by the risk-free rate.

In summary, in view of (7.9) for the underlying asset, as well as (7.12) and (7.13) for the options, we have a powerful valuation formula in the risk-neutral world for a financial instrument W_t, $t = 0, 1$ as follows:

$$W_0 = e^{-r} \mathbb{E}_0(\widetilde{W}_1). \tag{7.14}$$

What this formula means is that in the risk-neutral paradigm, you do not need to know the exact value of W_1 like you do about the deterministic cash C in (3.2) for the first principle of Quantitative Finance to be applicable. The expected value of W_1 computed under the risk-neutral probability p is good enough, as the market takes no view on which direction the financial instrument Q_0 is heading. Put simply, the variance of the outcome does not matter and no risk premium is required. If the dollar amount equivalent to W_0 is invested in the risk-free money market, the first principle of Quantitative Finance requires that its future value will be $e^r Q_0$. Therefore, the present value W_0 in (7.14) should be the expected value of $\widetilde{W}_1$ discounted by the risk-free rate. In the risk-neutral world, W_0 is the fair price that attracts equal numbers of buyers and sellers, in accordance to the third principle of Quantitative Finance.

7.4   Binomial Option Pricing

Obviously, using only one period to price options is an over simplification. But it provides the basic parts needed to price options on a more general setting. The key idea is to make the portfolio value invariant to both outcomes, i.e., remove the uncertainty arising from the randomness of coin tossing. To achieve this goal, the long position in the stock is required to hedge against a short position in the call option. The so-called delta-hedging ratio is defined as

$$x_0 = \frac{c_1^+ - c_1^-}{S_1^+ - S_1^-}, \tag{7.15}$$

where S_1^+ is the value S_1 of the underlying asset at time 1 in the up state and S_1^- is the value for the down state. Since $S_1^+ = uS_0$, $S_1^- = dS_0$, $c_1^+ = uS_0 - K$, and $c_1^- = 0$, the delta-hedging ratio (7.15) indeed yields the same result as (7.5):

$$x_0 = \frac{uS_0 - K}{(u - d)S_0}.$$

Moreover, under the risk-neutral probability p, (7.14) encapsulates the first principle of Quantitative Finance.

The multi-period version of the binomial option pricing scheme retains these critical features at each time period. However, the idea of hedging, i.e., making the portfolio indifferent to either outcome fails as soon as there are two periods. This is simply because there is a recombinant node, where the price S_2 is obtained by either dS_1^+ or uS_1^-, which are equal as $S_1^+ = uS_0$, $S_1^- = dS_0$, and $ud = 1$. Moreover, consider a node reached by a negative run such that after n periods, the underlying asset price is $d^n S_0$. This extreme low price $d^n S_0$ will surely make the long asset position in the asset-option portfolio beyond the realm of hedging with the call option.

7.4.1 *Replication of option's payoff*

A different idea is needed. We construct a portfolio comprising the underlying risky asset and the risk-free bond. This portfolio is constructed in such a way that it replicates the option's payoff at each node of the binomial tree. Since the option and this portfolio have the same payoff throughout the binomial tree, i.e., at every state of the binomial model, the third principle of Quantitative Finance requires them to have equal price at time 0. Otherwise, there will not be equal number of buyers and sellers. If the portfolio is more expensive than the option, then there will be more portfolio sellers and option buyers.

The initial cash amount or wealth is denoted by W_0. You buy x_0 shares of the underlying asset of the call option at the known price of S_0. The left-over cash is

$$M_0 := W_0 - x_0 S_0, \tag{7.16}$$

which is invested in the risk-free money market. One period later, the wealth W_1 will become

$$W_1 = \begin{cases} W_1^+ = x_0 S_1^+ + e^r M_0, & \text{blue outcome} \\ W_1^- = x_0 S_1^- + e^r M_0, & \text{red outcome} \end{cases}.$$

It is important to note that the two outcomes are anticipated at time 0, although which will eventually realize is unknown.

Consider again the one-period situation. The replication approach is to make the cash flow W_1 at time 1 equal the option's payoff c_1:

$$W_1 = x_0 S_1 + e^r M_0 = c_1.$$

To achieve this replication, using definition (7.16), we first rewrite the cash flow W_1 of the portfolio as

$$W_1 = e^r W_0 + x_0 (S_1 - e^r S_0)$$
$$= e^r (W_0 + x_0 (e^{-r} S_1 - S_0)).$$

We express the replication by matching each of the possible outcome:

$$W_0 + x_0 (e^{-r} S_1^+ - S_0) = e^{-r} c_1^+,$$
$$W_0 + x_0 (e^{-r} S_1^- - S_0) = e^{-r} c_1^-.$$

To arrive at this equalization, we need to find the values of x_0 and W_0. Multiplying the upward outcome by p and the downward outcome by $1 - p$, and after adding them together, we obtain

$$W_0 + x_0 \left(e^{-r} (p S_1^+ + (1-p) S_1^-) - S_0 \right) = e^{-r} (p c_1^+ + (1-p) c_1^-).$$

Because of (7.8), the sum of the two terms, $p S_1^+ + (1-p) S_1^-$, is equal to $e^r S_0$. Consequently,

$$W_0 = e^{-r} (p c_1^+ + (1-p) c_1^-).$$

In view of (7.12), W_0 is in fact the value of the option c_0 at time 0.

7.4.2 *Multi-period generalization*

An advantage of the replication approach is that it is generic. The one-period valuation argument applies to all the nodes in the binomial tree. Specifically, for each node that is not an ending node, the cash flow W_t at time t is

$$W_t = \begin{cases} W_t^+ = x_{t-1}S_t^+ + e^r M_{t-1}, & \text{blue outcome} \\ W_t^- = x_{t-1}S_t^- + e^r M_{t-1}, & \text{red outcome} \end{cases}.$$

The money market account M_t maturing at time $t+1$ is

$$M_t = W_t - x_t S_t, \qquad \text{for } t = 0, 1, 2, \ldots, T-1.$$

It is the fund left (or needed if M_t is negative) after taking a long position of x_t in the risky underlying asset at the price of S_t.

The delta-hedging ratio at time t for $t+1$ is

$$x_t = \frac{c_{t+1}^+ - c_{t+1}^-}{S_{t+1}^+ - S_{t+1}^-} = \frac{c_{t+1}^+ - c_{t+1}^-}{(u-d)S_t}. \tag{7.17}$$

Moreover, the risk-neutral pricing model is

$$c_t = e^{-r}\mathbb{E}_t(c_{t+1}). \tag{7.18}$$

What we require now is a proof that $W_t = c_t$ from time 0 up to time $T-1$. The method of the proof is forward induction: Assume that $W_t = c_t$ is true and show that $W_{t+1} = c_{t+1}$ also holds.

First, replication means that for the up state, i.e., $S_{t+1}^+ = uS_t$,

$$W_{t+1}^+ = x_t S_{t+1}^+ + e^r(W_t - x_t S_t) = e^r W_t + x_t S_t(u - e^r). \tag{7.19}$$

Substituting the delta-hedging ratio x_t (7.17) into (7.19), we obtain

$$W_{t+1}^+ = e^r W_t + \frac{(c_{t+1}^+ - c_{t+1}^-)(u - e^r)}{u - d}$$
$$= e^r W_t + (1-p)c_{t+1}^+ - (1-p)c_{t+1}^-.$$

In the second line, we have applied the fact that $1 - p = \dfrac{u - e^r}{u - d}$. In view of (7.18) and the forward induction assumption that $W_t = c_t$, we have

$$e^r W_t = e^r c_t = \mathbb{E}_t(c_{t+1}) = p c_{t+1}^+ + (1-p)c_{t+1}^-.$$

Hence,

$$W_{t+1}^+ = p c_{t+1}^+ + (1-p)c_{t+1}^+ = c_{t+1}^+.$$

Second, using the same method, you can also show that

$$W_{t+1}^- = pc_{t+1}^- + (1-p)c_{t+1}^- = c_{t+1}^-.$$

Accordingly, if $W_t^\pm = c_t^\pm$, then $W_{t+1}^\pm = c_{t+1}^\pm$. We have already shown that $t = 0$ is true, i.e., $W_0 = c_0$. At time $t = 1$, $W_1 = c_1$ must also be true, and so on. Thus, the proof by forward induction is complete.

In summary, for each t of the binomial tree, the risk-neutral valuation of a pair of future payoffs is

$$c_t = e^{-r}(pc_{t+1}^+ + (1-p)c_{t+1}^-) = e^{-r}\mathbb{E}(c_{t+1}). \qquad (7.20)$$

7.4.3 *Implementation of binomial option pricing model*

Having established the modeling foundation, we are now ready to apply the binomial model to price an option. The binomial option pricing model works as follows:

1. Generate a tree of N periods for the prices of the underlying asset.

   At each period t, the price S_t moves forward one period, resulting in $S_{n+1}^+ = uS_n$ and $S_{n+1}^- = dS_n$, for $n = 1, 2, \ldots, N$. The option matures at time T, so each period corresponds to a small time interval $t = T/N$ as N is taken to be a large number. This time interval is a fixed constant.

   The up and down factors depend on the rate of variance σ^2 of the underlying asset's return. The rate of variance σ^2 quantifies the degree of fluctuation exhibited by the return on the underlying asset. The variance for a time period t is $\sigma^2 t$, and the volatility is its square root $\sigma\sqrt{t}$. We set

$$u = e^{\sigma\sqrt{t}} \quad \text{and} \quad d = e^{-\sigma\sqrt{t}}.$$

2. Evaluate the option's payoff at each end node.
   Due to the recombinant property of the binomial tree, there are $N + 1$ end nodes. For each of these nodes, compute the option payoff at maturity. In the case of plain vanilla options,

the payoffs of a call and a put are, respectively,

$$c_N = \max(S_N - K, 0), \quad \text{and} \quad p_N = \max(K - S_N, 0).$$

3. Apply the one-period replication formula to obtain the option value at period n from a pair of option values at period $n + 1$.

Earlier, we have assumed that one period is one year, which allows the risk-free discount factor to be written as e^{-r}. In the multi-period framework, the duration t of each period is a fraction of a year. Since the interest rate is quoted on the annualized basis, the risk-free discount factor is generalized to e^{-rt}. Consequently, (7.20) is modified as follows:

$$c_t = e^{-rt}(pc_{n+1}^+ + (1 - p)c_{n+1}^-). \tag{7.21}$$

In this formula, the risk-neutral probability for an upward movement is modified from (7.10) to

$$p = \frac{e^{rt} - d}{u - d}. \tag{7.22}$$

The node in the binomial tree where c_n is evaluated is connected to the up and down nodes where c_{n+1}^+ and c_{n+1}^- have already been calculated. In this fashion, the payoffs at maturity are discounted period by period backward in time until the node for S_0.

Note from (7.11) that the risk-free factor e^{rt} must be smaller than the up factor u, i.e., $e^{rt} < e^{\sigma\sqrt{t}}$. It follows that the time interval t must satisfy

$$\sqrt{t} < \frac{\sigma}{r}.$$

7.4.4 A numerical example of binomial option pricing

Suppose the volatility of the return on an underlying asset is 73% per annum. The strike price of a put option is $28 for each unit of the underlying asset when its price is $30. The option matures 15 days later. The risk-free interest rate corresponding to the tenor of 15 days is 0.25% per annum.

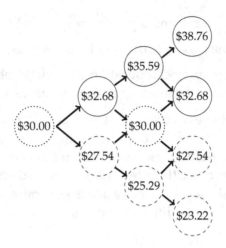

Fig. 7.3   Asset prices for all nodes in the three-period binomial tree.

We set the number of periods to 3 for pricing this option. So, with $N = 3$, the time interval t of each period is $5(= 15/3)$ days, or $5/365 = 1/73$ years. The up factor and down factors are, respectively,

$$u = e^{0.73 \times \sqrt{1/73}} = 1.08919624840487,$$

$$d = \frac{1}{u} = 0.918108193509203.$$

The risk-free discount factor is

$$e^{-rt} = e^{-0.0025/73} = 0.999965754011065.$$

Using these up and down factors, a binomial tree shown in Figure 7.3 is created, starting from $S_0 = \$30$. The binomial tree enumerates all the prices that could possibly realize at each node.

Given that the strike price of the put option is \$28, only the two end nodes in the tree, namely, $ud^2 S_0 = \$27.54$ and $d^3 S_0 = \$23.22$, are in the money. The put option values at these two nodes are \$0.46 and \$4.78, respectively, when the put option matures.

Working backward, you can find the corresponding put option value at every node in the tree. First, you need to compute the probability of an upward movement according to (7.22).

$$p = \frac{e^{rt} - d}{u - d} = \frac{e^{0.0025/73} - 0.918108193509203}{1.08919624840487 - 0.918108193509203}$$

$$= 0.478853147886451.$$

Combing the two non-zero option prices at the third period, i.e., $0.46 and $4.78, we obtain the second period option price p_2^-, which is

$$p_2^- = e^{-rt}(p \times \$0.46 + (1-p) \times \$4.78) = \$2.71.$$

The two option prices $0.46 and $0.00 give rise to the option price p_2^0 at the recombinant node in the second period:

$$p_2^0 = e^{-rt}(p \times \$0.00 + (1-p) \times \$0.46) = \$0.24.$$

The uppermost node in the second period is

$$p_2^+ = e^{-rt}(p \times \$0.00 + (1-p) \times \$0.00) = \$0.00.$$

Moving another step backward, we obtain the option price for the first period as follows:

$$p_1^- = e^{-rt}(p \times \$0.24 + (1-p) \times \$2.71) = \$1.53$$

and

$$p_1^+ = e^{-rt}(p \times 0 + (1-p) \times \$0.24) = \$0.12.$$

Finally, the put option at period 0 is

$$p_0 = e^{-rt}(p \times \$0.12 + (1-p) \times \$1.53) = \$0.86.$$

All these calculated values are enumerated in Figure 7.4.

7.5   From Binomial to Normal

In this section, we show how the continuous random variable can emerge from the discrete random variable in the asymptotic limit.

7.5.1   *Binomial probability*

The multiplicative random walk (7.4) in the context of multi-period binomial model takes the following form:

$$S_t = u^k d^{t-k} S_0.$$

This is one particular path from the starting point S_0 to point S_t that the drunken man has chanced upon. However, there are many other paths to reach S_t. For example, in Figure 7.1, three paths are

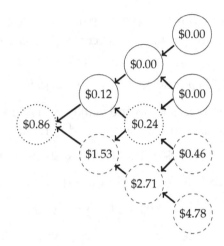

Fig. 7.4   Put option prices for all nodes in the three-period binomial tree.

possible to reach the same node $S_3 = u^2 d^1 S_0 = u S_0$, as there are three possible sequential outcomes in tossing a blue–red coin, i.e., $U_1\,U_2\,D_3$, $U_1\,D_2\,U_3$, and $D_1\,U_2\,U_3$.

What is the probability of reaching $S_t = u^2 d S_0$ in Figure 7.1? The answer is given by the binomial probability for the random number $\tilde{N}$ of obtaining the blue dot on top when tossing the blue–red coins T times. In this case, $\tilde{N} = 2$ and $T = 3$. Therefore the probability is

$$\mathbb{P}(3; \tilde{N} = 2) = \binom{3}{2} p^2 (1 - p)^1 = 3 p^2 (1 - p).$$

In general, the binomial probability of the number of "successes" in flipping the blue–red coin which turns up the blue dot is

$$\mathbb{P}(t; \tilde{N} = k) = \binom{t}{k} p^k (1 - p)^{t-k}, \tag{7.23}$$

where the binomial coefficient is

$$\binom{t}{k} := \frac{t!}{k!\,(t - k)!}.$$

Here, $\tilde{N}$ is a random variable, as the number of successes is uncertain before the t tosses are completed.

With the probability mass function (7.23) of the random variable $\widetilde{N}$ for the process of flipping the blue–red coin t times, we can compute the expected value at time 0 of $\widetilde{S}_t$ given S_0 as follows:

$$\mathbb{E}_0(\widetilde{S}_t) = \sum_{k=0}^{t} u^k d^{t-k} S_0 \mathbb{P}(t; \widetilde{N} = k).$$

Interestingly, we find that

$$\mathbb{E}_0(\widetilde{S}_t) = \sum_{k=0}^{t} u^k d^{t-k} S_0 \binom{t}{k} p^k (1-p)^{t-k}$$

$$= S_0 \sum_{k=0}^{t} \binom{t}{k} (up)^k (d(1-p))^{t-k}$$

$$= S_0 (up + d(1-p))^t.$$

The binomial theorem has been applied in the last step of this computation.

Moreover, using the one-period risk-neutral probability p, i.e., (7.10), we obtain

$$\mathbb{E}_0(\widetilde{S}_t) = S_0((u-d)p + d)^t = S_0 e^{rt}.$$

The reason for using (7.10) instead of (7.22) is that each time period we consider here is one unit of time. To gain further insight, notice that $up + d(1-p) = (u-d)p + d = e^r$, i.e., under the single-period risk-neutral probability p in (7.10), the average gross return over one period is simply the forward factor e^r.

In light of this result, the present value S_0 is the expected future value discounted by the risk-free discount factor e^{-rt}:

$$S_0 = e^{-rt} \mathbb{E}_0(\widetilde{S}_t). \tag{7.24}$$

This is the multi-period generalization of (7.8). It is important to emphasize that this result cannot be obtained if the risk-neutral probability is not utilized.

For convenience, we define a probability mass function $B(x)$ of a discrete variable x:

$$B(x) := \mathbb{P}(T; \widetilde{N} = x) = \frac{T!}{x!(T-x)!} p^x (1-p)^{T-x}. \tag{7.25}$$

It is the binomial probability of x number of successes in getting the blue dot on top out of T tosses. The large number T is the result of slicing the time period t into many tiny pieces of size δt, which is a very short duration. We write

$$T = \frac{t}{\delta t}.$$

It is noteworthy that T can be made arbitrarily large when δt is set at an arbitrarily small number. Even so, their product, i.e., $T \times \delta t$ is a non-zero finite number t.

In the application to option pricing, the success (blue dot on top) is mapped to a number $u = e^{\sigma\sqrt{\delta t}}$. The failure is mapped to its inverse $d = 1/u$. Under the risk-neutral probability p, the mean of this mapping — the random variable $\widetilde{\Lambda}_i$ in (7.4) — is, as computed before,

$$\mathbb{E}(\widetilde{\Lambda}_i) = up + d(1 - p) = e^{r\delta t}, \quad \text{for each } i.$$

Going further, we compute the variance of $\widetilde{\Lambda}_i$ as follows:

$$\begin{aligned}
\mathbb{V}(\widetilde{\Lambda}_i) &= (u - e^{r\delta t})^2 p + (d - e^{r\delta t})^2(1 - p) \\
&= p((u - e^{r\delta t})^2 - (d - e^{r\delta t})^2) + (d - e^{r\delta t})^2 \\
&= (e^{r\delta t} - d)(u + d - 2e^{r\delta t}) + (e^{r\delta t} - d)^2 \\
&= p(1 - p)(u - d)^2.
\end{aligned}$$

Given that δt is small, the variance $\mathbb{V}(\widetilde{\Lambda}_i)$ is well approximated by

$$\mathbb{V}(\widetilde{\Lambda}_i) \approx 4p(1 - p)\sigma^2\delta t.$$

In the standard discourse of the binomial model, however, the success is mapped to 1, and the failure to 0. Consequently, the mean is p and the variance is $p(1 - p)$. For T tosses, the mean is Tp, and the variance is $Tp(1 - p)$, since each toss is independent of the previous tosses. A feature of this standard mapping is that the mean Tp is the average number of success in T tosses.

7.5.2 *Normal probability density function*

In this subsection, we show that at the asymptotic limit, the binomial probability mass function becomes the normal density function. It is a specialized case of the general central limit theorem. The proof presented here is tailored specially for the binomial distribution.

We first apply natural logarithm on both sides of (7.25) to obtain

$$\ln(B(x)) = \ln(T!) - \ln(x!) - \ln((T-x)!) + x \ln p + (T-x) \ln(1-p).$$

Consider the case where x and hence T are very large, even infinite. We perform a Taylor expansion of $\ln(B(x))$ about the value x_0 where $\ln(B(x))$ is at its maximum.

$$\ln(B(x)) = \ln(B(x_0)) + \left.\frac{d \ln((B(x)))}{dx}\right|_{x=x_0} (x - x_0)$$

$$+ \frac{1}{2} \left.\frac{d^2 \ln((B(x)))}{dx^2}\right|_{x=x_0} (x - x_0)^2 + \cdots .$$

Sterling's formula allows the factorial to be approximated by

$$x! \approx e^{-x} x^x \sqrt{2\pi x}.$$

Taking the natural log, we obtain

$$\ln(x!) \approx x \ln x - x + \frac{1}{2} \ln(x) + \frac{1}{2} \ln(2\pi).$$

Since

$$\frac{d \ln(x!)}{dx} \approx \ln(x) + \frac{1}{2x},$$

and also because we are interested only in very large x, we can drop $1/(2x)$. Hence,

$$\frac{d \ln((B(x)))}{dx} \approx -\ln(x) + \ln(T - x) + \ln p - \ln(1 - p).$$

To find x_0, we set the above equation equal to zero. Solving this first-order condition, we obtain

$$\frac{d \ln((B(x)))}{dx} = 0 \quad \Longrightarrow \quad x_0 = Tp,$$

which is the mean of the binomial experiment involving T independent tosses of the blue–red coin. The probability of the blue dot facing up so that the Bernoulli random variable maps this outcome to 1 is p. Thus, we find that for the binomial distribution, at $x_0 = Tp$, the probability mass function $B(x)$ reaches its peak.

The second derivative with respect to x is

$$\frac{d^2 \ln((B(x)))}{dx^2} \approx -\frac{T}{x(T-x)}.$$

Evaluated at $x = x_0$, we obtain

$$\left.\frac{d^2 \ln((B(x)))}{dx^2}\right|_{x=x_0} \approx -\frac{1}{Tp(1-p)}.$$

It follows that the approximation of $\ln(B(x))$ by the Taylor expansion is

$$\ln(B(x)) \approx \ln(B(x_0)) - \frac{(x-x_0)^2}{2Tp(1-p)}. \tag{7.26}$$

We define $\varsigma^2 := Tp(1-p)\delta t = x_0(1-p)\delta t$, since $x_0 = Tp$. As noted earlier, δt is set in such a way that even if T goes to infinity, ς^2, which contains the product of T and δt, will still be a non-zero finite number. For the binomial probability of a random variable taking on the value of either 1 or 0 (instead of -1), the variance is $Tp(1-p)$ for T tosses of the blue–red coin. Since by definition the variance ς^2 is $\mathbb{E}(x^2) - \mu^2$, we consider $\mu^2 = (Tp)^2\delta t$, which is $\mu = x_0\sqrt{\delta t}$. Again, when $\delta t \longrightarrow 0$ and $T \longrightarrow \infty$, μ^2 remains a finite non-zero number as much as ς^2 is finite. Thus, the second term in (7.26) is rewritten as

$$\frac{(x-x_0)^2}{2Tp(1-p)} \times \frac{\delta t}{\delta t} = \frac{1}{2}\left(\frac{x\sqrt{\delta t} - x_0\sqrt{\delta t}}{\sqrt{x_0}\sqrt{1-p\sqrt{\delta t}}}\right)^2.$$

Next, we define a new variable y:

$$y := x\sqrt{\delta t}.$$

Then a function $f(y)$ *continuous* in y is obtainable from (7.26). Specifically, we define

$$f(y) := B(x_0) \exp\left(-\frac{1}{2}\left(\frac{y-\mu}{\varsigma}\right)^2\right).$$

To turn $f(y)$ into a probability density function, we must have

$$\int_{-\infty}^{\infty} f(y)\, dy = 1.$$

It can be readily shown that this condition is satisfied if and only if

$$B(x_0) = \frac{1}{\sqrt{2\pi}\,\varsigma}.$$

In conclusion, we find that

Binomial probability mass function $B(x)$

$\longrightarrow$ Normal probability density function $f(x)$,

when the number of periods T is large or when the time duration δt is made arbitrarily small. Moreover, if we define

$$z := (y - \mu)/\varsigma,$$

then we obtain the standard normal distribution with the probability density function:

$$g(z) = \frac{1}{\sqrt{2\pi}} \exp\left(-\frac{1}{2}z^2\right). \tag{7.27}$$

7.6 From Binomial to Black–Scholes

In this section, we follow the train of thoughts in [CRR79] (see also Lim [Lim11]) to show that in the asymptotic limit, the binomial pricing model converges to the Black–Scholes formula.

Let τ be the time to maturity of a European call option struck at K. We slice τ into n pieces and the duration of each tiny time interval is

$$\varepsilon := \frac{\tau}{n}.$$

Over this short time period, the risk-free forward factor R is

$$R = e^{r\varepsilon}.$$

The risk-neutral probability p of an upward movement in this setup is

$$p = \frac{R - d}{u - d} = \frac{e^{r\varepsilon} - e^{-\sigma\sqrt{\varepsilon}}}{e^{\sigma\sqrt{\varepsilon}} - e^{-\sigma\sqrt{\varepsilon}}}.$$

Since ε is a small quantity, we consider the approximation of p by Taylor expanding the exponentials up to the order of $\sqrt{\varepsilon}$. It follows that

$$p \approx \frac{1}{2}\left(1 + \left(\frac{r - \frac{1}{2}\sigma^2}{\sigma}\right)\sqrt{\varepsilon}\right) =: \hat{p}. \tag{7.28}$$

In this form, it is easy to understand that the risk-neutral probability p approaches $1/2$ as the tiny time duration ε approaches zero.

According to (7.20), the current call option price c_0 is the expected value of the call option payoff at period τ discounted by the risk-free rate.

$$c_0 = \frac{\mathbb{E}_0(c_\tau)}{R^\tau}.$$

Given that $S_\tau = u^x d^{n-x} S_0$ and $c_\tau = \max(u^x d^{n-x} S_0 - K, 0)$ for the call option at maturity, we write

$$\mathbb{E}_0(c_\tau) = \sum_{x=0}^{n} \binom{n}{x} p^x (1-p)^{n-x} \max(u^x d^{n-x} S_0 - K, 0).$$

Some of the end nodes are out of the money and they do not contribute to the call option premium. For those nodes that are in the money, suppose m is the smallest integer so that $u^m d^{n-m} S_0 - K > 0$. In other words,

$$m \gtrapprox \frac{\ln\left(\frac{K}{S_0}\right) - n \ln d}{\ln \frac{u}{d}}. \tag{7.29}$$

With respect to this smallest integer, the call option price c_0 becomes

$$c_0 = R^{-n} \sum_{x=m}^{n} \binom{n}{x} p^x (1-p)^{n-x} \left(u^x d^{n-x} S_0 - K\right)$$

$$= \sum_{x=m}^{n} \binom{n}{x} p^x (1-p)^{n-x} \frac{u^x d^{n-x} S_0}{R^n} - \frac{K}{R^n} \sum_{x=m}^{n} \binom{n}{x} p^x (1-p)^{n-x}. \tag{7.30}$$

7.6.1 *Probability of in-the-money* $\Phi(d_2)$

Recall that m is the smallest integer for the binomial nodes to be in the money when pricing a call option. To proceed further, we consider instead the probability $\mathbb{P}(x \leq m - 1)$. Subtract both sides of the inequalities in this probability by np, which is the average number of x for the upward movement. Also, divide both sides by the standard deviation of x, i.e., $\sqrt{np(1-p)}$. Then,

$$\mathbb{P}(x \leq m-1) = \mathbb{P}\left(\frac{x-np}{\sqrt{np(1-p)}} \leq \frac{m-1-np}{\sqrt{np(1-p)}}\right). \qquad (7.31)$$

By the central limit theorem elucidated in Section 7.5.2, as n increases to a large number,

$$\frac{x-np}{\sqrt{np(1-p)}} \longrightarrow \tilde{Z} \sim N(0,1). \qquad (7.32)$$

Keeping the Taylor expanded terms up to the order $\sqrt{\varepsilon}$, and by a straightforward calculation from (7.29), we obtain

$$m-1 \gtrapprox \frac{\ln\left(\frac{K}{S_0}\right) + (n-2)\sigma\sqrt{\varepsilon}}{2\sigma\sqrt{\varepsilon}}.$$

Using the approximate risk-neutral probability $\hat{p}$, (7.28), we find that the mean $n\hat{p}$ and the variance $n\hat{p}(1-\hat{p})$ are, respectively,

$$n\hat{p} = \frac{n}{2} + \frac{n\left(r - \frac{1}{2}\sigma^2\right)\varepsilon}{2\sigma\sqrt{\varepsilon}},$$

$$n\hat{p}(1-\hat{p}) = \frac{n}{4}\left(1 - \left(\frac{\left(r - \frac{1}{2}\sigma^2\right)}{\sigma}\right)^2 \varepsilon\right).$$

Furthermore,

$$m-1-n\hat{p} \gtrapprox \frac{\ln\left(\frac{K}{S_0}\right) - 2\sigma\sqrt{\varepsilon} - n\left(r - \frac{1}{2}\sigma^2\right)\varepsilon}{2\sigma\sqrt{\varepsilon}}.$$

Note that

$$\frac{1}{\sqrt{n\hat{p}(1-\hat{p})}} = \frac{2}{\sqrt{n}}\left(1 + \frac{1}{2}\left(\frac{\left(r - \frac{1}{2}\sigma^2\right)}{\sigma}\right)^2 \varepsilon\right) \approx \frac{2}{\sqrt{n}}.$$

As a result, with $\tau = n\epsilon$,

$$\frac{m - 1 - n\hat{p}}{\sqrt{n\hat{p}(1 - \hat{p})}} \gtrsim \frac{2}{\sqrt{n}} \times \frac{\ln\left(\frac{K}{S_0}\right) - 2\sigma\sqrt{\epsilon} - \left(r - \frac{1}{2}\sigma^2\right)n\epsilon}{2\sigma\sqrt{\epsilon}}$$

$$\gtrsim \frac{\ln\left(\frac{K}{S_0}\right) - \left(r - \frac{1}{2}\sigma^2\right)n\epsilon - 2\sigma\sqrt{\epsilon}}{\sigma\sqrt{n\epsilon}}$$

$$\gtrsim \frac{\ln\left(\frac{K}{S_0}\right) - \left(r - \frac{1}{2}\sigma^2\right)\tau}{\sigma\sqrt{\tau}} - \frac{2}{\sqrt{\tau}}\sqrt{\epsilon}.$$

Therefore, in the limit $\epsilon \longrightarrow 0$,

$$\frac{m - 1 - n\hat{p}}{\sqrt{n\hat{p}(1 - \hat{p})}} \longrightarrow \frac{\ln\left(\frac{K}{S_0}\right) - \left(r - \frac{1}{2}\sigma^2\right)\tau}{\sigma\sqrt{\tau}} =: d.$$

Combining all these results, (7.31) becomes

$$\mathbb{P}(x \leq m - 1) \longrightarrow \mathbb{P}(\tilde{Z} \leq d) = \frac{1}{\sqrt{2\pi}} \int_{-\infty}^{d} e^{-\frac{z^2}{2}} dz.$$

The second term involving the strike price in (7.30) sums from m to n, and the probability is $\mathbb{P}(x > m - 1)$ instead. Since

$$\mathbb{P}(x > m - 1) = 1 - \mathbb{P}(x \leq m - 1) = 1 - \mathbb{P}(\tilde{Z} \leq d),$$

we have, by the left-right symmetry of the normal distribution with respect to the mean,

$$\mathbb{P}(x > m - 1) = \mathbb{P}(\tilde{Z} \leq -d).$$

In other words, the probability of in the money $\mathbb{P}(x > m - 1)$ is equal to the probability of the standard normal random variable $\tilde{Z}$ being no larger than $-d$.

The term $-d$ can be recast as

$$-d = -\frac{\ln\left(\frac{K}{S_0}\right) - \left(r - \frac{1}{2}\sigma^2\right)\tau}{\sigma\sqrt{\tau}} = \frac{\ln\left(\frac{S_0}{K}\right) + \left(r - \frac{1}{2}\sigma^2\right)\tau}{\sigma\sqrt{\tau}} =: d_2.$$

(7.33)

It follows that

$$\mathbb{P}(\tilde{Z} \leq -d) = \mathbb{P}(\tilde{Z} \leq d_2) = \frac{1}{\sqrt{2\pi}}\int_{-\infty}^{d_2} e^{-\frac{z^2}{2}}\,dz =: \Phi(d_2).$$

In other words, when n increases to infinity,

$$\sum_{x=m}^{n}\binom{n}{x}p^x(1-p)^{n-x} \longrightarrow \Phi(d_2).$$

Accordingly, the second term in (7.30) approaches its limit:

$$\frac{K}{R^n}\sum_{x=m}^{n}\binom{n}{x}p^x(1-p)^{n-x} \longrightarrow Ke^{-r\tau}\Phi(d_2).$$

7.6.2   *Probability of in-the-money $\Phi(d_1)$*

For the first term in (7.30), we need to rewrite it to make it possible for applying the technique used earlier in Section 7.6.1. Consider therefore

$$p^* := \frac{u}{R}p.$$

By Taylor's expansion and using the approximate risk-neutral probability (7.28), we obtain

$$p^* \approx \frac{u}{R}\hat{p} = e^{\sigma\sqrt{\varepsilon}-r\varepsilon}\hat{p}$$

$$\approx \left(1 + \sigma\sqrt{\varepsilon} - \left(r - \frac{\sigma^2}{2}\right)\varepsilon + \cdots\right)\frac{1}{2}\left(1 + \left(\frac{r - \frac{1}{2}\sigma^2}{\sigma}\right)\sqrt{\varepsilon}\right)$$

$$\approx \frac{1}{2}\left(1 + \left(\frac{r - \frac{1}{2}\sigma^2}{\sigma}\right)\sqrt{\varepsilon} + \sigma\sqrt{\varepsilon} + \left(r - \frac{\sigma^2}{2}\right)\varepsilon - \left(r - \frac{\sigma^2}{2}\right)\varepsilon\right)$$

$$\approx \frac{1}{2}\left(1 + \left(\frac{r - \frac{1}{2}\sigma^2}{\sigma}\right)\sqrt{\varepsilon} + \sigma\sqrt{\varepsilon}\right)$$

$$\approx \hat{p} + \frac{1}{2}\sigma\sqrt{\varepsilon}.$$

Next, consider $(1 - p)d/R$. This term can be written as

$$(1 - p)\frac{d}{R} = \frac{1}{R}\left(\frac{ud - Rd}{u - d}\right)$$

$$= \frac{1}{R}\left(\frac{-Ru + ud + Ru - Rd}{u - d}\right)$$

$$= \frac{1}{R}\left(\frac{-uR + ud + R(u - d)}{u - d}\right)$$

$$= \frac{1}{R}\left(R - \left(\frac{uR - ud}{u - d}\right)\right)$$

$$= 1 - \frac{u}{R}p$$

$$= 1 - p^*$$

With this preparation, we are now ready to write the first term in (7.30) as

$$S_0 \sum_{x=m}^{n} \binom{n}{x} p^{*x}(1 - p^*)^{n-x}.$$

This expression is exactly of the same form as the second term in (7.30), when S_0 is replaced by KR^{-n} and p by p^*. Therefore, we can apply the same technique used in Section 7.6.1.

Since $p^* \approx \hat{p} + \frac{1}{2}\sigma\sqrt{\varepsilon}$ and in view of (7.28), we obtain

$$p^* \approx \frac{1}{2}\left(1 + \left(\frac{r + \sigma^2/2}{\sigma}\right)\sqrt{\varepsilon}\right) =: \hat{p}^*.$$

With respect to this approximate probability $\hat{p}^*$, the mean and variance are, respectively,

$$n\hat{p}^* = \frac{n}{2} + \frac{n\left(r + \frac{1}{2}\sigma^2\right)\varepsilon}{2\sigma\sqrt{\varepsilon}},$$

$$n\hat{p}^*(1 - \hat{p}^*) = \frac{n}{4}\left(1 - \left(\frac{(r + \frac{1}{2}\sigma^2)}{\sigma}\right)^2\varepsilon\right) \approx \frac{n}{4}.$$

Thus, we find that $r - \frac{1}{2}\sigma^2$ in the mean $n\hat{p}$ and variance $n\hat{p}(1 - \hat{p})$ of Section 7.6.1 has been replaced by $r + \frac{1}{2}\sigma^2$.

Starting from (7.29), it can be verified that

$$m - 1 - n\hat{p}^* \gtrsim \frac{\ln\left(\frac{K}{S_0}\right) - 2\sigma\sqrt{\varepsilon} - n\left(r + \frac{1}{2}\sigma^2\right)\varepsilon}{2\sigma\sqrt{\varepsilon}}.$$

It follows that

$$\frac{m - 1 - n\hat{p}^*}{\sqrt{n\hat{p}^*(1 - \hat{p}^*)}} \gtrsim \frac{\ln\left(\frac{K}{S_0}\right) - \left(r + \frac{1}{2}\sigma^2\right)\tau}{\sigma\sqrt{\tau}} - \frac{2}{\sqrt{\tau}}\sqrt{\varepsilon}.$$

Again, in the limit $\varepsilon \longrightarrow 0$,

$$\frac{m - 1 - n\hat{p}^*}{\sqrt{n\hat{p}^*(1 - \hat{p}^*)}} \longrightarrow \frac{\ln\left(\frac{K}{S_0}\right) - \left(r + \frac{1}{2}\sigma^2\right)\tau}{\sigma\sqrt{\tau}} =: d^*.$$

The term $-d^*$ can be recast as

$$-d^* = -\frac{\ln\left(\frac{K}{S_0}\right) - \left(r + \frac{1}{2}\sigma^2\right)\tau}{\sigma\sqrt{\tau}} = \frac{\ln\left(\frac{S_0}{K}\right) + \left(r + \frac{1}{2}\sigma^2\right)\tau}{\sigma\sqrt{\tau}} =: d_1.$$

$$(7.34)$$

Now, the first term involving the underlying asset price S_0 in (7.30) also sums from m to n. The probability of interest is still $\mathbb{P}(x > m - 1)$. As explained in Section 7.6.1, the probability of in the money is $\mathbb{P}(Z \leq -d^*)$. Consequently, by the central limit theorem in the form of (7.32),

$$\mathbb{P}(\tilde{Z} \leq -d^*) = \mathbb{P}(\tilde{Z} \leq d_1) = \frac{1}{\sqrt{2\pi}} \int_{-\infty}^{d_1} e^{-\frac{z^2}{2}} dz =: \Phi(d_1).$$

In other words, when n increases to infinity,

$$\sum_{x=m}^{n} \binom{n}{x} p^{**x}(1 - p^*)^{n-x} \longrightarrow \Phi(d_1).$$

Having all the pieces in place, we conclude that the binomial pricing model converges to a continuous model involving the normal distribution when the number of periods n becomes infinitely large:

$$c_0 = S_0 \sum_{x=m}^{n} \binom{n}{x} p^{**x}(1 - p^*)^{n-x} - Ke^{-r\tau} \sum_{x=m}^{n} \binom{n}{x} p^x(1 - p)^{n-x}$$

$$\longrightarrow S_0\Phi(d_1) - Ke^{-r\tau}\Phi(d_2).$$

$$(7.35)$$

The limit turns out to be the Black–Scholes formula [BS73] for pricing a European call option with maturity τ and a strike price K. In conclusion, when the number of periods n is very large, equivalently when the interval ε is very small,

Binomial option pricing model

$\longrightarrow$ Black–Scholes pricing formula.

7.6.3 Numerical comparison to the binomial pricing model

It is interesting to compare the put option price produced by the Black–Scholes formula against the value computed in Section 7.4.4.

First, we derive the Black–Scholes formula for the European put option by applying the put–call parity:

$$p_0 = c_0 - S_0 + Ke^{-r\tau}.$$

Substituting in the Black–Scholes call option price

$$c_0 = S_0\Phi(d_1) - Ke^{-r\tau}\Phi(d_2), \tag{7.36}$$

we obtain

$$p_0 = (1 - \Phi(d_2))Ke^{-r\tau} - (1 - \Phi(d_1))S_0. \tag{7.37}$$

In these pricing formulas,

$$\Phi(x) := \frac{1}{\sqrt{2\pi}}\int_{-\infty}^{x} e^{-\frac{v^2}{2}}\, dv. \tag{7.38}$$

For normal distribution, the left–right symmetry with respect to the mean allows us to write, for any d,

$$1 - \Phi(d) = \mathbb{P}(\tilde{Z} > d) = \mathbb{P}(\tilde{Z} \le -d) = \Phi(-d).$$

Consequently, we obtain

$$p_0 = Ke^{-r\tau}\Phi(-d_2) - S_0\Phi(-d_1). \tag{7.39}$$

For the Black–Scholes pricing model, we first calculate d_1 and d_2.

$$d_1 = \frac{\ln\left(\frac{S_0}{K}\right) + \left(r + \frac{1}{2}\sigma^2\right)\tau}{\sigma\sqrt{\tau}};$$

$$d_2 = \frac{\ln\left(\frac{S_0}{K}\right) + \left(r - \frac{1}{2}\sigma^2\right)\tau}{\sigma\sqrt{\tau}}.$$

It is noteworthy that

$$d_2 = d_1 - \sigma\sqrt{\tau}.$$

Using the same option data in Section 7.4.4, we have

$$d_1 = \frac{\ln(30/28) + (0.0025 + 0.5 \times 0.73^2) \times 15/365}{0.73 \times \sqrt{15/365}}$$

$$= 0.540898114734428,$$

$$d_2 = d_1 - 0.73 \times \sqrt{15/365} = 0.392911628864941.$$

The cumulative function of the standard normal distribution produces

$$\Phi(-d_1) = 0.29428890521348 \quad \text{and} \quad \Phi(-d_2) = 0.34719237616266.$$

Inserting these numbers into (7.39), we find that $p_0 = \$0.89$, which is \$0.03 more expensive than the put option premium computed by the three-period binomial pricing model.

7.7   Exercises

Q1. For the one-dimensional random walk model (7.1), a return to the origin S_0 at time n occurs if $S_n = 0$. Note that a return to the origin can only happen if n is an even number.

(a) Show that the probability of a return to the origin at time $2m$ for any non-negative integer m is given by

$$p_{2m} = \frac{1}{2^{2m}} \binom{2m}{m}.$$

Note that $p_0 = 1$.

(b) First return to the origin is said to have occurred at time $2m$ if $m > 0$, and $S_{2k} \neq 0$ for all $k < m$. Denote the probability of the first return to the origin by f_{2m}. For $n \geq 1$, show that the probabilities p_{2k} and f_{2k} are related as follows:

$$p_{2k} = f_0 p_{2n} + f_2 p_{2(n-1)} + \cdots + f_{2n} p_0,$$

where $f_0 = 0$.

Q2. Instead of using the put-call parity, start from

$$\mathbb{E}_0(p_\tau) = \sum_{x=0}^{n} \binom{n}{x} p^x (1-p)^{n-x} \max\left(K - u^x d^{n-x} S_0, 0\right).$$

(a) Go through the same steps in Section 7.6 to derive the Black-Scholes pricing formula for the put option.

(b) Show that the Black-Scholes pricing formulas for put and call satisfies the put-call parity.

Chapter 8

The Black–Scholes Model

8.1 Introduction

Truly revolutionary ideas are few. As alluded to in Chapter , Black and Scholes's 1973 paper on option pricing [BS73] is so ground breaking that it becomes the genesis of Quantitative Finance. This chapter aims to provide a detailed discussion on their brilliant idea.

In Chapter 6.9, we have demonstrated how the normal distribution emerges as the asymptotic limit of the discrete binomial distribution when the time interval is infinitesimally small while the number of intervals is infinitely large. The Black–Scholes pricing formula (7.36) for a plain vanilla call option is also obtained as the limit of the binomial model.

It is nonetheless important to understand how Black and Scholes derived the equation that is named after them since their 1973 seminal paper [BS73]. Solving the Black–Scholes partial differential equation to obtain the pricing formula (7.36) as its solution is also an interesting exercise in itself.

In this chapter, we trace the origin of the Brownian motion and the theory of its stochastic dynamics by Einstein and Bachelier, though the latter might not be aware of the Brownian motion. Remarkably, Bachelier did his mathematical analysis of the Brownian motion 5 years earlier than Einstein. An interesting result of their highly original papers is the heat equation and the identical scaling law for the root mean square motion. Truly amazing is the fact that in Einstein's theory, molecules are the objects of investigation whereas in Bachelier's thesis, speculators collectively as price changers are the subjects of interest. Yet, despite the fundamental difference between molecules, which cannot think, and speculators, who are supposedly capable to think rationally, the resulting Brownian motion dynamics from two different approaches are identical.

8.2 Einstein's Theory of Brownian Motion

Brownian motion is an important and useful model in Quantitative Finance. A discovery by Robert Brown — a Scottish botanist — Brownian motion is the random movement of microscopically visible particles suspended in a fluid. In a note originally printed as part of a privately circulated pamphlet, Brown gave an account of the microscopical observations he made in the summer of 1827.[1] Einstein in his 1905 paper [Ein05] examined the statistical dynamics of the continuous jittery motion that Brown had discovered.

The framework of Einstein theory has n particles suspending in a liquid. Over a short period of time τ, the x coordinate of a particle will be displaced by a random amount ϵ, either positive or negative. Intriguingly, this framework is strikingly similar to Bachelier's [Bac00]. In this section, ϵ refers to the x-axis position of the Brownian particle. In the theory of speculation, ϵ is the deviation from the true price.

Consider next the infinitesimal number dn of particles experiencing a displacement that lies between ϵ and $\epsilon + d\epsilon$ in the time interval τ. It is postulated that

$$dn = n\phi(\epsilon)d\epsilon,$$

where $\phi(\epsilon)$ is a probability density function of ϵ. The probability for a particle to be found in the interval between ϵ and $\epsilon + d\epsilon$ is $\phi(\epsilon)d\epsilon$. For n particles, dn is therefore n times this probability.

---

[1] Brown's note was reprinted in the *Edinburgh New Philosophical Journal* (pp. 358–371, July–September, 1828).

Moreover, the probability density function $\phi(\epsilon)$ is assumed to be symmetric:

$$\phi(\epsilon) = \phi(-\epsilon).$$

In other words, positive and negative ϵ values are equally likely to realize. This assumption effectively excludes any odd-number moment to complicate Einstein's theory. In other words,

$$\int_{-\infty}^{\infty} \epsilon^j \phi(\epsilon) d\epsilon = 0,$$

for any odd number j.

Let $g(x, t)$ be the number of particles per unit volume. The object of interest is the distribution of the particles at a time $t + \tau$, i.e., $g(x, t + \tau)$, from the distribution at time t, i.e., $g(x, t)$. We first consider

$$g(x, t + \tau) dx = \left(\int_{-\infty}^{\infty} g(x + \epsilon, t + \tau) \phi(\epsilon) d\epsilon \right) dx. \qquad (8.1)$$

This expression suggests that $g(x, \cdot)$ is the sum of all possible values of $g(x + \epsilon, \cdot)$ weighted by the probability $\phi(\epsilon) d\epsilon$.

Now, since τ is very small, we have

$$g(x, t + \tau) \approx g(x, t) + \tau \frac{\partial g(x)}{\partial t}.$$

On the other hand, we perform Taylor's expansion to obtain

$$\int_{-\infty}^{\infty} g(x + \epsilon, t + \tau) \phi(\epsilon) d\epsilon$$

$$= g(x, t) \int_{-\infty}^{\infty} \phi(\epsilon) d\epsilon + \frac{\partial g}{\partial x} \int_{-\infty}^{\infty} \epsilon \phi(\epsilon) d\epsilon$$

$$+ \frac{\partial^2 g}{\partial x^2} \int_{-\infty}^{\infty} \frac{\epsilon^2}{2} \phi(\epsilon) d\epsilon + \cdots$$

$$\approx g(x, t) + \frac{\partial^2 g}{\partial x^2} \int_{-\infty}^{\infty} \frac{\epsilon^2}{2} \phi(\epsilon) d\epsilon.$$

By the assumption of $\phi(\epsilon) = \phi(-\epsilon)$, only the even-order moments contribute to the expansion. Moreover, probabilities sum to 1 and therefore $\int_{-\infty}^{\infty} \phi(\epsilon) d\epsilon = 1$.

Setting

$$C_d := \frac{1}{2\tau} \int_{-\infty}^{\infty} \epsilon^2 \phi(\epsilon) d\epsilon, \tag{8.2}$$

and by virtue of (8.1), we obtain the well-known partial differential equation of diffusion, also known as the heat equation:

$$\frac{\partial g}{\partial t} = C_d \frac{\partial^2 g}{\partial x^2}. \tag{8.3}$$

In light of this equation, C_d is identified as the coefficient of diffusion.

Now, suppose the motion of each particle starts at the point x for which the x-coordinate coincides with the center of gravity of n particles. For $x \neq 0$ and $t = 0$, the initial conditions are

$$g(x,0) = 0, \quad \text{and} \quad \int_{-\infty}^{\infty} g(x,0) dx = n.$$

The solution is

$$g(x,t) = \frac{n}{\sqrt{4\pi C_d}} \frac{\exp\left(-\frac{x^2}{4 C_d t}\right)}{\sqrt{t}}. \tag{8.4}$$

This claim can be verified by showing that the solution (8.4) satisfies the heat equation, (8.3).

With this solution, it is straightforward to compute the variance:

$$\int_{-\infty}^{\infty} x^2 g(x,t) dx = 2 C_d t. \tag{8.5}$$

This derivation requires the fact that $\int_{-\infty}^{\infty} x^2 \exp(-\frac{x^2}{2}) dx = \sqrt{2\pi}$. So, from (8.5), the root mean square displacement is proportional to the square root of time. This result is an important characterization of the Brownian motion.

8.3　Bachelier's Probability Law

In his 1900 doctoral thesis, Bachelier derives the probability density function that turns out to be exactly the one found by Einstein independently. Bachelier has in mind the deviation of the quoted price or market price from the true price. He sets forth a coordinate system where the true price of an asset is at the origin. The deviation or spread from the true price can in principle ranges from $-\infty$ to ∞.

For convenience, the spread or difference is just called the market (quoted) price. Let $p_{x,t_1}\, dx$ denote the probability that, at time t_1 from time 0, the market price x is to be found in the infinitesimal interval $(x, x + dx]$. Similarly, $p_{z-x,t_2}\, dz$ is the probability that the market price is at $(z - x, z - x + dz - dx]$.

What is the probability that the market price is in $(z, z + dz]$ at time $t_1 + t_2$? If the price movement is independent, the said probability must be the product of these two probabilities:

$$p_{x,t_1} p_{z-x,t_2}\, dxdz.$$

At time t_1, the market price could be located in any of the infinitesimal interval dx between $-\infty$ and ∞. The probability $p_{z,t_1+t_2}\, dz$ of the price z being quoted at time $t_1 + t_2$ is

$$p_{z,t_1+t_2}\, dz = \int_{-\infty}^{\infty} p_{x,t_1} p_{z-x,t_2}\, dxdz.$$

Therefore,

$$p_{z,t_1+t_2} = \int_{-\infty}^{\infty} p_{x,t_1} p_{z-x,t_2}\, dx. \tag{8.6}$$

With A and B denoting two constants with respect to x (but may vary with time t), the solution for (8.6) is postulated to be

$$p_{x,\cdot} = \frac{A}{\sqrt{2\pi}} \exp\left(-\frac{B^2 x^2}{2}\right).$$

Being a probability function, it must be that (see Q1)

$$1 = \int_{-\infty}^{\infty} p_{x,\cdot}\, dx = \frac{A}{\sqrt{2\pi}} \int_{-\infty}^{\infty} \exp\left(-\frac{B^2 x^2}{2}\right) dx.$$

As a result, $A = B$.

When the true price $x = 0$, we have

$$p_0 = \frac{A}{\sqrt{2\pi}} \quad \text{or} \quad B = A = p_0\sqrt{2\pi}.$$

Therefore the probability function becomes

$$p_{x,\cdot} = p_0 \exp(-\pi p_0^2 x^2). \tag{8.7}$$

Let p_1 and p_2 be the quantities corresponding to p_0 and with respect to times t_1 and t_2, respectively. We evaluate (8.6) in light of (8.7):

$$p_{z,t_1+t_2} = \int_{-\infty}^{\infty} p_1 \exp(-\pi p_1^2 x^2) p_2 \exp(-\pi p_2^2 (z-x)^2) dx.$$

Noting that z is a constant in the integral, we have

$$p_{z,t_1+t_2} = p_1 p_2 \exp(-\pi p_2^2 z^2) \int_{\infty}^{\infty} \exp\left(-\pi(p_1^2 + p_2^2)x^2 + 2\pi p_2^2 z\, x\right) dx.$$

By completing the square, we write

$$p_{z,t_1+t_2} = \frac{p_1 p_2}{\sqrt{p_1^2 + p_2^2}} \exp\left(-\pi p_2^2 z^2 + \frac{\pi p_2^4 z^2}{p_1^2 + p_2^2}\right) \int_{-\infty}^{\infty} e^{-\pi u^2} du,$$

where the variable has been transformed to

$$u := x\sqrt{p_1^2 + p_2^2} - \frac{p_2^2 z}{\sqrt{p_1^2 + p_2^2}}.$$

Since the integral $\int_{-\infty}^{\infty} e^{-\pi u^2} du = 1$, we obtain

$$p_{z,t_1+t_2} = \frac{p_1 p_2}{\sqrt{p_1^2 + p_2^2}} \exp\left(-\pi \frac{p_1^2 p_2^2}{p_1^2 + p_2^2} z^2\right).$$

If we write $t_3 = t_1 + t_2$ and define

$$p_3 := \frac{p_1 p_2}{\sqrt{p_1^2 + p_2^2}}, \tag{8.8}$$

then the same functional form (8.7) for the probability function is evident:

$$p_{z,t_3} = p_3 \exp(-\pi p_3^2 z^2).$$

Hence, the solution for (8.6) is obtained.

Going further, we define, for $i = 1, 2$, the function $f(t_i)$ as follows:

$$p_i := \frac{f(t_i)}{\sqrt{2\pi}}.$$

Inspired by (8.8) and squaring both sides, we obtain

$$f^2(t_1 + t_2) = \frac{f^2(t_1) f^2(t_2)}{f^2(t_1) + f^2(t_2)}.$$

The function $f(t_1 + t_2)$ is symmetric in t_1 and t_2. Partial differentiation with respect to t_1 is therefore equal to the partial differentiation with respect to t_2. Accordingly,

$$\frac{f'(t_1)}{f^3(t_1)} = \frac{f'(t_2)}{f^3(t_2)}.$$

As usual, $f'(t)$ denotes the differentiation with respect to t. We see the separation of variables in this equation and thus the ratio is a constant C. If follows that

$$f'(t) = C f^3(t). \tag{8.9}$$

It is easy to verify that the solution of (8.9) is

$$f(t) = \sqrt{2\pi}\, p_0 = \frac{D}{\sqrt{t}},$$

where D is a constant. In accordance to (8.7), the probability density function is

$$p(x, t) = \frac{D}{\sqrt{2\pi t}} \exp\left(-\frac{D^2 x^2}{2t}\right). \tag{8.10}$$

The expected value of x^2, i.e., variance $\sigma^2(t)$, is found to be

$$\sigma^2(t) = \int_{-\infty}^{\infty} x^2 \frac{D}{\sqrt{2\pi}\sqrt{t}} \exp\left(-\frac{D^2 x^2}{2t}\right) dx = \frac{t}{D^2}.$$

It is important to note that the variance $\sigma^2(t)$ is proportionate to time t. In other words, the square root of the mean of squared displacement from 0 is proportional to the square root of elapsed time.[2]

$$\sigma(t) = \frac{1}{D}\sqrt{t}.$$

Remarkably, this result of Bachelier is 5 years earlier than Einstein's ground breaking investigation on the Brownian motion [Ein05].

For a unit time $t = 1$, we define $\sigma^2 := \sigma^2(1)$ as the rate of variance. The constant D is thus given by

$$D = \frac{1}{\sigma}.$$

Consequently, the probability function is

$$p(x,t) = \frac{1}{\sqrt{2\pi t}\,\sigma} \exp\left(-\frac{x^2}{2\sigma^2 t}\right). \qquad (8.11)$$

Notably, (8.11) satisfies the heat equation:

$$\frac{\partial p(x,t)}{\partial t} = \frac{\sigma^2}{2}\frac{\partial^2 p(x,t)}{\partial x^2}.$$

In light of (8.3), this property of $p(x,t)$ allows $\sigma^2/2$ to be interpreted as the diffusion coefficient C_d in (8.2). When σ is large, it means that x has a lot of heat to diffuse to a large value in absolute terms, i.e., the amplitude of fluctuation is large. It also means that to forecast the range of values that x might take is a lot harder, and with much lesser certainty. Interestingly, Bachelier names σ *le coefficient d'instabilité*. Simply put, x is more uncertain the larger is the volatility σ.

8.4 Mathematical Brownian Motion

Despite the fact that Bachelier is a mathematician, his PhD thesis is not written in the definition–lemma–theorem–corollary format. But

---

[2]Bachelier computes instead what he refers to as the "total positive expectation," $\int_0^\infty xp(x,t)\,dx$. Using (8.10), it is straightforward to find that the total positive expectation is $\frac{1}{\sqrt{2\pi D}}\sqrt{t}$, i.e., proportional to the square root of time elapsed.

to introduce stochastic calculus, it is necessary to define the Brownian motion mathematically.

First, we define a stochastic process to be a collection of random variables $\widetilde{X}_t$ indexed by $t \in \mathfrak{R}$. A Brownian motion is a continuous stochastic process $\widetilde{B}_t$ that satisfies the following requirements:

1. $B_0 = 0$.
2. For $t > s$, the probability $\mathbb{P}\left(\widetilde{B}_t - B_s\right)$ is independent of the past history up to time s.
3. Moreover, $\widetilde{B}_t - B_s$ follows the normal distribution with mean 0 and variance $t - s$.

$$\widetilde{B}_t - B_s \sim N(0, t - s).$$

The first condition sets the origin of the coordinate system. The second condition is a statement about the invariance of the system with respect to a translation in the time coordinate. Namely, having the same statistical distribution, the increment $\triangle \widetilde{B}_t := \widetilde{B}_{t+dt} - B_t$, as a random variable, is the same as $\triangle \widetilde{B}_{t+s}$ for all t. Also, the system has zero memory since each $\triangle \widetilde{B}_t$ is independent. Consequently, the correlation between $\triangle \widetilde{B}_t$ and $\triangle \widetilde{B}_{t+s}$ vanishes when $s \neq 0$.

Next, we consider the uniform partition, $\{t_i\}_{i=0}^n$, of time t from time 0 into n intervals:

$$\triangle t_i := t_i - t_{i-1} = \frac{t}{n},$$

where $t_i < t_{i+1}$, $t_0 = 0$ and $t_n = t$. With respect to this partition, the quadratic variation of the sample path $\widetilde{B}_{t_i}$ for the integers $i = 0$ to $i = n$ is defined as

$$\widetilde{Q}(t) := \lim_{n \to \infty} \sum_{i=1}^n \left(\widetilde{B}_{t_i} - \widetilde{B}_{t_{i-1}}\right)^2 = \lim_{n \to \infty} \sum_{i=1}^n (\triangle \widetilde{B}_{t_i})^2.$$

The expected quadratic variation of the sample path is,

$$\mathbb{E}\left(\widetilde{Q}(t)\right) = \lim_{n \to \infty} \sum_{i=1}^n \mathbb{E}\left(\left(\widetilde{B}_{t_i} - \widetilde{B}_{t_{i-1}}\right)^2\right) = \lim_{n \to \infty} \sum_{i=1}^n (t_i - t_{i-1}) = t.$$

$$(8.12)$$

Notice that $\mathbb{E}\left(\widetilde{B}_{t_i} - \widetilde{B}_{t_{i-1}}\right) = 0$, so the expected quadratic variation is in fact the variance of $\widetilde{B}_{t_i} - \widetilde{B}_{t_{i-1}}$.

Before calculating the variance of the quadratic variation, we need to know the expression of the fourth-order moment. Toward this end, we consider

$$\sigma^2 t = \frac{1}{\sqrt{2\pi t}\,\sigma} \int_{-\infty}^{\infty} x^2 \exp\left(-\frac{x^2}{2\sigma^2 t}\right) dx.$$

The integrand is made up of two functions, x and $x \exp(-\frac{x^2}{2\sigma^2 t})$. We perform the integration by parts:

$$\int^x f(u)g(u)\,du = \int^x f(u)\,du\; g(x) - \int^x \int^u f(s)\,ds\; \frac{dg}{du}\,du.$$

We thus obtain

$$\sigma^2 t = \frac{1}{\sqrt{2\pi t}\,\sigma} \left(\frac{x^2}{2} x \exp\left(-\frac{x^2}{2\sigma^2 t}\right) \Big|_{-\infty}^{\infty} \right.$$

$$\left. - \int_{-\infty}^{\infty} \frac{x^2}{2} \left(\exp\left(-\frac{x^2}{2\sigma^2 t}\right) - \frac{x^2}{\sigma^2 t} \exp\left(-\frac{x^2}{2\sigma^2 t}\right) \right) dx \right).$$

$$(8.13)$$

The first term in (8.13) is zero because its exponential term vanishes at a much faster rate than x^3 as x approaches infinity. Therefore, we have

$$\sigma^2 t = -\frac{1}{\sqrt{2\pi t}\,\sigma} \int_{-\infty}^{\infty} \frac{x^2}{2} \exp\left(-\frac{x^2}{2\sigma^2 t}\right) dx$$

$$+ \frac{1}{\sqrt{2\pi t}\,\sigma} \int_{-\infty}^{\infty} \frac{x^4}{2\sigma^2 t} \exp\left(-\frac{x^2}{2\sigma^2 t}\right) dx. \qquad (8.14)$$

Note that the first term of (8.14) is equal to $-\sigma^2 t/2$. Re-arranging the terms, we obtain

$$\frac{3}{2}\sigma^2 t = \frac{1}{\sqrt{2\pi t}\,\sigma} \int_{-\infty}^{\infty} \frac{x^4}{2\sigma^2 t} \exp\left(-\frac{x^2}{2\sigma^2 t}\right) dx. \qquad (8.15)$$

In other words, we have obtained an analytical expression for the integral, which is the expected value of the fourth moment:

$$\mathbb{E}(\tilde{X}^4) = \frac{1}{\sqrt{2\pi t}\,\sigma} \int_{-\infty}^{\infty} x^4 \exp\left(-\frac{x^2}{2\sigma^2 t}\right) dx = 3\sigma^4 t^2. \qquad (8.16)$$

The variance of the quadratic variation is

$$\lim_{n\to\infty} \sum_{i=1}^{n} \mathbb{V}((\widetilde{B}_{t_i} - \widetilde{B}_{t_{i-1}})^2) = \lim_{n\to\infty} \sum_{i=1}^{n} (\mathbb{E}((\widetilde{B}_{t_i} - \widetilde{B}_{t_{i-1}})^4)$$
$$- \mathbb{E}((\widetilde{B}_{t_i} - \widetilde{B}_{t_{i-1}})^2)^2).$$

Note that the second term is the square of the expected quadratic variation (8.12). For the first term, it is (8.16) with $\sigma = 1$ and t changed to $\triangle t_i$. Accordingly, with respect to the uniform partition, the variance of the quadratic variation is zero:

$$\mathbb{V}(\widetilde{Q}(t)) = \lim_{n\to\infty} \sum_{i=1}^{n} (3(t_i - t_{i-1})^2 - (t_i - t_{i-1})^2)$$

$$= \lim_{n\to\infty} \sum_{i=1}^{n} 2(t_i - t_{i-1})^2$$

$$= \lim_{n\to\infty} \sum_{i=1}^{n} 2\frac{t^2}{n^2}$$

$$= \lim_{n\to\infty} 2\frac{t^2}{n} = 0.$$

A random variable for which the variance is zero implies that the variable is not really random after all. In that case, the mean of the "random" variable is simply the variable itself. Therefore, the quadratic variation $Q(t)$ is equal to its mean:

$$Q(t) = \mathbb{E}(\widetilde{Q}(t)) = t.$$

This is an important result, suggesting that

$$(\triangle B_{t_i})^2 = \triangle t_i.$$

In the limit $n \to \infty$, we write

$$(dB(t))^2 := \lim_{n\to\infty} (\triangle B_{t_i})^2 \longrightarrow dt. \tag{8.17}$$

8.5 Itô Calculus

Modern calculus is said to be invented independently by Leibniz and Newton in the 17th century. The Taylor expansion of a function

$f(x)$ of a variable x in the Leibniz–Newton calculus is

$$df(x+dx) = f(x) + \frac{df}{dx}dx + \frac{1}{2}\frac{d^2f}{dx^2}(dx)^2 + \cdots .$$

Since $(dx)^2$ and the higher-order terms are negligible,

$$df(x) := f(x+dx) - f(x) = \frac{df}{dx}dx + \frac{1}{2}\frac{d^2f}{dx^2}(dx)^2 + \cdots$$

$$= \frac{df}{dx}dx. \tag{8.18}$$

But for the Brownian motion, we see from (8.17) that $\left(dB(t)\right)^2$ is not negligible. In fact, it is asymptotically equal to dt.

According to Wiener [Wie23], a fundamental property of a *random* variable such as $\widetilde{B}(t)$ at time t is that it cannot be differentiated by the standard Leibniz–Newton machinery. But thanks to stochastic calculus or Itô calculus, we can not only study the sample paths $\widetilde{B}(t)$ of a Brownian motion, but also the function of $\widetilde{B}(t)$. As alluded to in Chapter , the very first application of Itô's stochastic calculus by Black and Scholes in their 1973 paper on option pricing is said to be the dawn of Quantitative Finance.

Kiyoshi Itô is a mathematician and a man of "enormous curiosity and determination to understand the world." In the preface of his book [Str03], Stroock writes,

> No matter what the topic, Itô is driven to master it in a way that enables him to share his insights with the rest of us. Certainly the most renowned example of Itô's skill is his introduction of stochastic differential equations to explain the Kolmogorov–Feller theory of Markov processes.

Intriguingly and fortunately, Itô was not drafted as a soldier before and during the second World War. As a Statistics Officer of the Statistical Bureau of the Cabinet, Itô published the nascent form of the calculus that would be named after him. The Japanese journal in which the seed of Itô calculus was planted is a hand-written mimeographed journal [Ito42]. In that 1942 paper, Itô successfully constructed the sample path of a stochastic process directly as the unique solution of a stochastic differential equation (see Fukushima [Fuk07]).

In Section 7 of [Ito42] on indefinite integrals, we find the equivalent of the following stochastic differential equation:

$$df(\tilde{X}_t) = \frac{df(x)}{dx}\bigg|_{x=\tilde{X}_t} d\tilde{X}_t + \frac{1}{2}\frac{d^2 f(x)}{dx^2}\bigg|_{x=\tilde{X}_t} (d\tilde{X}_t)^2, \tag{8.19}$$

where $\tilde{X}_t$ is the Itô process with functions f_t and g_t:

$$d\tilde{X}_t = g_t\, dt + f_t\, d\tilde{B}_t. \tag{8.20}$$

It is important to understand that the differentiation is by the usual Leibniz–Newton calculus; the functional form of $f(x)$ is the focus. After differentiation, the resulting differential will then take the random variable $\tilde{X}_t$ as its argument. In comparison to the Leibniz–Newton calculus (8.18), the Itô calculus has an "extra" second term. Namely, $(d\tilde{X}_t)^2$ cannot be ignored because of the nature of quadratic variation (8.17) discussed earlier.

As an application example of this remarkable Itô formula (8.19), consider the following stochastic differential equation:

$$d\tilde{S}_t = \tilde{S}_t(\mu_t\, dt + \sigma_t\, d\tilde{B}_t). \tag{8.21}$$

Next, consider the log function of S_t. According to the Itô formula (8.19),[3] we have

$$d(\ln(\tilde{S}_t)) = \frac{1}{S_t}d\tilde{S}_t - \frac{1}{2}\frac{1}{S_t^2}(d\tilde{S}_t)^2.$$

The Itô formula is mistakenly called Itô lemma by some. Itô himself calls it formula. This misnomer of "lemma" ought to be eradicated.

Now, the square of (8.21) is

$$(d\tilde{S}_t)^2 = \tilde{S}_t^2\sigma_t^2(d\tilde{B}_t)^2 = S_t^2\sigma_t^2 dt, \tag{8.22}$$

because $(dt)^2$ is negligible and $d\tilde{B}_t\, dt$ is zero since $\mathbb{E}(d\tilde{B}_t) = 0$. Consequently,

$$d(\ln(\tilde{S}_t)) = \left(\mu_t - \frac{1}{2}\sigma_t^2\right) dt + \sigma_t d\tilde{B}_t. \tag{8.23}$$

---

[3]The English translation of Itô's trailblazing work [Ito42] appears in Itô *et al.* [IVS87].

The integral form of this stochastic differentiation equation is

$$\widetilde{S}_t = S_0 \exp\left(\int_0^t \left(\mu_s - \frac{1}{2}\sigma_s^2\right) ds + \int_0^t \sigma_s d\widetilde{B}_s\right).$$

When μ_t and σ_t are constant, we obtain the geometric Brownian motion:

$$\widetilde{S}_t = S_0 \exp\left(\left(\mu - \frac{1}{2}\sigma^2\right) t + \sigma\widetilde{B}_t\right). \tag{8.24}$$

With no loss of generality, $B_0 = 0$ at time $t = 0$. Because of the Brownian noise $\widetilde{B}_t$, the asset price $\widetilde{S}_t$ is also random.

The Itô formula for a two-variable function $\theta(t, x)$ is

$$d\theta(t, \widetilde{X}_t) = \frac{\partial\theta}{\partial t}dt + \frac{\partial\theta}{\partial x}d\widetilde{X}_t + \frac{1}{2}\frac{\partial^2\theta}{\partial x^2}(dX_t)^2. \tag{8.25}$$

As noted before, it is important to emphasize that all the differentials are with respect to the functional form of $\theta(t, x)$. For the Itô process , we obtain

$$d\theta(t, \widetilde{X}_t) = \left(\frac{\partial\theta}{\partial t} + \frac{\partial\theta}{\partial x}g_t + \frac{1}{2}\frac{\partial^2\theta}{\partial x^2}f_t\right) dt + \frac{\partial\theta}{\partial x}f_t\, d\widetilde{B}_t.$$

The mathematical proof of this extremely useful formula appears in an introductory book by H.-H. Kuo [Kuo06], which is dedicated to Itô. The preface in Kuo's book contains an interesting insight on the Itô integral; equally interesting is Kuo's personal stories about Itô.

8.6   Black–Scholes Equation

With these preparations, we are ready to derive the Black–Scholes equation [BS73]. We must state upfront that there are several derivation methods. Discussed here is a simple method.

We assume that S_t is a geometric Brownian motion parameterized by two constants, the rate of drift μ and the variance σ^2:

$$\frac{dS_t}{S_t} = \mu \, dt + \sigma \, dB_t.$$

We construct a portfolio P_t comprising the option $O(t, S_t)$ and δ units of the underlying asset S_t.

$$P_t = O(t, S_t) + \delta S_t. \tag{8.26}$$

The brilliant idea of Black and Scholes is that, by adjusting δ, the portfolio can be made risk-free. By the first principle of Quantitative Finance, any risk-free asset must increase at the risk-free rate r. So after a short period $\triangle t$, the portfolio will have increased by an amount of $P_t r \triangle t$. It is as if the principal sum P_t is deposited at the risk-free bank and $P_t r \triangle t$ is the interest earned over a short time period $\triangle t$.

In view of (8.26), the change in portfolio must be, with the abbreviation $O_t := O(t, S_t)$,

$$\triangle \widetilde{P}_t = \triangle O_t + \delta \triangle \widetilde{S}_t = P_t r \triangle t. \tag{8.27}$$

It is important to note that the time period $\triangle t$ is such that S_t is known at the beginning of the period, but unknown at the end of period, as in any one-period model. In the limit $\triangle t \to 0$, we have

$$dP_t = dO_t + \delta \, d\widetilde{S}_t = r(O_t + \delta \, S_t) dt.$$

For the right side of the equation above, (8.26) has been applied.

Since the option $O := O(t, S_t)$ is a function of the stochastic process S_t, we apply the Itô formula (8.25) to obtain

$$\frac{\partial O}{\partial t} dt + \left(\frac{\partial O}{\partial S_t} + \delta \right) d\widetilde{S}_t + \frac{1}{2} \frac{\partial^2 O}{\partial S_t^2} (dS_t)^2 = r(O + \delta S_t) dt.$$

Equivalently, in view of (8.22),

$$\left(\frac{\partial O}{\partial t} + \frac{1}{2} \sigma^2 S_t \frac{\partial^2 O}{\partial S_t^2} \right) dt + \left(\frac{\partial O}{\partial S_t} + \delta \right) d\widetilde{S}_t = r(O + \delta S_t) dt. \tag{8.28}$$

Once again, it warrants a reminder that the differentiation is with respect to the functional form of $O(t, S_t)$.

Since the portfolio is risk-free, it means that the random term $d\tilde{S}_t$ should be absent. To bring about this non-random outcome, you set the hedge ratio δ in such a way that

$$\delta = -\frac{\partial O}{\partial S_t}. \tag{8.29}$$

Substituting this δ into (8.28), you obtain the Black–Scholes equation for the option:

$$\frac{\partial O}{\partial t} + rS_t \frac{\partial O}{\partial S_t} + \frac{1}{2}\sigma^2 S_t \frac{\partial^2 O}{\partial S_t^2} - rO = 0. \tag{8.30}$$

This method of derivation is based on the idea of delta hedging, i.e., removing the stochastic element $d\tilde{S}_t$ from the portfolio by buying and selling the underlying asset. Interestingly, in the context of delta-hedging, the second derivative term in the Black–Scholes equation (8.30) is in fact the rate at which the P&L is generated from delta-hedging the option.

As an illustration, consider the two-period binomial world. The risk-free portfolio P_t at time t_0 is given by

$$P_0 = O_0 + \delta_0 S_0.$$

At time t_1, on the up state,

$$S_1 = S_0 e^{\sigma\sqrt{\Delta t}}.$$

We must re-balance the hedge ratio by a certain amount. According to the chain rule,

$$\Delta\delta = \frac{\partial \delta}{\partial S}\Delta S = -\frac{\partial^2 O}{\partial S^2}(S_1 - S_0). \tag{8.31}$$

So at time t_1, the cash flow is $c_1 = -\Delta\delta \times S_1$. Suppose at time t_2, the underlying asset goes back down. Then,

$$S_2 = S_1 e^{-\sigma\sqrt{\Delta t}} = S_0,$$

resulting in the opposite re-balancing $\triangle \delta_1 = -\triangle \delta$. The cash flow is $c_2 = \triangle \delta\, S_0$.

The P&L from rebalancing is the sum of these two cash flows:

$$P\&L = c_1 + c_2 = -\triangle \delta (S_1 - S_0).$$

From (8.31),

$$P\&L = \frac{\partial^2 O}{\partial S^2}(S_1 - S_0)^2 = S_0^2 \frac{\partial^2 O}{\partial S^2}(e^{\sigma\sqrt{\triangle t}} - 1)^2.$$

Taylor's expansion of the exponential leads to

$$e^{\sigma\sqrt{\triangle t}} = 1 + \sigma\sqrt{\triangle t} + \text{ higher-order terms, i.e., } \left(\sqrt{\triangle t}\right)^3 + \cdots.$$

We find that

$$P\&L = S_0^2 \frac{\partial^2 O}{\partial S^2}\sigma^2 \triangle t.$$

The rate of P&L is therefore

$$\frac{P\&L}{2\triangle t} = \frac{1}{2}S_0^2\sigma^2 \frac{\partial^2 O}{\partial S^2},$$

which is precisely the second derivative term in (8.30).

8.7 Black–Scholes Equation is the Heat Equation

Interestingly, the Black–Scholes equation is in fact the heat equation. Suppose $g(t, S)$ solves the Black–Scholes partial differential equation (8.30) with terminal condition:

$$h(S) = \max(S - K, 0).$$

This $h(S)$ is the payoff function of a European call option maturing at time T. The strike price is denoted by K.

We begin by making the substitution:

$$g(t, S) = e^{rt}\, u(t, S), \tag{8.32}$$

using the chain rule,

$$\frac{\partial g}{\partial t} = rg + e^{rt}\frac{\partial u}{\partial t}.$$

The first term in the above equation cancels out the term rg in (8.30). Accordingly, we obtain the equation that the function u must satisfy:

$$\frac{\partial u}{\partial t} + rS\frac{\partial u}{\partial S} + \frac{1}{2}\sigma^2 S^2\frac{\partial^2 u}{\partial S^2} = 0. \tag{8.33}$$

Next, we make the substitutions:

$$y = \ln S, \qquad \theta = T - t.$$

Recall that T is the original time to maturity. Therefore, θ is the remaining time to maturity. These changes of variables are motivated by the following considerations:

- The underlying process described by the variable S is a geometric Brownian motion and hence $y = \ln S$ is a Brownian motion with a drift.
- The evolution of the system is backward from the time of maturity. Being equal to 1, the coefficient of $\frac{\partial u}{\partial t}$ is positive in (8.33). So to get to the heat equation, we have to use a substitution to reverse time.

Since

$$\frac{\partial u}{\partial \theta} = -\frac{\partial u}{\partial t}, \quad \frac{\partial u}{\partial S} = \frac{\partial u}{\partial y}\frac{dy}{dS} = \frac{1}{S}\frac{\partial u}{\partial y},$$

and

$$\frac{\partial^2 u}{\partial S^2} = \frac{\partial}{\partial S}\left(\frac{1}{S}\frac{\partial u}{\partial y}\right) = -\frac{1}{S^2}\frac{\partial u}{\partial y} + \frac{1}{S^2}\frac{\partial^2 u}{\partial y^2}.$$

Substituting these results into (8.33), we find

$$-\frac{\partial u}{\partial \theta} + \left(r - \frac{1}{2}\sigma^2\right)\frac{\partial u}{\partial y} + \frac{1}{2}\sigma^2\frac{\partial^2 u}{\partial y^2} = 0. \tag{8.34}$$

The first partial derivative with respect to y does not go away, unless $r = \sigma^2/2$, which is too restrictive.

To counter the drift, which is linear in time, we make the variable transformations as follows:

$$z = y + \left(r - \frac{1}{2}\sigma^2\right)\theta, \quad \tau = \theta.$$

Under the new coordinate system (z, τ), we have the relations

$$\frac{\partial u}{\partial y} = \frac{\partial u}{\partial z}\frac{\partial z}{\partial y} = \frac{\partial u}{\partial z},$$

$$\frac{\partial u}{\partial \tau} = \frac{\partial u}{\partial y}\frac{\partial y}{\partial \tau} + \frac{\partial u}{\partial \theta}\frac{\partial \theta}{\partial \tau} = -\left(r - \frac{1}{2}\sigma^2\right)\frac{\partial u}{\partial y} + \frac{\partial u}{\partial \theta}.$$

Consequently, (8.34) becomes the heat equation:

$$-\frac{\partial u}{\partial \tau} + \frac{1}{2}\sigma^2\frac{\partial^2 u}{\partial z^2} = 0. \tag{8.35}$$

Again, we find that $\sigma^2/2$ is the diffusion coefficient. Accordingly, we have proven that the Black–Scholes equation is the heat equation.

8.8 Solution of the Heat Equation

To solve the heat equation, we need to perform one more variable transformation:

$$\zeta = \frac{z}{\sigma},$$

which results in the canonical form

$$\frac{\partial u}{\partial \tau} = \frac{1}{2}\frac{\partial^2 u}{\partial \zeta^2}.$$

In the following, we demonstrate that the solution $u(\tau, \zeta)$ with the initial condition $u_0(x)$ is given by

$$u(\tau, \zeta) = \frac{1}{\sqrt{2\pi\tau}}\int_{-\infty}^{\infty} u_0(x)\exp\left(-\frac{(\zeta - x)^2}{2\tau}\right)dx. \tag{8.36}$$

First, we shift the x axis, i.e., $x \to x + \zeta$. So at $\tau = 0$,

$$\lim_{\tau \to 0}\frac{1}{\sqrt{2\pi\tau}}\int_{-\infty}^{\infty} u_0(x)\exp\left(-\frac{(\zeta - x)^2}{2\tau}\right)dx$$

$$= \int_{-\infty}^{\infty} u_0(x + \zeta) \lim_{\tau \to 0} \left(\frac{\exp\left(\frac{-x^2}{2\tau}\right) dx}{\sqrt{2\pi\tau}} \right)$$

$$= u_0(\zeta).$$

This is because the term $\exp\left(\frac{-x^2}{2\tau}\right)$ vanishes much faster than $\sqrt{\tau}$ as $\tau \to 0$. So, no integration is to be done over x, and the function u_0 becomes not dependent on x.

Next, it is straightforward to verify that

$$\frac{\partial}{\partial \tau} \left(\frac{\exp\left(\frac{-(\zeta-x)^2}{2\tau}\right)}{\sqrt{\tau}} \right) = \frac{1}{2\sqrt{\tau}} \left(\frac{(\zeta - x)^2}{\tau^2} - \frac{1}{\tau} \right) \exp\left(-\frac{(\zeta - x)^2}{2\tau} \right)$$

$$= \frac{1}{2\sqrt{\tau}} \frac{\partial^2}{\partial \zeta^2} \left(\exp\left(-\frac{(\zeta - x)^2}{2\tau} \right) \right).$$

It then follows that

$$\frac{\partial u}{\partial \tau} = \frac{\partial}{\partial \tau} \int_{-\infty}^{\infty} u_0(x) \left(\frac{\exp\left(\frac{-(\zeta-x)^2}{2\tau}\right)}{\sqrt{\tau}} \right) \frac{dx}{\sqrt{2\pi}}$$

$$= \frac{1}{2\sqrt{\tau}} \frac{\partial^2}{\partial \zeta^2} \frac{1}{\sqrt{2\pi}} \int_{-\infty}^{\infty} u_0(x) \exp\left(-\frac{(\zeta - x)^2}{2\tau} \right) dx$$

$$= \frac{1}{2} \frac{\partial^2 u}{\partial \zeta^2}.$$

In this way, we have shown that a general solution of the heat equation is (8.36).

8.9　Solution of the Black–Scholes Equation

In this section, we follow the train of thoughts of Privault [Pri13]. To solve the Black–Scholes partial differential equation (8.30), we consider the function $g(t, y)$ and the variable transformations:

$$g(t, y) := e^{rt} O(T - t, e^{\sigma y - \omega t}), \tag{8.37}$$

where

$$\omega := r - \frac{1}{2}\sigma^2. \tag{8.38}$$

The variable transformation $t \to T - t$ and $y \to e^{\sigma y - \omega t}$ is motivated by the functional form of the geometric Brownian motion. It is noteworthy that the constant risk-neutral drift rate ω corresponds to the "physical" drift rate $\mu - \sigma^2/2$ for $d \ln(S_t)$ in (8.23), which is the infinitesimal log return.

As in Section 8.7, the function $g(t, y)$ (8.32) is involved in solving the canonical form of the heat equation in Section 8.8:

$$\frac{\partial g}{\partial t} = \frac{1}{2}\frac{\partial^2 g}{\partial y^2}.$$

Notice that the variance σ^2 is not in this canonical form as it has been "absorbed" in the definition (8.37). The initial condition becomes

$$g(0, y) = h(e^{\sigma y}). \tag{8.39}$$

As a matter of fact, the heat equation has many different solutions. In general, the solution of a partial differential equation depends critically on the initial condition and the boundary condition. Different initial and boundary conditions will give rise to different solutions even though the partial differential equation is the same. The initial condition (8.39) may look simple but it dictates the specific form of the solution to the heat equation.

Using the Black–Scholes equation (8.30), we shall now demonstrate that (8.37) is a solution of the canonical heat equation. First, we recognize that the variable y and the underlying asset price S_t are related by way of variable transformation motivated by the assumption of geometric Brownian motion for the underlying asset dynamics:

$$S_t := e^{\sigma y - \omega t}. \tag{8.40}$$

Next, we perform a direct differentiation of (8.37) with respect to t and obtain

$$\frac{\partial g}{\partial t}(t, y) = e^{rt}\left(r\,O(T - t, S_t) - \frac{\partial O}{\partial t}(T - t, S_t) - \omega S_t \frac{\partial O}{\partial S_t}(T - t, S_t)\right).$$

Note that the first two terms on the right side of the equation also appear in (8.30). Accordingly, we have

$$r O - \frac{\partial O}{\partial t} = r S_t \frac{\partial O}{\partial S_t} + \frac{\sigma^2}{2} S_t^2 \frac{\partial^2 O}{\partial S_t^2},$$

leading to

$$\frac{\partial g}{\partial t}(t,y) = e^{rt} \left(\frac{\sigma^2}{2} S_t^2 \frac{\partial^2 O}{\partial S_t^2}(T - t, S_t) + \frac{\sigma^2}{2} S_t \frac{\partial O}{\partial S_t}(T - t, S_t) \right),$$

since $r - \omega = \sigma^2/2$ in view of the definition (8.38).

On the other hand,

$$\frac{\partial g}{\partial y}(t,y) = e^{rt} \sigma e^{\sigma y - \omega t} \frac{\partial O}{\partial S_t}(T - t, e^{\sigma y - \omega t}),$$

and the second-order partial derivative is obtained as

$$\frac{1}{2} \frac{\partial^2 g}{\partial y^2}(t,y) = e^{rt} \left(\frac{\sigma^2}{2} e^{\sigma y - \omega t} \frac{\partial O}{\partial S_t} + \frac{\sigma^2}{2} e^{2(\sigma y - \omega t)} \frac{\partial^2 O}{\partial S_t^2} \right)$$

$$= e^{rt} \left(\frac{\sigma^2}{2} S_t \frac{\partial O}{\partial S_t} + \frac{\sigma^2}{2} S_t^2 \frac{\partial^2 O}{\partial S_t^2} \right),$$

in view of the definition (8.40) for S_t. Therefore, we see from these direct calculations that the canonical heat equation has $g(t,y)$ as its solution.

An important step toward finding the solution for the Black–Scholes equation is to perform another variable transformation of (8.37). Let

$$s := T - t,$$

and rewrite the definition (8.40) as

$$y = \frac{\omega(T - s) + \ln S_t}{\sigma}. \tag{8.41}$$

Accordingly,

$$O(s, S_t) = e^{-r(T-s)} g \left(T - s, \frac{\omega(T - s) + \ln S_t}{\sigma} \right).$$

This is a subtle technique to get the time back to move forward.

Now, we need to involve the initial condition $\psi(y) := h(e^{\sigma y})$. Given the functional form of the solution to the heat equation, (8.36), we can write

$$O(t, S_t) = e^{-r(T-t)} \frac{1}{\sqrt{2\pi(T-t)}} \int_{-\infty}^{\infty} \psi(z) \exp\left(-\frac{(y-z)^2}{2(T-t)}\right) dz$$

$$= e^{-r(T-t)} \frac{1}{\sqrt{2\pi(T-t)}} \int_{-\infty}^{\infty} \psi(z+y) \exp\left(-\frac{z^2}{2(T-t)}\right) dz$$

$$= e^{-r(T-t)} \frac{1}{\sqrt{2\pi(T-t)}} \int_{-\infty}^{\infty} h(S_t e^{\sigma z + \omega(T-t)})$$

$$\times \exp\left(-\frac{z^2}{2(T-t)}\right) dz. \tag{8.42}$$

In the second step, we have shifted the variable, i.e., $z \to z + y$. The third equality is because, in conjunction with (8.41),

$$\psi(z+y) = h(e^{\sigma(z+y)}) = h(S_t e^{\sigma z + \omega(T-t)}).$$

It follows that, with $T - t$ denoted by τ, and since $h(H) = \max(H - K, 0)$ for the call option struck at the price K, we obtain

$$O(t, S_t) = e^{-r\tau} \frac{1}{\sqrt{2\pi\tau}} \int_{-\infty}^{\infty} \max(S_t e^{\sigma x + \omega\tau} - K, 0) \exp\left(-\frac{x^2}{2\tau}\right) dx. \tag{8.43}$$

The integration range starts from

$$S_t e^{\sigma x + \omega\tau} - K > 0.$$

Equivalently,

$$x > \frac{\ln(K/S_t) - \omega\tau}{\sigma} = -\frac{\ln(S_t/K) + \omega\tau}{\sigma} = -\sqrt{\tau}d_2,$$

where

$$d_2 = \frac{\ln\left(\frac{S_t}{K}\right) + \left(r - \frac{1}{2}\sigma^2\right)\tau}{\sigma\sqrt{\tau}},$$

which is (7.33). Consequently,

$$O(t, S_t) = e^{-r\tau} \frac{1}{\sqrt{2\pi\tau}} \int_{-\sqrt{\tau}d_2}^{\infty} (S_t e^{\sigma x + \omega\tau} - K) \exp\left(-\frac{x^2}{2\tau}\right) dx$$

$$= S_t e^{-r\tau} \frac{1}{\sqrt{2\pi\tau}} \int_{-\sqrt{\tau}d_2}^{\infty} e^{\sigma x + \omega\tau} \exp\left(-\frac{x^2}{2\tau}\right) dx$$

$$- Ke^{-r\tau} \frac{1}{\sqrt{2\pi\tau}} \int_{-\sqrt{\tau}d_2}^{\infty} \exp\left(-\frac{x^2}{2\tau}\right) dx.$$

In the first integral, given the definition of ω, (8.38), all the exponents can form a complete square:

$$-r\tau + \sigma x + r\tau - \frac{\sigma^2\tau}{2} - \frac{x^2}{2\tau} = -\frac{(x - \sigma\tau)^2}{2}.$$

The first term $-r\tau$ is from the discounting term outside the integral. It cancels the $r\tau$ term in the definition of ω.

Let $w := x - \sigma\tau$. Then the first integral becomes

$$S_t \frac{1}{\sqrt{2\pi\tau}} \int_{-\sqrt{\tau}d_2 - \sigma\tau}^{\infty} \exp\left(-\frac{w^2}{2\tau}\right) dw.$$

After another variable transformation $v = w/\sqrt{\tau}$, the first integral involving S_t is given by

$$S_t \frac{1}{\sqrt{2\pi}} \int_{-d_2 - \sigma\sqrt{\tau}}^{\infty} e^{-\frac{v^2}{2}} dv.$$

It follows that

$$O(t, S_t) = S_t \frac{1}{\sqrt{2\pi}} \int_{-d_2 - \sigma\sqrt{\tau}}^{\infty} e^{-\frac{v^2}{2}} dv - Ke^{-r\tau} \frac{1}{\sqrt{2\pi}} \int_{-d_2}^{\infty} e^{-\frac{v^2}{2}} dv.$$

Given that $d_2 + \sigma\sqrt{\tau} = d_1$, which is (7.34), we obtain, finally, the solution of the Black–Scholes equation (8.30):

$$O(t, S_t) = S_t(1 - \Phi(-d_1)) - Ke^{-r\tau}(1 - \Phi(-d_2))$$
$$= S_t\Phi(d_1) - Ke^{-r(T-t)}\Phi(d_2),$$

where $\Phi(x)$ is given by (7.38). Clearly, the solution $O(t, S_t)$ of the heat equation with the "initial condition" of max $(S_T - K, 0)$ is none other than (7.35), the price of a European call option.

8.10 The Derman–Taleb Approach to Option Pricing

To present a balanced account, we now turn to the critique of the Black–Scholes model by Derman and Taleb [DT05]. Their main concern is that the Black–Scholes model requires dynamical hedging, i.e., keep changing the hedge ratio whenever the price of the underlying asset changes. As in (8.29), the hedge ratio δ in fact is not static. The reason is because the delta of the option, Δ defined by

$$\Delta := \frac{\partial O}{\partial S_t}$$

is time dependent, and therefore $\delta = -\Delta$ is also time dependent. Moreover, the Black–Scholes model is not discrete in time and therefore, in principle, requires continuous hedging.

In reality, it is costly to perform dynamical hedging, i.e., buying and selling the underlying asset to maintain equality with a dynamic Δ. In practice, this is what Derman and Taleb [DT05] have to say:

> ... a trading desk must deal with transactions costs, liquidity constraints, the need for choosing price evolution models and the uncertainties that ensue, the confounding effect of discontinuous asset price moves, and, last but by no means least, the necessity for position and risk management software.

Practitioners know from bitter experience that dynamic hedging is a much more fragile procedure. So the brilliant idea mentioned in Section 8.6 is not practical after all!

Despite these shortcomings, the Black–Scholes pricing formulas are robust. In fact, Derman and Taleb show that it is possible to obtain the Black–Scholes formulas using a different approach, which does not rely on dynamic hedging at all.

To understand the Derman–Taleb approach, we first note that the integral in (8.42) is the expected value of the option payoff function $h(\cdot)$ under the risk neutral measure and under the assumption that the underlying asset price is a log normal random variable. The first principle of Quantitative Finance suggests that the expected future cash flow or payoff is to be discounted to obtain its present value. In the case of the European call option, with $\tau = T = t$,

$$c(t, S_t) = e^{-r\tau} \mathbb{E}\big(\max(S_t - K, 0) \big).$$

Suppose for a moment the expectation is not under the risk-neutral measure. So instead of ω (see (8.38)), we define

$$\lambda := \mu - \frac{\sigma^2}{2}.$$

In this definition, μ is the rate of drift of the underlying asset. To compute $\mathbb{E}\big(\max(S_t - K, 0) \big)$, given the assumption of log normality for the underlying asset's price, we have the parallel to (8.43) with ω replaced by λ:

$$\mathbb{E}(\max(S_t - K, 0))$$

$$= \frac{1}{\sqrt{2\pi\tau}} \int_{-\infty}^{\infty} \max\left(S_t \, e^{\sigma x + \lambda\tau} - K, 0\right) \exp\left(\frac{-x^2}{2\tau}\right) dx.$$

By the same logic, we arrive at

$$\mathbb{E}\big(\max(S_t - K, 0) \big) = S_t \frac{1}{\sqrt{2\pi\tau}} \int_{-\sqrt{\tau}d_-}^{\infty} e^{\sigma x + \lambda\tau} \exp\left(\frac{-x^2}{2\tau}\right) dx$$

$$- K \frac{1}{\sqrt{2\pi\tau}} \int_{-\sqrt{\tau}d_-}^{\infty} \exp\left(\frac{-x^2}{2\tau}\right) dx,$$

where

$$d_- := \frac{\ln\left(\frac{S_t}{K}\right) + \left(\mu - \frac{1}{2}\sigma^2\right)\tau}{\sigma\sqrt{\tau}}.$$

It follows that

$$\mathbb{E}\big(\max(S_t - K, 0) \big) = e^{\mu\tau} S_t \Phi(d_+) - K\Phi(d_-),$$

where

$$d_+ := \frac{\ln\left(\frac{S_t}{K}\right) + \left(\mu + \frac{1}{2}\sigma^2\right)\tau}{\sigma\sqrt{\tau}}.$$

Consequently,

$$c(t, S_t) = e^{-r\tau}(e^{\mu\tau} S_t \Phi(d_+) - K\Phi(d_-)). \qquad (8.44)$$

The analogous formula for a European put $p(S_t, t)$ is given by

$$p(t, S_t) = e^{-r\tau}\mathbb{E}\big(\max(K - S_t, 0)\big)$$
$$= e^{-r\tau}\big(K\Phi(-d_-) - S_t e^{\mu\tau}\Phi(-d_+)\big). \qquad (8.45)$$

Now, the forward contract F expiring at time T is effectively a long position in a call c and a short position in a put p with the same strike price K, i.e., $F_T = c_T - p_T$. At time t before maturity, the marked-to-market fair value of F_t is (see Q1 in Chapter 5.8),

$$F_t = S_t - Ke^{-r\tau}.$$

On the other hand, using the current prices of the call $c(t, S_t)$, (8.44), and the put $p(t, S_t)$, (8.45), we obtain

$$F_t = e^{-rt}(S_t e^{\mu\tau} - K).$$

Invoking the third principle of Quantitative Finance, these two forward contracts must be equal. The only way to achieve equality is to set $\mu = r$. Hence, d_+ becomes identical to d_1, d_- to d_2, and the probability measure becomes risk neutral. Accordingly, the Black–Scholes formulas for European calls and puts are obtained.

In this remarkably simple derivation, dynamic hedging is not needed at all. The Derman–Taleb approach, though elegant, is completely silent on how the option *should* be hedged. Traders know from *far* bitter experience that an un-hedged call option is naked and fully exposed to the market risk. Therefore, in practice, some form of hedging is still required unless you purely speculate on your view about the future of the underlying asset.

The intriguing thing about option hedging is that

$$\delta = -\Delta$$

in fact is the minimum variance hedge for the portfolio P comprising the option and the underlying, (8.26) (see Q8). In other words, $\mathbb{V}(\triangle P)$ will have the smallest variance if the hedge ratio is the negative of the option's delta denoted by Δ. So, we have gone a full circle back to the Black–Scholes model.

8.11 Exercises

Q1. Show that

$$\frac{1}{\sqrt{2\pi}} \int_{-\infty}^{\infty} \exp\left(-\frac{B^2 x^2}{2}\right) dx = \frac{1}{B}.$$

Hint: Perform a variable transformation $y = Bx$.

Q2. Although the European put option price can be obtained from the put-call parity, it is nonetheless a useful exercise to derive it directly from the heat equation. Starting from the analogue of (8.43). i.e.,

$$\varphi(t, S_t) = e^{-r\tau} \frac{1}{\sqrt{2\pi\tau}} \int_{-\infty}^{\infty} \max\left(K - S_t\, e^{\sigma x + \omega\tau}, 0\right)$$

$$\times \exp\left(-\frac{-x^2}{2\tau}\right) dx$$

for the plain vanilla European put option, go through the same steps of calculation to obtain

$$\varphi(t, S_t) = K e^{-r(T-t)} \Phi(-d_2) - S_t \Phi(-d_1).$$

Q3. Show that

$$\frac{1}{2}\left(d_1^2 - d_2^2\right) = \ln\left(\frac{S_t}{K}\right) + r(T - t).$$

Q4. Using the result in Q3, show that

$$S_t \Phi'(d_1) - K e^{-r(T-t)} \Phi'(d_2) = 0,$$

where

$$\Phi'(x) := \frac{d\Phi(x)}{dx} = \frac{1}{\sqrt{2\pi}} e^{-\frac{x^2}{2}}.$$

Q5. From (8.29), we see that δ is the negative of the partial differential of the option with respect to the underlying asset, which is the delta Δ. In symbols,

$$\Delta := \frac{\partial O}{\partial S_t}.$$

Using the result in Q4, show that the delta of the European call option is $\Phi(d_1)$.

Q6. Show that the delta of the European put option is $-\Phi(-d_1)$.

Q7. What is the financial interpretation of d_2?

Q8. Treating $\triangle \widetilde{P}_t$ in (8.27) as a random variable, show that if the hedge ratio δ is the negative delta Δ of the option, then the variance of the change in portfolio $\triangle \widetilde{P}_t$ is a minimum with respect to the hedge ratio.

Epilogue

It is appropriate that the eight-chapter story of introductory Quantitative Finance ends with the beginning of Quantitative Finance: The first application of probability theory and stochastic calculus to solve the option pricing problem in Chapter 8.

As a synopsis of the story, Chapter provides the philosophical underpinning of the story line. Moving on from a brief introduction to four major asset classes in Chapter 1.6, the three principles of Quantitative Finance are articulated in Chapter 3 as a set of guides to select models that are useful from the practitioners' standpoint. With the three-principle approach, hopefully you have already found coherency through the lens of Quantitative Finance to look at the real world of return, risk, and the financial products that need to be priced and hedged.

Chapter 3.10 focuses on fixed income securities and explains how the yield curve could be modeled with the three principles. For reasons stated in the preface, I have avoided mentioning the qualitative "theories" of the yield curves typically found in the Economics & Finance textbooks. Instead, guided by the three principles, a novel parsimonious model to describe the yield curve from 1- to 10-year maturities is proposed.

Derivatives with linear payoffs are presented in Chapter 4.8 along with an emphasis on the importance of discount factors, and the way they are computed in practice. The financial products discussed include currency forward contracts, forward rate agreements, interest rate swaps, and cross-currency interest rate swaps. These financial instruments are powerful tools frequently used by banks to manage their assets and liabilities.

The next three chapters from Chapter 5.8 to Chapter 8 are devoted to derivatives with the simplest nonlinear payoffs, i.e., plain vanilla options. Hopefully you have found the third principle particularly useful for deriving the bounds that must be observed by the put and call premiums. Moreover, several properties concerning the shapes of the option price functions are obtained. Put-call parity, put-call inequalities for American options, and box spread parity are also obtainable from the three principles. The ideas and concepts related to the binomial and the Black–Scholes models are presented in the last two chapters from the perspectives of the three principles of Quantitative Finance.

Having discussed the Black–Scholes model in detail, we recognize that the volatility input into the Black–Scholes pricing formula is a quantity assumed (wrongly) to be non-time-dependent. The reality, however, is the very opposite. Not only is the volatility varying with time, the volatility dynamics is stochastic as well. The wrong assumption is the ugly beast in many models of Quantitative Finance.

The beauty, however, is the way the Black–Scholes pricing formula is applied in practice, and also in academic research. Instead of using it as much to price an option, the Black–Scholes formula is employed rather as a translator for obtaining an implied volatility from the language of option prices spoken in the option markets. As the name suggests, implied volatility is the volatility that you reverse engineer from an observed option price.

The computational procedure used popularly for the purpose of reverse engineering by practitioners and academics alike is the Newton–Raphson method of root finding. On this note, it is obvious that quants need to apply computer programming proficiently in order to perform the algorithmic implementation of many numerical methods. Treating the Black–Scholes formula and the observed option price as a nonlinear function of the volatility, the well-known Newton–Raphson method iteratively finds a more accurate implied volatility that better matches the market price. Interestingly, despite sharing the same underlying asset, the evidence is overwhelming that the implied volatility varies from one option to the other.

On the other hand, in the Black–Scholes model, the annualized volatility must be the same for all options regardless of whether they are put or call, or of different strike prices, or with different maturities. The simple reason is that the volatility in the Black–Scholes model is the volatility of the underlying asset return. Given that the geometric Brownian motion is assumed, there can only be one and only one volatility common to all these options.

Therefore, the empirical evidence of non-unique implied volatility suggests that the Black–Scholes model is scientifically wrong. In the history of astronomy, several models of the planetary motions had appeared prior to Kepler's model. But they all failed to explain the phenomena in the solar system as correctly and accurately compared to Kepler's model. The Black–Scholes model is very much like these pre-Kepler models, which are flawed in a few dimensions. But that does not mean that the Black–Scholes model is useless.

On the contrary, practitioners use the Black–Scholes formula to back out the implied volatilities and plot them against the strike prices. The plot shows a dependence of the implied volatility on the strike price and this dependence is known as the volatility smile or the volatility skew. Option traders sometimes use the volatility smile as a simple device to trade a chain of options with different strike prices. Whenever a local spike appears in the smile curve, they will sell (buy) the option with the upward (downward) spike because that option is likely to be overpriced (underpriced) relative to the other options. Consequently, the smile curve tends to become smoother. This application of the Black–Scholes model by traders is certainly beyond the inventors' imagination. And that, is the beauty of Quantitative Finance.

Sadly, unlike the fairy tale of *Beauty and the Beast* where the Beast is transformed into the handsome prince with the happily-ever-after ending, the beast of Quantitative Finance is still hopelessly under the magic spell. But like Belle in this French fairy tale, a good quant practitioner knows the creative way to draw out the beautifully handsome ones inside the Beast.

Bibliography

[Bac00]   M. Louis Bachelier, *Théorie de la spéculation*, Annales Scientifiques de l'École Normale Supérieure **17** (1900), 21–86.

[Ber92]   Peter L. Bernstein, *Capital ideas: The improbable origins of modern Wall Street*, The Free Press, 1992.

[Ber05]   Jeremy Bernstein, *Bachelier*, American Journal of Physics **73** (2005), 395–398.

[Bil06]   Randall S. Billingsley, *Understanding arbitrage: An intuitive approach to financial analysis*, Pearson Education, 2006.

[BIS96]   BIS, *Central bank survey of foreign exchange and derivatives market activity 1995*, Tech. report, Bank for International Settlements, 1996.

[BJN00]   Mark Britten-Jones and Anthony Neuberger, *Option prices, implied processes, and stochastic volatility*, Journal of Finance **55** (2000), 839–866.

[Bla86]   Fischer Black, *Noise*, Journal of Finance **41** (1986), 529–543.

[Box79]   George E. P. Box, *Robustness in the strategy of scientific model building*, Robustness in Statistics: Proceedings of a Workshop (Robert L. Launer and Graham N. Wilkinson, eds.), Academic Press, 1979.

[BS73]   Fischer Black and Myron Scholes, *The pricing of options and corporate liabilities*, Journal of Political Economy **81** (1973), 637–654.

[CRR79]   John C. Cox, Stephen A. Ross and Mark Rubinstein, *Option pricing: A simplified approach*, Journal of Financial Economics **7** (1979), 229–263.

[Der04]   Emanuel Derman, *My life as a quant: Reflections on physics and finance*, John Wiley & Sons, 2004.

[Der11]   Emanuel Derman, *Models behaving badly*, Free Press, 2011.

[DJRVD09]   Abe De Jong, Leonard Rosenthal and Mathijs Van Dijk, *The risk and return of arbitrage in dual-listed companies*, Review of Finance **13** (2009), 495–520.

[dlV57]   Penso Joseph de la Vega, *Confusión de confusiones, 1688* Baker Library, Harvard Graduate School of Business Administration, 1957.

[DR07]   Ramon P. DeGennaro and Cesare Robotti, *Financial market frictions*, Economic Review **92** (2007), no. 3, 1–16.

[DT05]   Emanuel Derman and N. Nassim Taleb, *The illusions of dynamic replication*, Quantitative Finance **5** (2005), no. 4, 323–326.

[Duf01]   Darrell Duffie, *Dynamic asset pricing theory*, third edn., Cambridge University Press, 2001.

[Ein05]   Albert Einstein, *Über die von der molekularkinetischen theorie der wärme geforderte bewegung von in ruhenden flssigkeiten suspendierten teilchen.*, Annalen der Physik **17** (1905), 549–560.

[FD99]   Kenneth A. Froot and Emil M. Dabora, *How are stock prices affected by the location of trade?*, Journal of Financial Economics **53** (1999), 189–216.

[FF04]   Eugene F. Fama and Kenneth R. French, *The capital asset pricing model: Theory and evidence*, Journal of Economic Perspectives **18** (2004), 25–46.

[FGR12]   Rik Frehen, William N. Goetzmann and K. Geert Rouwenhorst, *New evidence on the first financial bubble*, Yale ICF Working Paper No. 09-04, July 2012.

[Fis07]   Irving Fisher, *The rate of interest*, The Macmillan Company, 1907.

[Fra49]   John Francis, *Chronicles and characters of stock exchange*, The Church of England Quarterly Review **27** (1849), 128–154.

[Fuk07]   Masatoshi Fukushima, *On the works of Kiyosi Itô and stochastic analysis*, Japanese Journal of Mathematics **2** (2007), no. 1, 45–53 (English).

[GS80]   Stanford J. Grossman and Joseph E. Stiglitz, *On the impossibility of informationally efficient markets*, American Economic Review **79** (1980), 393–408.

[GSW06]   Refet S. Gurkaynak, Brian Sack and Jonathan H. Wright, *The U.S. Treasury yield curve: 1961 to the present*, Tech. report, Divisions of Research & Statistics and Monetary Affairs, Federal Reserve Board, Washington D.C., 2006, Finance and Economics Discussion Series 2006-28.

[Gut46]   Harry G. Guthmann, *The American Finance Association*, Journal of Finance **1** (1946), no. 1.

[Har03]   Larry Harris, *Trading and exchange: Market microstructure for practitioners*, Financial Management Association Survey and Synthesis Series, Oxford University Press, 2003.

[Hul12]   John C. Hull, *Options, futures, and other derivatives*, eighth edn., Prentice Hall, 2012.

[Ito42]   Kiyoshi Ito, *Differential equations determining a Markoff process* (*original Japanese: Zenkoku Sizyo Sugaku Danwakai-si*), Journal of Pan-Japan Mathematics collegium **244** (1942), no. 1077, 1352–1400.

[IVS87]   K. Itô, S.R.S. Varadhan and D.W. Stroock, *Kiyosi Itô selected papers*, Springer-Verlag, 1987.

[Key36]   John Maynard Keynes, *The general theory of employment, interest, and money*, Palgrave Macmillan, 1936.

[Kuo06]   Hui-Hsiung Kuo, *Introduction to stochastic integration*, Springer, 2006.

[Lim11]   Kian Guan Lim, *Probability and finance theory*, World Scientific Publising, 2011.

[Low00]   Roger Lowenstein, *When genius failed: The rise and fall of long-term capital management*, first edn., Random House, 2000.

[LT03]   Owen A. Lamont and Richard H. Thaler, *Anomalies: The law of one price in financial markets*, Journal of Economic Perspectives **17** (2003), 191–202.

[Mar52]   Harry M. Markowitz, *Portfolio selection*, Journal of Finance **7** (1952), 77–91.

[McD13]   Robert L. McDonald, *Derivatives markets*, third edn., Pearson, 2013.

[Meh05]   Perry Mehrling, *Fischer Black and the revolutionary idea of finance*, John Wiley & Sons, 2005.

[Mer73]   Robert C. Merton, *Theory of rational option pricing*, Bell Journal of Economics and Management Science **4** (1973), 141–183.

[MH04]   Benoit B. Mandelbrot and Richard L. Hudson, *The (mis)behavior of markets: A fractal view of risk, ruin, and reward*, Basic Books, 2004.

[Mil88]   Merton H. Miller, *The Modigliani–Miller propositions after thirty years*, Journal of Economic Perspectives **2** (1988), no. 4, 99–120.

[Mil99]   Merton H. Miller, *The history of finance: An eyewitness account*, Journal of Portfolio Management **25** (1999), no. 4, 95–101.

[MM58]   Franco Modigliani and Merton H. Miller, *The cost of capital, corporation finance and the theory of investment*, The American Economic Review **48** (1958), no. 3, 261–297 (English).

[Moo29]   Justin H. Moore, *Handbook of financial mathematics*, Prentice Hall, 1929.

[New86]   Isaac Newton, *Philosophiæ naturalis principia mathematica*, Philosophical Transactions of the Royal Society, 1686.

[NP14]   Grégoire Naacke and Eleanor Peniston, *WFE/IOMA derivatives market survey 2013: Final report*, Tech. report, World Federation of Exchanges and International Options Market Association, 2014.

[NS87]   Charles R. Nelson and Andrew F. Siegel, *Parsimonious modeling of yield curves*, Journal of Business **60** (1987), 473–489.

[Pat10]   Scott Patterson, *The quants: How a new breed of math whizzes conquered Wall Street and nearly destroyed it*, Crown Business, 2010.

[Pea05]   Karl Pearson, *The problem of the random walk*, Nature **72** (1905), 294.

[Per88]   André F. Perold, *The implementation shortfall: Paper versus reality*, Journal of Portfolio Management **14** (1988), 4–9.

[Pri13]   Nicolas Privault, *Stochastic finance: An introduction with market examples*, Chapman and Hall/CRC, 2013.

[Ree99]   Christopher Reed, *The damn'd South Sea*, Harvard Magazine, vol. May–June, Harvard Magazine Inc., 1999.

[Ros08]   Stephen A. Ross, *Finance*, The New Palgrave Dictionary of Economics Second Edition **3** (2008), 329–333.

[Roy56]   *Royal Statistical* Society, *Proceedings of the meeting*, Journal of the Royal Statistical Society Series A (General) **119** A, no. 2, 1956.

[Sha64]   William F. Sharpe, *Capital asset prices: A theory of market equilibrium under conditions of risk*, Journal of Finance **19** (1964), 425–442.

[Som70]   Arnold Sommerfeld, *To Albert Einstein's seventieth birthday*, Albert Einstein: Philosopher-Scientist (Paul Armor Schilpp, ed.), The Library of Living Philosophers, vol. 7, MJF Books, 1970.

[Ste12]   Ian Stewart, *In pursuit of the unknown: 17 equations that changed the world*, Basic Books, 2012.

[Sto00]   Hans R. Stoll, *Friction*, Journal of Finance **55** (2000), 1479–1513.

[Str03]   D.W. Stroock, *Markov processes from K. Itô's perspective*, Annals of Mathematics Studies, vol. 155, Princeton University Press, 2003.

[Sum85]   Lawrence H. Summers, *On economics and finance*, Journal of Finance **40** (1985), 633–635.

[Tal07]   Nassim Nicholas Taleb, *The black swan: The impact of the highly improbable*, Random House, May 2007.

[TK67]   Edward O. Thorp and Sheen T. Kassouf, *Beat the market: A scientific stock market system*, Random House, 1967.

[Tre61]   Jack L. Treynor, *Toward a theory of market value of risky assets*, Unpublished, 1961.

[Tri09]   Pablo Triana, *Lecturing birds on flying: Can mathematical theories destroy the financial markets?*, John Wiley & Sons, 2009.

[Var87]   Hal R. Varian, *The arbitrage principle in financial economics*, Journal of Economic Perspectives **1** (1987), no. 2, 55–72.

[vKMMG10]   Karsten von Kleist, Carlos Mallo, Philippe Mesny and Serge Grouchko, *Report on global foreign exchange market activity in 2010*, Tech. report, Bank for International Settlements, 2010.

[Wie23]   Norbert Wiener, *Differential space*, Journal of Mathematical Physics **2** (1923), 131–174.

Index